PENGUIN BOOKS

GOLDEN DOOR TO AMERICA

Professor Abraham J. Karp is himself an immigrant, having arrived in the United States from Poland at the age of nine. He graduated from Yeshiva University and received his rabbinical degree from The Jewish Theological Seminary, where he also received the degree of Doctor of Divinity.

He has served as a rabbi for a quarter-century, the last sixteen years at Temple Beth El in Rochester, New York. While so doing, he also taught as a visiting professor at Dartmouth College, The Hebrew University of Jerusalem, and The Jewish Theological Seminary. Since 1972 he has been Professor of History and Religious Studies at the University of Rochester, and he was recently designated the first holder of the Philip S. Bernstein Professorship of Jewish Studies. He is a fellow of the Institute of Contemporary Jewry of The Hebrew University, Jerusalem.

He has written and edited six other books and numerous articles, and has been the president of the American Jewish Historical Society.

GOLDEN DOOR TO AMERICA

The Jewish Immigrant Experience

ABRAHAM J. KARP

PENGUIN BOOKS

Penguin Books Ltd, Harmondsworth,
Middlesex, England
Penguin Books, 625 Madison Avenue,
New York, New York 10022, U.S.A.
Penguin Books Australia Ltd, Ringwood,
Victoria, Australia
Penguin Books Canada Limited, 2801 John Street,
Markham, Ontario, Canada L3R 1B4
Penguin Books (N.Z.) Ltd, 182–190 Wairau Road,
Auckland 10, New Zealand

First published in the United States of America in
the Jewish Heritage Classics Series by
The Viking Press 1976
Published in Penguin Books 1977

LIBRARY OF CONGRESS CATALOGING IN PUBLICATION DATA
Main entry under title:
Golden door to America.
Reprint of the 1976 ed. published by
The Viking Press, New York, in series:
The Jewish heritage classics.
Bibliography: p. 263.
Includes index.
1. Jews in the United States—Biography.
2. Jews in the United States—Social conditions.
3. United States—Biography. 4. United States—
Emigration and immigration—Personal narratives.
I. Karp, Abraham J. II. Series: The Jewish
heritage classics.
[E184.J5G6225 1977]   920′.0092′92073
ISBN 0 14 00.4544 9   77-7998

Printed in the United States of America by
Offset Paperback Mfrs., Inc., Dallas, Pennsylvania
Set in VIP Times Roman

Page 272 constitutes an extension of this copyright page.

Send these, the homeless, tempest-tossed to me.·
I lift my lamp beside the golden door.

—EMMA LAZARUS

Preface

In *A Dreamer's Journey* the American Jewish teacher and philosopher Morris Raphael Cohen describes his parents in a letter addressed to his granddaughter. They were, he said, "of that heroic generation that tore up their roots in their old homeland, and unaided and with no equipment other than their indomitable faith and courage, built new homes in this land and raised up children who have made invaluable contributions to the life of this country in the fields of art, science, industry, education, and philanthropic work."

In the pages that follow, the story of the arrival and early years of that heroic generation is retold through documents, reports, descriptions, and reminiscences—both their own and by those who preceded them through "the golden door" to America.

That experience begins with the movement of Jews from the Old World to the New. Beginning with a slow trickle of immigrants, mainly of Spanish and Portuguese origin (Sephardim), in the middle and late seventeenth century, the real story of the Jewish immigrant takes shape only after the more substantial flow of arrivals from Germany and western Europe during the nineteenth century. With the veritable tidal waves of new arrivals from eastern Europe in the late nineteenth and early twentieth centuries, American Jewry and the American Jewish community came into its own. The ensuing tension brought on by the interaction of the settled community guarding its power and prerogatives and the exploding energies of the newcomers bent on exercising new-found freedom and opportunities in service of their own interests, is an important aspect of this period.

Once the Jews arrived in America, transformations began to take place. Internal tensions in families and individuals were created by the conflict between the desire to become part of the New World and the need to retain the ways of the Old. The immigrant was a person beset by all manner of hardship in keeping himself and his family alive; hand in hand with the driving necessity to nurture the body went the age-old Jewish concern with learning and matters of the spirit. The network of mutual-aid organizations created to help the new arrivals is also discussed. The perplexities, pains, joys, sorrows, and achievements of the American Jewish immigrant are movingly summed up in a series of vignettes taken from the life stories and observations of Della R. Adler, Abraham Goldberg, poet Ephraim Lisitzky, and philosopher Morris Raphael Cohen.

One despairs at doing justice to this heroic generation, and no attempt is made here to carry the story beyond the early years of adjustment, or to explore fully all the achievements or transformations of American acculturation, or to evaluate the experience. The emphasis here is on the saga itself; the material is rich, varied, massive. The difficulty is not in what is available, but in what one is forced to omit.

The experience of the immigrant was sporadic, and so the picture must be: not a composed photograph providing precise detail, but an impressionistic painting of dabs and jots of color to which distance gives form and definition. The Jewish immigrants, and those who knew them, best tell the story.

The debts of gratitude for this volume are many. The truly heroic men and women who dared the unknown fashioned the experiences and vignettes set down here. Observers, students, critics, children, grandchildren and great-grandchildren, who have remembered, unearthed, and recorded, have offered insight and understanding into the immigrant experience.

While many individuals assisted along the way in bringing this book

into being, I wish to express to Lily Edelman, director of B'nai
B'rith's Commission on Adult Jewish Education, my special appreciation for her help in giving this volume a measure of editorial direction
and cohesion which it might otherwise have lacked.

A.J.K.

Contents

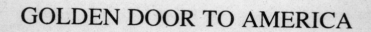

GOLDEN DOOR TO AMERICA

Introduction: The Making
of the American Jew

The story of the Jew in America begins with an act of will. The first Jewish community in what is now the United States was founded in early September 1654, by four men, six women, and thirteen young people. The twenty-three arrived in New Amsterdam from Recife, Brazil, having been forced to leave that city when it was recaptured by the Portuguese from the Dutch. While most Jews returned to Amsterdam, where freedom and prosperity were still possible, some chose to remain in the New World.

The immigration of Jews to America in the seventeenth and eighteenth centuries was part of the general movement of the center of the Occidental world from the Mediterranean to the Atlantic. The discoveries of the sixteenth century turned the attention of nations and men to the promise of the Americas. Tales and evidence of the great wealth of the new continents began to fill the dreams of the daring and raise the hopes of the hungry. The population of Europe was growing at an unprecedented rate, and new frontiers were needed. America became the goal and destination, the Atlantic a route to new hope and new life.

European Jews had engaged in mercantile endeavors. In the later Middle Ages, the rise of a European middle class had pushed the Jews of western and southern Europe out of their favored position in trade and commerce. Looking for new frontiers as merchants and financiers, they had found opportunity in eastern Europe in the fifteenth and sixteenth centuries. They settled in Poland, Lithuania, the Ukraine, and the western provinces of Russia, where they prospered economically and flourished spiritually.

In 1648 the Chmielnicki uprising devastated Polish Jewry. While Eastern Europe continued to have the largest concentration of Jews, many now began to turn their gaze westward to the mercantile cities of northwestern Europe. The direction of Jewish migration was now reversed as Jews from Poland and Russia began to arrive in the cities of North Germany, Holland, and England. Here they found Jews of Spanish origin whose ancestors had been driven from Spain and Portugal at the end of the fifteenth century. Some had made their way to northern Europe where they were joined by former Marranos, who could now live openly as Jews in the Protestant countries. In Amsterdam and London, Jews established thriving communities. Sephardi and Ashkenazi communities remained separate and apart. It was only in America that distinctions were erased.

The immigration westward had now turned toward the Americas, which the mercantile nations were opening for exploitation. From the beginning this new area of opportunity was settled by both Sephardim and Ashkenazim. Indeed, there were Ashkenazi Jews among the twenty-three who came to New Amsterdam from Brazil, where they had enjoyed a thriving communal life under benevolent Dutch rule.

The twenty-three refugees who arrived in New Amsterdam were met by at least two coreligionists. Some Jews had come to the colony in the summer of 1654 to engage in trade. Since the Dutch West India Company was promoting immigration to New Netherlands, the Jews of Holland considered themselves included among those invited to make a home in the New World.

The twenty-three were refugees, with no legal right to settle. Indeed, Governor Peter Stuyvesant and his Council ordered them to depart. The Jews of Amsterdam, among them some major shareholders in the Dutch West India Company, supported the refugees' right to remain, and won the cause for the twenty-three. More Jews arrived from Holland. Some found the atmosphere of New Amsterdam economically and politically oppressive, and returned home. The Jews did have to struggle for the minimal rights to engage in trade, to own property, to keep watch and ward, and to gain citizenship. These rights were granted only after petition and pressure in the colony, and with help from affluent Dutch Jews. The rights to work at crafts, to hold public office, to build a synagogue or to engage in public religious services were never won in New Amsterdam. These came later, under British rule of the renamed colony of New York.

Colonial history demonstrates that the conditions of freedom and tolerance existing in the mother country were seldom exported to the colonies. The colonial overseers and settlers were generally not of the more enlightened segment of the population. The dangers and insecurity of colonial enterprise made men suspicious and intolerant of the stranger. Only the Dutch Protestants were really welcome in New Amsterdam. Pleading against extending rights to the Jews, Governor Stuyvesant wrote to the Company's Directors in Amsterdam in October 1655, "Giving them liberty, we cannot refuse the Lutherans and the Papists."

What was true of New Amsterdam was true of the other colonies as well. Old World prejudices had been transplanted to the New. Most of the colonies were organized by particular groups or sects for themselves and their coreligionists—to the exclusion of Jews and others.

Certain factors and forces unique to the New World, however, did operate to mitigate anti-Jewish sentiments and lay the foundation first for the tolerance, later for the freedom granted to Jews as to all other new Americans. An immigrant society, no matter how meticulously planned or controlled, inevitably becomes a diversified community made up of individuals and groups from different countries and of different beliefs. At first the "different" might have been resented and rejected as intruders; but soon, because they were needed, they were grudgingly accepted. Land was plentiful in colonial America; human beings were not. People with skills, organizational ability, daring and imagination were a precious commodity. The expanding frontier society offered opportunities for economic growth and success. In an expanding society where wealth is looked on as a social good, men of enterprise became respected and esteemed members of their communities, were accepted socially, and could wield political power and influence.

The Jews of colonial America, along with other segments of the population, were the beneficiaries of the opportunities which an open frontier society provided. Being largely in mercantile enterprises, they were in a position to benefit from a constantly expanding frontier and population. Jewish religious development was fostered in the general atmosphere of colonial America, where religion pervaded all of life. Many of the colonies had been founded by religious groups, some for religious purposes. In all, religious forms were adhered to and religion esteemed. Religious leaders were an important part of the establishment.

The hazard for Jews was the small size and dispersion of the community. The necessities of life made intermarriage acceptable in deed, if not formally approved by the community. There was considerable social integration in the frontier communities and Jews became, through marriage, members of some of America's socially elite families. Though many remained practicing, participating Jews in their lifetime, their children most often entered the majority society.

During the first three decades of the Republic, the Jewish population increased from fewer than two thousand to about three thousand, while the general population trebled. During the next three decades, 1820–1850, the general population doubled, but the Jewish population, through accelerated immigration, soared to some fifty thousand— a seventeenfold increase.

The condition of Jews in Western and Central Europe was described in a letter published in the *Deutsches Museum* of June 1783, addressed to the President of the Continental Congress, followed by a plea "to be permitted to become subjects of these thirteen provinces," in return for which they "would gladly contribute twofold taxes."

Following a period of freedom and hope after the French Revolution, the Congress of Vienna—convened in 1814–1815 to restore Europe to its pre-Napoleonic ways—set off a wave of reaction which brought suffering to the Jews. Newly granted rights were revoked and new oppressive measures enacted and enforced. The social upheaval which the Napoleonic wars engendered caused a population flow from German rural areas to urban centers with attendant political and economic consequences for the Jewish townsmen. The unsuccessful revolutions of 1830 and 1848, and the reaction which afterward set in, gave further cause for Jewish uneasiness.

In the 1830s and particularly in the 1840s Jews arrived on American shores in significant numbers, mainly from Bavaria. They founded congregations and communities in Boston, Hartford, New Haven, Albany, Syracuse, Rochester, Buffalo; Baltimore, Columbia, Augusta, Mobile, New Orleans, and Galveston; Cincinnati, Cleveland, Chicago, Louisville, Milwaukee, Pittsburgh, Columbus, and Indianapolis. The DeSola-Lyons Calendar of 1854 listed ten congregations in the new state of California.

The Jews of the early Republic remained largely merchants, a term inclusive of the international trader and the large-scale land speculator as well as the small storekeeper and peddler. Later, Jews became "mechanics"—carpenters, tailors, watchmakers. In 1838 a group of Jews from New York City established an agricultural settlement in Ulster County, which they named "Scholem."

The German Jewish immigration introduced large-scale peddling as a transitional occupation. Each peddler looked for a suitable place to establish a business and settle down: "From pack-on-back to store to department store" describes the economic career of a number of them. In 1820, the American Jewish community had been largely native-born, English-speaking, small in number and rapidly assimilating. By 1850, it was largely a German-speaking, immigrant community beginning to establish those institutions and organizations which would give it structure and identity and lay the foundation for the future.

New waves of Jewish immigrants followed on the heels of the political and civic reaction which took place in the middle-European countries after the Revolution of 1848, letting loose anti-Jewish sentiments in Bohemia, Slovakia, Hungary, Posen, and Upper Silesia. The traditional anti-Semitism of Bavaria continued to find expression in a wide variety of Jewish legal disabilities. Small wonder that the Jewish population of the United States increased from some 50,000 people to approximately 150,000 in the decade from 1850 to 1860.

Among the new immigrants were a growing number of Jews from eastern Europe. The Russian suppression of the Polish uprising of 1860–1863, in which Jews had taken part in significant numbers, gave the latter new cause to leave the Polish provinces. Many of the so-called German Jewish immigrants came from the areas on the border between the eastern and western European communities—Posen, Silesia, Bohemia, and Slovakia. Thus, American Jewry in the three decades following the mid-century was comprised chiefly of immigrants from the "German" countries of central Europe, with a significant admixture from Russia, Poland, and Romania.

Once arrived in the New World, the American Jew joined other Americans in moving westward. Individual Jews could be found in many pioneer settlements, and Jewish communities began to dot the entire map of expanding America. Los Angeles was typical of the new frontier communities, with eight Jews in 1850, six from Germany and two from Poland, all under thirty, single, and merchants. A decade later, there were a hundred Jews living there.

By 1860 some Jews were laying the foundation for what later would become great fortunes. The manufacture of clothing, which became the chief Jewish economic enterprise, was beginning. A few successful merchants were entering the larger worlds of high finance.

Simultaneously, the Jewish communities were establishing institutions to care for human needs, organizations, social clubs, literary societies, and congregations. Fraternal orders, whose secret ritual shared with "brothers" substituted for the intimacy of family life, provided sickness and death benefits for their members and for bereaved families.

The first of the fraternal orders, the Independent Order of B'nai B'rith, was organized in New York in 1843. Soon lodges spread throughout the country and eventually the world. The orders Kesher

Shel Barzel, Free Sons of Israel, B'nai Abraham, and B'nai Moshe soon followed. These not only served the needs of the member brothers, but often spearheaded social welfare endeavors and served to unite the scattered Jewish communities through correspondence, conventions, and joint enterprises.

A dozen years after the Jewish Foster Home for orphans and neglected children of Philadelphia was established, the Jewish community met to dedicate a Jewish hospital. B'nai B'rith had initiated the movement, with 700 persons pledging five dollars per annum. Jewish foster homes and hospitals also existed at that time in New Orleans, New York, and Cincinnati.

The decades of the Civil War and Reconstruction saw a decrease in immigration. The first attempt at a Jewish population survey, undertaken by the Board of Delegates of American Israelites in 1877, placed the number of Jews in the United States at 230,257.

But a new wave of immigration was set in motion by the throwing of the bomb that took the life of Alexander II, "Czar of all the Russias," in March 1881. The assassination touched off pogroms in more than a hundred Jewish communities, followed by restrictive laws aimed at eliminating Jews from economic and civic life. Physical persecution, political oppression, and economic disabilities brought two and one-half million Jews from eastern Europe to American shores in the half century from 1880 to 1930.

During the first half of the nineteenth century, all manner of restrictive, oppressive measures had been enacted against Russia's Jews. Young boys were forced into long-term military service; Jews were expelled from many communities and restricted to the western provinces; a whole series of laws, decrees, and enactments regulated Jewish communal, cultural, and religious life.

In the second half of the century, Czar Alexander II, in an attempt to modernize Russian society, undertook reforms designed to integrate the Jew into Russian economic, social, and civil life. "Useful" Jews were permitted to reside in areas which heretofore had been closed to them. Some Jews were admitted to the universities and the professions. It seemed that a bright day was beginning to dawn for Russian Jewry.

The hope was short-lived. Though emancipated in the early 1860s, the peasants were not provided with the means of fending for themselves. They began to crowd the cities, competing with Jewish merchants and artisans. Their plight intensified the revolutionary movement, and this in turn aroused reactionary forces. The abortive Polish revolution of 1863 led to attempts at "Russification" of the Polish provinces and the growth of a Russian chauvinistic nationalism. Jews were accused of economic domination and exploitation. A pogrom in Odessa dramatized the precarious Jewish situation, resulting in the migration of 40,000 east European Jews to America between 1870 and 1880.

The 1870s were but a prelude. The pogroms following Czar Alexander's assassination were justified in Russian government circles as resulting from the Russian populace's reaction to Jewish economic oppression. Indeed, the government felt it had to "shield the Russian population against this harmful Jewish activity." The "Temporary Laws" of May 31, 1882 (known as the "May Laws") forbade Jews to settle in villages; gave villages the right to drive out Jews already living in them; expelled many Jews from such cities as St. Petersburg, Moscow, Kiev; limited the number of Jews in secondary schools and universities; prohibited Jews from entering the legal profession and participating in local government.

The "strong man" of Russian politics at the time, Constantine Pobedonostsev, advocated a police state guided by the Russian Orthodox Church. He had a formula for the solution of the Jewish problem in Russia: one-third of the Jews were to be permitted to die; one-third to convert to Christianity; one-third to emigrate. The Jews took his third plank most seriously. The mass migration begun in the 1880s was brought to an end for Russian Jews by the Revolution of 1917, and for Polish Jews by the restrictive American immigration law of 1924.

In the decade 1880–1890, some 200,000 Jews emigrated from Eastern Europe; by the next decade the number doubled. The great majority came from Russia-Poland, but an appreciable number came from Galicia, Hungary, and Romania.

America was ready to receive them. With the end of the depression of the early 1870s, the country was again expanding, geographically and economically. Industries needed new labor, and the new laboring class needed purveyors of food and clothing. The Jewish immigrants became small merchants and clothing workers to supply the needs. In small towns across the country they opened stores; in the large cities they entered the shops. Peddling continued to be the lot of many, especially those arriving without a craft or trade.

"Happy were they who knew a trade in the old country," wrote immigrant Bernard Weinstein in *Yiddische Yunions in America*. "The tailors, the joiners, and other artisans would obtain employment very quickly. But the bulk of the Jewish immigrants had no vocation."

The clothing shop swallowed up the immigrant, no matter what his state or status in the Old World. "Former Yeshiva students, sales clerks, insurance agents, semi-intellectuals, teachers, bookkeepers, sons-in-law of the well-to-do, storekeepers, merchants, etc., became cloak operators," wrote Dr. B. Hoffman in his *Fufzig yahr klokmacher yunion* (Fifty Years of the Cloak Maker Union).

By and large, the immigrant Jews were looked upon as poor and ignorant masses, even by the sympathetic observer. To the average American, they were pitiful remnants of a peculiar race, rejected by God for its obstinacy, despised by man for its avarice. America was a Christian nation, imbued with the Christian folklore of the Wandering Jew. What better example of this strange, driven wanderer than the bearded, gabardined, impoverished member of this stiff-necked race, now coming in such numbers as to raise the specter of an invasion?

Nor did their well-established Jewish brethren embrace them without reserve. For many they were an annoyance and a threat; for the more compassionate, an object of pity and concern. It is to the credit of the "native" Jew that immigrant relief organizations were established to accept, help, and even welcome the new arrivals. Some felt they were welcoming brothers; most sought to help the immigrants become established and Americanized so that they would not long remain a burden and an embarrassment to the community.

The structured, ordered life of the *shtetl* was replaced by the socially fluid, economically frenetic, and religiously lax life of the American urban center. The change brought disorientation and disintegration in its wake. Life had been difficult in eastern Europe, but withal each man had his place in the family, his name in the community, his seat in the synagogue. Here he was depersonalized, dehumanized—bereft of family, devoid of status.

Added to the normal problems and plight of every immigrant were the anti-Jewish sentiments and acts of the "native" population (mainly immigrants who had arrived a generation earlier), and the discrimination against east European Jews by their west European brethren.

And yet, the new American Jew proved equal to the challenge. His religious laws and values helped in the struggle for physical survival. James B. Reynolds, head worker of the University Settlement House of New York, spoke of the Jewish qualities which impressed him most: "intellectual avidity . . . intensity of feeling, high imagination . . . the extremest idealism, with an utter disregard of the restraining power of circumstance and conditions . . . a character often full of imagination, aspiration and appreciation."

Those qualities of imagination, aspiration, and appreciation fashioned cultural institutions and created cultural values of unusual quality. What drove the immigrants on was the faith that work and will would lift them and especially their children to an easier life in better surroundings. In the meanwhile, workers organized labor unions to demand better conditions, and if necessary to fight for them through public persuasion and the strike. Leaders rose to the fore, meetings were held, a literature was fashioned, and the Jewish immigrant entered American life as a leading actor in the movement for economic justice and societal betterment.

"Perhaps one third of the Jews in the United States are still orthodox, another third neglect religion except on the greatest days of the
religious year . . . another third are in various stages of Reform
. . ." James Parton wrote in 1870. The east European immigration
which followed added to the first two groups, and introduced a new
phenomenon in Jewish religious life in America—the active an-
tireligionists. The latter, comprised of socialists, anarchists, and a variety of freethinkers, launched all manner of antireligious projects. Periodicals in Yiddish and Hebrew launched regular and sustained attacks,
and books and pamphlets were published to argue the falsity of religious doctrine, and to portray organized religion as a regressive, reactionary force serving those elements in society which oppose truth,
suppress freedom, and exploit fellow human beings. Religious laws
and customs were scoffed at and religious leaders attacked in spoken
and written word. Perhaps the most dramatic antireligious projects
were the Yom Kippur balls, held on *Kol Nidre* night, "to eat, drink
and make merry," while most other Jews were observing the day in
prayer and fasting.

Abraham Cahan, himself an immigrant and by then a political
and cultural leader of the New York ghetto, wrote a laudatory appreciation of "The Russian Jew in America" in *The Atlantic Monthly,* July
1898:

*The poor laborer . . . will pinch himself to keep his child at col-
lege, rather than send him to a factory. . . . At least 500 of 1677
students at the New York City College, where tuition and books are
free, are Jewish boys from the East Side. . . .*

In all, cultural life on New York's Lower East Side at the turn of
the century was vital and varied, giving promise of even greater
growth and activity. The Yiddish theater was already becoming a significant cultural force. Periodicals, books, and pamphlets of quality

were beginning to appear in Hebrew.

Thanks to the Franco-Prussian War of 1870 and the Russo-Turkish War in 1877, a Yiddish press was established. The lithographed *Yiddische Zeitung* began to appear in 1870, *Die Post* a year later, the *Israelitische Presse* of Chicago soon after. The language of the early press was a Germanized Yiddish; their social view was conservative and favorable to religion; their existence was precarious, their appearance weekly, monthly, or "on occasion." The daily *Yiddisches Tageblatt* was established in 1885, attaining wide readership and influence until 1928, when it merged with the *Morgen-Zhurnal*. The *Tageblatt* represented the Orthodox viewpoint; its competitors, *Der Volksadvocat* and *Die Volkzeitung,* were critical of the religious "establishment." The *New Yorker Yiddische Folkzeitung* attempted to speak for both socialism and the nascent Jewish nationalism represented by the *Hibat Zion* movement. Since the Yiddish papers were not only sources of opinion but also literary forums, Morris Rosenfeld, the "poet of the ghetto," began his literary career in 1886. The 1890s saw the beginning of the famed *Forverts,* which in time, under the editorship of Abraham Cahan, became the largest Yiddish newspaper in the world, and still appears daily. The outstanding Yiddish journal of literature and thought, *Die Zukunft* (still appearing monthly) began its life in 1892. Its most distinguished editor was the poet, Abraham Liesin. The socialist *Zukunft* was preceded by two years by the anarchist *Freie Arbeiter Shtimme,* which continues its appearance to date.

Beginning with the 1860s, contributions by American Jews began to appear in European Hebrew periodicals. *Ha-Magid* (published in Lyck, East Prussia) of 1864, for example, contained reports and articles from San Francisco, St. Louis, Detroit, Chicago, and New York.

Emek Rephaim by M. E. Holzman, the second Hebrew book to be published in America (1865), is a vigorous and at times vitriolic attack against American Reform rabbis, notably Max Lilienthal and Isaac M. Wise. "A sect has arisen in Israel who attempted to form a code of worship . . . men who call themselves Doctors, and who are in fact destroyers of all that is sacred." *Tuv Taam* (1875), another early Hebrew title, by Aaron Zebi Friedman, was a "vindication of the Jewish mode of slaughtering animals for food called *shehita,*" written in response to an accusation by the Society for the Prevention of Cruelty to Animals that the Jewish method of slaughtering was "cruelty, needlessly inflicted."

Zvi Hirsch Bernstein, a pioneer of both the Yiddish and Hebrew press in America, who arrived after the abortive Polish uprising of 1863, published the first Hebrew newspaper, *Ha-Zofeh ba-Arez ha-Chadashah,* from 1871 to 1876. The periodical served the new immigrants as a tie to the Old World, and helped introduce them to the New.

The second east European immigration, that of the 1880s, produced a Hebrew reading public large enough to encourage the establishment of three Hebrew weeklies in New York. Michael L. Rodkinson, who later translated the Talmud into English, published *Ha-Kol.* Ephraim Deinard, bibliographer and polemicist, whose bibliographical acumen and enterprise helped establish the major Jewish libraries in America, put out thirty-two issues of *Ha-Leumi,* and Wolf Schur began the publication of *Ha-Pisgah.* Schur continued his publication efforts in Chicago, Boston, and Baltimore, undaunted by financial difficulties and undiscouraged by indifference and rebuff to his promotion of early Zionism, and his combatting of assimilatory tendencies in American Jewish life.

In the last two decades of the nineteenth century, to the largely west European, German-speaking, religiously Reform, rapidly assimilating community of merchants and artisans was added an east European, Yiddish-speaking Orthodox or militantly antireligious, culturally separated community of shopworkers and small storekeepers. Though they were united by shared historic memories, a common religious heritage, and a mutuality of concern and responsibility, the separation wrought by differences of language, customs, culture, and economic status seemed more pronounced, real, and immediate. Recrimination abounded. The German Jews saw their Russian brethren as indigent refugees burdened by their barbarian culture and appalling manners.

They were an object of pity and a source of embarrassment. They did not tire of informing their American neighbors that these were "different Jews." At the same time they gave freely of their time and substance to help the Russian Jew become established, educated, and "Americanized." Russian Jews accused the Germans of being economic exploiters, cultural apostates, and religious renegades. But this did not prevent them from taking pride in a political triumph, academic accomplishment, professional distinction, or economic success which came to a member of the often berated and always envied German Jewish community.

As the nineteenth century turned into the twentieth, American Jewry was divided into two communities. At the time the differences seemed so strong that many thought them to be permanent. Others believed that as the immigrant became a resident the schism would heal, and the mutually shared heritage and interests and the overriding consciousness of the unity of Jewish identity would forge a unified and united American Israel.

Meanwhile, immigration continued to be the single most important factor in the American Jewish historic experience. Some 600,000 Jews came to the United States during the last two decades of the nineteenth century. Three times that number arrived in the first two decades of the twentieth. This great immigration wave was temporarily halted by World War I, and was brought to a virtual end by the restrictive immigration laws of 1924. Some ninety-five percent of the immigrants originated in eastern Europe. Most came directly to America: some had remained for shorter or longer periods in west European countries. The rise of Hitler in 1933 precipitated a migration of German Jews to America in significant numbers, and some 150,000 came here in the years following World War II.

The 50,000 Jews of America in 1850 constituted one percent of world Jewry. The million Jews in 1900 were ten percent of the world's Jews. America's five million Jews made up almost half of world Jewry in 1945. At the turn of the century the Jews constituted some one percent of the population of the United States. Within two decades it had risen to three percent, where it has remained to date.

The increase in immigration from eastern Europe was due not so much to worsening conditions in that part of the world as to other factors. The Jews of Russia were far more disadvantaged, discriminated against, and oppressed in the half century before 1870 than in the half century which followed. But in the later years, America offered more opportunities for urban, artisan immigrants; increased communication spread the knowledge about America and its opportunities to the remotest villages; improved means of transportation made the journey seem less fraught with danger; and the earlier immigrants were now subsidizing the later emigration. A good deal of the latter consisted of families which were being reunited—wife and children joining the head of the family, younger brothers and sisters brought over by the first to arrive. In the years 1900–1925, almost one-half of the Jewish immigrants were women, though women constituted no more than one-third of the non-Jewish immigrants. In the same years, children comprised one quarter of the immigrants, twice as many as among non-Jews.

The high percentage of women and children among Jewish immigrants had something to do with the fact that the Jew came to America to stay. Among other European people, a man would go to the New World to "make his fortune" and then return home to his town in Russia, Poland, Italy, or Hungary. The dollars he brought back enabled him to establish a firm economic base for himself and his family. In the years 1908–1925 the remigration percentage was more than fifty percent for Romanians, Magyars, Italians, and Russians. At that same time the percentage of Jews returning to the Old World was only five percent relative to those arriving in the New World. Even more striking is the percentage of returnees to Poland between 1919–1922, when that nation had been restored to independent sovereignty: Poles, 369.5 percent; Ukranians, 56.5 percent; Jews, 0.5 percent.

It was only in comparison to conditions in eastern Europe that America was considered home and haven. In truth, Jews were beset here by economic discrimination, social exclusion, and a pervasive anti-Semitism usually genteel but on occasion overt and blatant. Many neighborhoods, hotels, clubs, and jobs were closed to them. In the first decades of the century the specter of the Jewish international financial conspiracy to dominate the world was raised. After World War I, the fear of the Jewish bolshevik conspiracy to subjugate the Christian world was widely disseminated and discussed by some very "respectable" persons and groups. "The International Jew and his satellites, as the conscious enemies of all that Anglo-Saxons mean by civilization . . ." was "exposed" in Henry Ford's *The Dearborn Independent,* and reprinted in pamphlets, under the title *The International Jew,* which received the widest circulation. The notorious *The Protocols of the Elders of Zion* was published in 1920 to alert America to the Jewish plot, fostered by bolshevists and Zionists, to control the world. American Jews came to know Protestant ministers and Catholic priests who spewed anti-Semitism.

Discrimination and accusations were of course not new experiences for the Jew. But here in America, more than anywhere else, they could be countered and fought in the press, in the court of public opinion as well as of law. Individual Jews and Jewish leaders stood ready to enter the fray. Jewish organizations formed to protect the Jew and defend Judaism were able to invoke the American tradition of rights and freedom, to quote the classic American documents and the words of great Americans, and to enlist the friendship and help of leading Americans who stood vigilant against the importation of Old World prejudices to the New World.

To the land "conceived in liberty" came the immigrant Jews seeking the unalienable rights proclaimed by the Declaration of Independence. They sought little more than the right to *life*—personal security and economic opportunity. Their children waged a valiant battle to secure *liberty*—political and social equality, the right to choose where to live, and the opportunity to work according to one's competence. It was a resolute struggle which gave courage and example to others seeking similar rights and opportunities.

Life secured, liberty established, the generations which followed turned to the Declaration's third promise, *the pursuit of happiness*. In this they have joined other Americans, as the nation enters its third century, on a journey with a goal but no ending.

The immigrants seeking a home found a haven. Their children and their children's children have turned haven into home. This is the story of the generations of American Jews, the story of America itself.

PART ONE

Jews on the Move

1. Early Trickle: 1654–1830

Two weeks after the arrival in New Amsterdam of the twenty-three Jewish refugees from Recife, Brazil, Governor Peter Stuyvesant wrote his employers, the Dutch West India Company in Amsterdam. His letter was dated September 22, 1654:

. . . The Jews who have arrived would nearly all like to remain here, but learning that they (with their customary usury and deceitful trading with the Christians) were very repugnant to the inferior magistrates, as also to the people having the most affection for you; the Deaconry also fearing that owing to their present indigence they might become a charge in the coming winter, we have, for the benefit of this weak and newly developing place and the land in general, deemed it useful to require them in a friendly way to depart; praying also most seriously, in this connection, for ourselves as also for the general community of your worships, that the deceitful race,—such hateful enemies and blasphemers of the name of Christ,—be not allowed further to infect and trouble this new colony, to the detraction of your worships and the dissatisfaction of your worships' most affectionate subjects.

The Amsterdam Jewish community lost little time in interceding on behalf of their coreligionists. Calling themselves "the merchants of the Portuguese Nation residing in" Amsterdam, they sent a petition to the Directors of the West India Company in January 1655. After pointing out the poverty and inability of the Recife Jews to return to Spain or Portugal "because of the Inquisition," they stressed the economic and trade benefits that would accrue to the Company were the Jews allowed to remain in New Amsterdam:

Yonder land is extensive and spacious. The more of loyal people that go to live there, the better it is in regard to the population of the country as in regard to the payment of various excises and taxes which may be imposed there, and in regard to the increase of trade, and also to the importation of all the necessaries that may be sent there.

Your Honors should also consider that the Honorable Lords, the Burgomasters of the City and the Honorable High Illustrious Mighty Lords, the States-General, have in political matters always protected and considered the Jewish nation as upon the same footing as all the inhabitants and burghers. Also it is conditioned in the treaty of perpetual peace with the King of Spain that the Jewish nation shall also enjoy the same liberty as all other inhabitants of these lands.

The telling argument followed:

Your Honors should also please consider that many of the Jewish nation are principal shareholders in the Company. They having always striven their best for the Company, and many of their nation have lost immense and great capital in its shares and obligations. . . .

As foreign nations consent that the Jewish nation may go to live and trade in their territories, how can your Honors forbid the same and refuse transportation to this Portuguese nation who reside here and have been settled here well on to sixty years, many also being born here and confirmed burghers, and this to a land that needs people for its increase?

The profit motive prevailed, and permission was granted by the Company for the Recife Jews to remain in New Amsterdam. On April 25, 1655, Governor Stuyvesant received its decision:

We would have liked to effectuate and fulfill your wishes and request that the new territories should no more be allowed to be infected by people of the Jewish nation, for we foresee therefrom the same difficulties which you fear, but after having further weighed and considered the matter, we observe that this would be somewhat unreasonable and unfair, especially because of the considerable loss sustained by this nation, with others, in the taking of Brazil, as also because of the large amount of capital which they still have invested in the shares of this company. Therefore after many deliberations we have finally decided and resolved to apostille upon a certain petition presented by said Portuguese Jews that these people may travel and trade to and in New Netherland and live and remain there, provided the poor among them shall not become a burden to the company or to the community, but be supported by their own nation. You will now govern yourself accordingly.

Less than a century later, in 1733, the London Jewish community—specifically, three leading members of its Sephardic community—helped dispatch to the new colony of Georgia two groups of London Jews: one made up of forty Sephardim, another of twelve Ashkenazi families. Their motive was a mixture of philanthropy and self-interest: Georgia would serve to relieve the London Jewish magnates of the burden of caring for an ever-increasing number of Jewish poor, and at the same time the existence of an outpost of coreligionists might be economically useful in the future. Contact was maintained: for example, in 1737 Benjamin de Menasseh Mendes sent the Jewish community in Savannah a second Torah, "a Hanukia and a quantity of books for the use of the Congregation."

Two years later, the Reverend S. Quincy described the Jews in a letter from Savannah to his superiors in London's Church of England:

We have here two sorts of Jews, Portuguese and Germans. The first having professed Christianity in Portugal or the Brazils, are more lax in their way, and dispense with a great many of their Jewish Rites, and two younger men, the Sons of a Jew Doctor, Sometimes come to Church, and for these reasons are thought by some people to be Christians but I cannot find that they really are So, only that their education in these Countries where they were oblig'd to appear Christians makes them less rigid and stiff in their way. The German Jews, who are thought the better sort of them [i.e. better Jews], are a great deal more strict in their way and rigid observers of their Law. . . . They all in general behave themselves very well, and are industrious in their business. . . .

The fullest contemporary description of Jewish life in Savannah is found in a letter from the Reverend Bolzius to a fellow minister, the Reverend Johann Heinrich Gallenberg in Halle, dated February 21, 1738. Not only were the Jews resistant to conversion to Christianity but there was strife between the Spanish-Portuguese and the more recent arrivals from Germany.

The Spanish and Portuguese Jews are not so strict insofar as eating is concerned as the others are. They eat, for instance, the beef that comes from the warehouse or that is sold anywhere else. The German Jews, on the other hand, would rather starve than eat meat they do not slaughter themselves.

The German Jews have in Savannah the same liberties as any Englishman. They drill with a rifle, as all the soldiers do. They have no other profession besides farming or dealing in small trade. The latter comes easier to them than the former. They even have a doctor, who has the permission of the Trustees to cure them when they are sick.

The Jews use at their service, which they are holding in an old and miserable hut, men and women separated, the same ceremonies which I have seen in Berlin. A boy speaking several languages and especially good in Hebrew is their reader and he is paid for his services. There are not more than two families who can speak Jewish-German. . . . [t]he Spanish and Portuguese Jews are against the German Jews and they are going to protest the petition by the German Jews to build a synagogue. The German Jews would like to be on good terms with us Salzburgers, and they have done us small favors time and again. But as far as their religion is concerned, they have been obstinate and there is very little that we could do about it.

As the plight of Jews in central Europe worsened, more thought was given to the possibilities for a better life in the New World. The June 1783 issue of *Deutsches Museum* contained an article in the form of a

"Memorial Sent by German Jews to the President of the Continental Congress." While it is doubtful that such a letter was ever sent, its vision of what the new nation, "the thirteen united provinces," the United States, could offer German Jews is enlightening. The author remains unknown, though it has been suggested that the philosopher Moses Mendelssohn might have written it or at least had a hand in its composition.

Many of us . . . have learned with much satisfaction, from the peace made by the mighty American States with England, that wide tracts of land had been ceded to them which are as yet almost uninhabited, . . . and we ask no more than to be permitted to become subjects of these thirteen provinces, and would gladly contribute two-fold taxes for their benefit if we can only obtain permission to establish colonies at our own cost and to engage in agriculture, commerce, arts and sciences. Do we not believe in the same God as the Quakers do? Can our admission become more dangerous and precarious than that of the Quakers? Supposing that two thousand families of us would settle in a desert of America and convert it into a fertile land, will the old inhabitants of the provinces suffer by it? Let the conditions be stated to us, gracious President, under which you will admit us; we will then consider whether we can accept and keep them. . . .

The problems of Jewish life in early America are described in a letter written in 1791 by Rebecca Samuel of Petersburg, Virginia, to her parents in Hamburg, Germany, from *American Jewry,* edited by Jacob R. Marcus. While hailing America as a "wonderful country . . . for the comman man," she announces the family's intention to move to Charleston, South Carolina, in order to be able to live in a more Jewish atmosphere.

Dear parents, I know quite well you will not want me to bring up my children like Gentiles. Here they cannot become anything else. Jewishness is pushed aside here. There are here [in Petersburg] ten or twelve Jews, and they are not worthy of being called Jews. We have a shohet here who goes to market and buys terefah [nonkosher] meat and then brings it home. On Rosh Ha-Shanah [New Year] and on Yom

Kippur [*Day of Atonement*] *the people worshipped here without one sefer torah* [*Scroll of the Law*], *and not one of them wore the tallit* [*prayer shawl*] *or the* arba kanfot [*the small set of fringes worn on the body*], *except Hyman and my Sammy's godfather. The latter is an old man of sixty, a man from Holland. He has been in America for thirty years already; for twenty years he was in Charleston, and he has been living here for four years. He does not want to remain here any longer and will go with us to Charleston. In that place there is a blessed community of three hundred Jews.*

You can believe me that I crave to see a synagogue to which I can go. The way we live now is no life at all. We do not know what the Sabbath and the holidays are. On the Sabbath all the Jewish shops are open; and they do business on that day as they do throughout the whole week. But ours we do not allow to open. With us there is still some Sabbath. You must believe me that in our house we all live as Jews as much as we can.

As for the Gentiles (?), we have nothing to complain about. For the sake of a livelihood we do not have to leave here. Nor do we have to leave because of debts. I believe ever since Hyman has grown up that he has not had it so good. You cannot know what a wonderful country this is for the common man. One can live here peacefully. Hyman made a clock that goes very accurately, just like the one in the Buchenstrasse in Hamburg. Now you can imagine what honors Hyman has been getting here. In all Virginia there is no clock [*like this one*], *and Virginia is the greatest province in the whole of America, and America is the largest section of the world. Now you know what sort of a country this is. It is not too long since Virginia was discovered. It is a young country. And it is amazing to see the business they do in this little Petersburg. At times as many as a thousand hogsheads of tobacco arrive at one time, and each hogshead contains 1,000 and sometimes 1,200 pounds of tobacco. The tobacco is shipped from here to the whole world. . . .*

All the people who hear that we are leaving give us their blessings. They say that it is sinful that such blessed children should be brought up here in Petersburg. My children cannot learn anything here, nothing Jewish, nothing of general culture. My Schoene [*my daughter*],

God bless her, is already three years old. I think it is time that she should learn something, and she has a good head to learn. I have taught her the bedtime prayers and grace after meals in just two lessons. I believe that no one among the Jews here can do as well as she. And my Sammy (born in 1790), God bless him, is already beginning to talk.

While some Christians were interested in encouraging Jewish immigration for purposes of proselytism, others promoted schemes for more utilitarian purposes. One such was W. D. Robinson, a non-Jew of Philadelphia, who published, in 1819 in London, a *Memoir Addressed to Persons of the Jewish Religion in Europe, on the Subject of Emigration to, and Settlement in, One of the Most Eligible Parts of the United States of North America.*

His motivations are unclear. Robinson was a man of vision, and the return of Jews to their Biblical pursuits on the soil of the New World may have excited his imagination. But he was a practical man as well. He was interested in South American trade and had even attempted gunrunning. In any case, his proposal for a large-scale agricultural settlement for Jews, which went unanswered, offers some insights on the status of Jewish immigration in the early nineteenth century:

. . . . Much may be expected from the Jews when placed beyond the reach of want or persecution. They are an industrious, abstemious, and persevering race of people; and when urged by necessity, or animated by hope, they are, unquestionably, capable of making the same exertions as any other part of mankind. Where are the Jewish parents who would not feel delight in beholding their children pursuing the honourable and useful labours of agriculture, in preference to the wretched and menial occupations in which they are now generally engaged? Where is the individual of this class whose bosom would not throb with satisfaction, when he contemplates an establishment of his own brethren, in a country where all can enjoy the same privileges and blessings as the natives themselves? Can it be supposed, that if a prospect so interesting were unfolded to their view, they would be so blind as not to perceive its advantages? Would they not soon contrast their present degraded and persecuted situation with that which awaits

them? No sooner would the first settlement be formed, and its benign effects made known by those who are partakers in it, than we should find thousands of distressed applicants praying to be removed from their hovels to the land of plenty and toleration. Even from the metropolis of the British empire, many families would emigrate, for, notwithstanding, by the laws of Great Britain, and the liberal spirit of British subjects, the Jews are there more secure and happy than in any other part of Europe, they are, nevertheless, excluded from certain political, as well as personal privileges, enjoyed by other classes in society. Besides these considerations, there exist a great number of Jews in London, in wretched condition, who find it difficult to earn a subsistence by occupations of the most degrading kind.

If a Jewish settlement should be established in the United States, on the enlarged scale here laid down, it does not require the gift of prophecy to foresee the result. In a very few years such a settlement would become known to the Jews in every quarter of the globe, and we should find thousands flocking to it, who never before dreamt that such an asylum could be procured in any part of the civilized world. We should behold Jewish agriculture spreading through the American forests; Jewish towns and villages adorning the banks of the Mississippi and Missouri, and the arts, commerce, and manufactures, would advance with the same rapidity in this new settlement, as has been exemplified in all the other agricultural regions of the United States. . . .

Even before the publication of the Robinson *Memoir,* the grand visionary of early American Israel, Mordecai Manual Noah, had published his own call of welcome to potential Jewish immigrants.

Noah was born in Philadelphia in 1785, his father an immigrant from Germany, his mother descended from an early Sephardi American family. He had spent his formative years in Philadelphia, Charleston, and New York, making his living through pen and politicking. From 1813 to 1815 he had served as Consul in Tunis, and on his return became editor of the *National Advocate,* owned by his uncle Naphtali Phillips, a Tammany leader. Noah himself became something of a political force in New York, serving as Sheriff, Surveyor of the

Port, and Associate Justice of the Court of Sessions. He was a moderately successful playwright and a much quoted political writer and essayist.

His Jewish interests were wide and strong. A leading member of the Shearit Israel (Spanish-Portuguese) congregation, he was also a founder of B'nai Jeshurun, the first Ashkenazi congregation in New York. He apparently had a good knowledge of Jewish history and lore, and was always ready to offer his opinion in these fields. His continuing interest, which gave a basic unity to his conception of Jewish life and destiny, was combined with an abiding faith and driving zeal for the reconstitution of a Jewish state. Later he called for a restoration of the Jews in their ancient homeland in Palestine, but his first vision of a new Jewish commonwealth was in America. Appearing in the *Koblenzer Anzeiger* on July 2, 1819, it is nothing less than a manifesto for territorial Zionism, the establishment of a "new Jewish state" in the United States:

Children of Israel, my beloved brethren who believe in Moses and the prophets.

God's people have spread all over the world after leaving their own old country. From that time on they have been subjected to persecution and oppression in all countries, wherever they settled among foreign peoples. This persecution and oppression will not cease despite the sympathy of many good men unless the Jews choose to assimilate totally among the peoples with whom they live, giving up their own glorious nationality. To exterminate Jews from the face of the earth—this is the goal of all their adversaries. But the Jews should not heed all the arguments to which they are exposed. The time has come for this great people, weakened and suppressed during its exile, to gather again and raise itself up . . . the abundance of spiritual powers and wealth possessed by the Jews enables them to choose for themselves a new fatherland where they will be free to preserve their nationality; through a speedy development of their ethical and physical powers, they will be able to advance and become one of the leading nations of the world. Old Palestine, the cradle of your forefathers, is in the hands of the rough Muslims whose regime excludes all political and civil freedom. The Jews cannot, therefore, go to Palestine for the purpose of restoring their former national glory and achieving independence. But another glorious country is beckoning to them from afar. Free America, with its immeasurably vast stretches of land, surpassing almost all other countries in its natural resources and fertility, welcomes the suppressed peoples of the old world escaping from religious fanaticism and party strife. Where in all the world can another country be found so suitable for extended commerce and for growing rich as America, whose geographical situation makes her a center of navigation and a hub of world trade.

The Congress in Washington, which has already wisely agreed to a suggested plan for the restoration of the Jews, will readily assign an appropriate portion of land for settlement for the purpose of creating a new Jewish state. Under the protection of the great American Union this state could equal Palestine in size, but would have many advantages.

When I think of the brilliant new era of national glory awaiting one of the oldest peoples, a people which has retained its religion and the ancestral traditions through all suffering and distress, and which has diligently preserved its national conscience—when I think of all that— there rises within me a prayer: may they not be tardy in beginning this honorable work and complete it speedily with united powers.

In 1820 Noah followed his call with a petition to the legislature of the state of New York to sell him Grand Island, near Buffalo, for the establishment of a Jewish commonwealth. A committee reported favorably on the request, but no bill was passed. A year later he proposed a Jewish settlement in Newport, Rhode Island.

In the columns of the *National Advocate,* which he edited, Noah continued to propagate his vision of a Jewish state in America. From time to time other newspapers took up his proposal and gave it publicity and approval, as in the case of the New York *Commercial Advertiser,* October 16, 1822:

THE JEWS

We hastily mentioned some days ago that Mr. Noah had received an appointment from his European brethren. To prevent a construction being placed upon it which facts will not warrant, we took occasion to make inquiry of him relative to the report, and learn that it was a diploma from Berlin, constituting him extraordinary member and correspondent for the United States, of the society for the advancement of science and knowledge among the Jews—which diploma was accompanied by a letter highly complimentary to this country. It seems (as we are informed) that the project originally started by Mr. Noah of bringing a colony of Jews to this country to settle in Grand Island, or some other part of the Union, has created a profound interest among this ancient and persecuted people. The conclusion of the continental war has brought back to their coffers an immense sum in cash with which the armies of Europe were supplied, and the same is now lying useless, or producing a very trifling interest. The agency which they exercised in those wars—the importance and political weight of their great bankers, the wealth of the agriculturalists—are singularly contrasted with the national oppression under which they live; and as this people advance in the higher departments of knowledge, they cannot but turn their attention to this happy land, where perfect freedom awaits them.

The wealth and enterprise of the Jews would be a great auxiliary to the commercial and manufacturing, if not agricultural, interests of the United States. A new generation, born in more enlightened times, and having the benefit of education, would be free from those errors generally imputed to the Jews, and participating in the blessings of liberty, would have every inducement to become valuable members of society. That toleration and mildness upon which the Christian religion is founded, will lend its influence to the neglected children of Israel, who, in the United States, can find a home undisturbed—land which they dare call their own; laws which they will assist in making; magistrates of which they may be of the number; protection, freedom, and as they comport themselves respect and consideration. We shall not be surprised if the views which shall be spread before them should lead to a valuable emigration of these people; and when they perceive one of their brethren honored with the highest executive office of the metropolis of the Union, and exercising a jurisdiction over Christians with Christian justice, they will be satisfied of the practical utility of

those institutions which proclaim equal freedom and privileges to all.
We have obtained a copy of the letter addressed to Mr. Noah, and
herewith subjoin it.

This supportive editorial was occasioned by a letter which Noah had
received from the Verein für Kultur und Wissenschaft der Juden, an
organization of some seventy young Jewish intellectuals in Germany
founded "to improve the social condition of the Jews" and to stem the
conversions to Christianity which were then plaguing the Berlin Jewish community. Responding to Noah's call for emigration to free
America, the society had commended his efforts, hailed the "public
freedom" and "general happiness" in America, and asked specific information about Jews in America. It had invited the establishment of a
branch society in America that would join with the European parent
body in "promoting the emigration of European Jews to the United
States." Of the signatories to the letter, Leopold Zunz became the
leading figure in the development of Judische Wissenschaft in Germany; Moses Moser became a businessman scholar; Eduard Gans, the
president, converted to Christianity to gain a professorship at the University of Berlin; and Leo Wolf, a physician, later emigrated to
America.

Noah was finally able to persuade a friend to buy a section of Grand
Island, and set about to dedicate it in a worthy manner. Booming can-
non announced the day of dedication, September 15, 1825. Military
and Masonic formations led a grand march to a local church, where
the dedication took place. (There were not enough boats to convey the
assembled multitude to Grand Island.) And "Mordecai Manuel Noah,
Citizen of the United States of America, late Consul of the said States
for the City and Kingdom of Tunis, High Sheriff of New York, Coun-
sellor at Law, and by the grace of God Governor and Judge of Israel,"
established a Jewish community and invited the emigration of the Jewish youth of the world to it. He levied a poll tax of three *shekels* or one
Spanish dollar

. . . upon each Jew throughout the world, for the purpose of defraying
the various expenses of reorganizing the government, of aiding emigrants
in the purchase of agricultural implements, providing for their imme-

diate wants and comforts, and assisting their families in making their first settlements . . . in furtherance of the laudable objects connected with the restoration of the people and the glory of the Jewish nation.

All that remains of the proposed Jewish commonwealth, which Noah named *Ararat,* are the newspaper accounts and the cornerstone which is now in a Buffalo museum.

Another, more poetic invitation to fellow Jews was published in *Fancy's Sketch Book.* The verses were written in 1833 by Penina Moise, an author and educator living in Charleston, South Carolina:

TO PERSECUTED FOREIGNERS
Penina Moise

Fly from the soil whose desolating creed,
Outraging faith, makes human victims bleed.
Welcome! where every Muse has reared a shrine,
The aspect of wild Freedom to refine.

Upon *our* Chieftain's brow no crown appears;
No gems are mingled with his silver hairs,
Enough that Laurels bloom amid its snows,
Enriched with these, the sage all else foregoes.

If thou art one of that oppressed race,
Whose pilgrimage from Palestine we trace,
Brave the Atlantic—Hope's broad anchor weigh,
A Western Sun will gild your future day.

Zeal is not blind in this our temp'rate soil;
She has no scourge to make the soul recoil.
Her darkness vanished when our stars did flash;
Her red arm grasped by Reason dropt the lash.

Our Union, Liberty and Peace imparts,
Stampt on our standards, graven on our hearts,
The first, from crush'd Ambition's ruin rose,
The last, on Victory's field spontaneous grows.

> Rise, then, elastic from Oppression's tread,
> Come and repose on Plenty's flowery bed.
> Oh! not as Strangers shall your welcome be,
> Come to the homes and bosoms of the free!

But neither poetry, emigration schemes, nor restoration projects brought Jews in large numbers to the shores of America. In 1840, the Jews of the United States numbered no more than 15,000. What urging and invitation could not effect in the decades before, tragic circumstances and dire need were to accomplish in the years following.

2. The Flow of German Jews:
1830–1880

I n the years from 1840 to 1850, the Jewish population of the United States rose from 15,000 to 50,000. By the next decade it had more than tripled. The tenfold expansion in twenty years was due both to worsening political and economic conditions for the Jew in post-Napoleonic Europe and to a rapidly expanding America which opened welcoming doors to needed populations. The Jewish newcomers were part of an unprecedented surge which saw immigration figures rise from 138,393 (1820–1830) to 2,799,423 (1850–1860). By the 1830s, immigrants from Germany began to join those from Great Britain. Among these were an ever-increasing number of Jews, largely from Bavaria and later from areas north and east of it. An emancipation in which reality did not match promise, an economy which became ever more restrictive to a rising Jewish professional and mercantile class, a resurgence of a xenophobic nationalism—all contributed to the decision of many young Jews to seek fortune and future in the new land of freedom and promise.

Articles in the *Allgemeine Zeitung des Judentums* * reported on the

* Unless otherwise noted, the translations on pages 36–40 are by Dr. Rudolf Glanz, and are reproduced with YIVO's permission from his article entitled "Source Materials on the History of Jewish Immigration to the United States 1800–1880" in *YIVO Annual* VI, 1951, pp. 73–156.

growing emigration and followed its development. Two selections from issues published in September 1837 describe the phenomenon:

[*From Bavaria*] . . . They are emigrating, indeed. *We have young men who have completed their apprenticeship and journeymen's years of travel just as precisely as any one of another faith, who can legally prove possession of no inconsiderable fortune, who meet all the requirements that may be made of them, and yet cannot obtain letters of protection and domicile on account of their registration number. What should such people do, who have sacrificed half their fortune in legal proceedings in order to obtain their object?* . . .

. . . What else should they do but seek a new fatherland, where they should exercise the profession they had learned, to show off their wares, their knowledge and their learning. A young man, capable and a professional, applied to his district court . . . in the Retzat district for a certificate of protection. It was denied to him at the first tribunal as well as repeatedly at the higher ones. He made a last attempt to obtain it, but simultaneously annexed his petition to have his passport permitting him to go abroad drawn up. . . . The petitioner received the latter and emigrated.

Jews were in the vanguard of emigration from Germany, actually leaving while Christians were still making up their minds. The February 14, 1839 *Allgemeine Zeitung* published the following comment from Germany: "Wuerzburg, Jan. 16 (Private communication). The departures to America on the part of Jews of our district, I fear, will be very numerous. In the *Intelligenzblatt* No. 8 of this year, already *eight Jewish emigrants* have been brought to public notice. By all accounts, many Christian families, too, have made up their minds to do likewise." There were other differences as well between Jewish and Christian emigration. On May 4, 1839, a further comment from Germany was published:

Wuerzburg, April 12 (Private communication) . . . An interesting observation strikes the observer in looking over the names of those listed for emigration. When comparing the gentile with the Jewish emigrants one finds that the former have more family groups than single persons, the latter by far more single persons than families. From this one might also draw a conclusion as to the motives for emigration. The Jewish emigration appears to be due less to greed for gain than to the consciousness of being unable in any other way to achieve independence or to found a family.

Although the emigrants left filled with hope, emigration caused particular hardship to the small Jewish communities left behind. Also, the German press voiced jubilation over the number of Jews departing, evoking bitter rejoinders. The *Allgemeine Zeitung* printed communications concerning this situation, as seen in two reports published March 30 and April 2, 1839:

Wuerzburg, March 10 (Private communication). It was possible to foresee that emigration would not be inconsiderable this year; but unfortunately it was far greater than had been surmised! I say unfortunately because in our condition this will work perceptible disadvantages. Many a small community may easily be compelled to give up public worship and its school, because it may be unable to pay the teachers and religious functionaries, unless certain provisions are made by the state. From certain places, in which there are 30–40 Jewish families, 15–20 persons or more are leaving, and, at that, mostly young and hard-working people. At Riedenburg, a village in the province of Brueckenau, an old man of eighty-five has decided to migrate to America.

Munich, March 10 (Private communication). Cases of emigration to America are ever and ever increasing in number. As often, and that is almost daily, as good letters come in from the emigrants, more people make up their minds anew to take up their wanderer's staff. From tiny Hagenbach, a townlet in central Franconia, twelve young men are leaving after Passover. In Warnbach nearby there are almost no young folks to be found any longer, save those who are without means. . . . Besides, not only artisans and merchants are emigrating but also men of the learned class, since the prospects for rabbinical or medical positions are not particularly bright owing to the vast number of candidates.

Indeed we hear that many papers are jubilant over the departure of such large groups of Jews and they express the joyous and pious wish that those remaining behind may follow those who have gone ahead; but we reply to them that to get rid of a companionship like theirs involves for us at least the exercise of self-control and self-denial, which cost the emigrants few tears, and which will some day perhaps give them some happy hours.

Occasionally the *Allgemeine Zeitung* published warnings about anti-Semitism in America that was directed at the new immigrants:

Boston, Nov. 15 (Private communication) [published January 9, 1841]
. . . There are men here also who would exploit the Jew-hatred which echoes so abundantly here from Europe. There are starving journalists, who cannot get a job. The drawback is indeed the enormously increased and ever-swelling immigration from Europe. There is, on the one hand, a large number of such Europeans who, for lack of profitable activity, turn their eyes toward the tranquility of their industrious neighbors and do not shrink from attempts to sow the seeds of suspicion of natives among the multitude. On the other hand, there come over also many Jewish individuals who are not in the least familiar with the spirit of American life and qualified for it, a circumstance to be deplored but which cannot be of the least consequence as soon as one weighs the enormous number of Christians who immigrate and know and comprehend just as little about what they find here and what they are here to do . . . Recently several journals have busied themselves extensively with the Jews, that is with those who have immigrated and are immigrating. One newspaper, the Volksfreund, *published in Lancaster, in the state of Ohio, is seeking to stir up the most hateful things. It charges that Jews do not engage in working in the fields, that when they come to America, they peddle or pose as scholars, preachers and poets (!); that they had had an inclination toward perpetrating fraud on the Christians, that marriages between Jews and Christians are not tolerated (!), that they cannot become good Republicans, and that they should be dispatched to Palestine (!), for which a society should be formed. . . .*

New York, Sept. 20 [1850]. Who would believe that the wild appetite for Jew-baiting crosses over even to North America? And who brings it there? Irish emigrants or rather dregs. . . . The Weserzeitung *reports the following: A shocking event occurred last Sunday. It was the eve of the great Day of Atonement of the Jews and they all were in the synagogue. The house in which the synagogue is situated is occupied both by Jews and by Irish families. During the gathering of the congregation some one brought a street woman into the rear building: a short time later a rumor spread that the Jews had murdered a Gentile girl for their holiday. About 10:30 a crowd of some 500 men burst into the house, broke down the doors and literally pulled from their beds the sleeping women, one of whom was in childbed next to a sick husband. A most shocking riot was perpetrated; everyone who resisted was knocked down, a little box of jewelry to the amount of 63 dollars was stolen from a peddler. The remarkable thing about the affair is that three Irish policemen were the leaders of this raging mob, and the tumult thereby acquired a sort of official character, whereas, after all, the authorities had remained totally ignorant of this riot.*

However, more favorable conditions were reported elsewhere, as noted in the 1846 *Wiener Jahrbuch fuer Israeliten:* "Prosperity is growing day by day; those who had immigrated as beggars are rich after 6–10 years; and the name German Jew has become here a name of honor and a guarantee of integrity and honesty. The congregation in Baltimore, which consists mostly of Germans, and particularly of Bavarians, dedicated a new, magnificent synagogue on October 26." But in 1873, the murder of a peddler was reported in the weekly paper, *Die Deborah* (no. 21):

The Deutsche Zeitung *of Baton Rouge, Louisiana reports:*
"THREE NEGROES LYNCHED. *Last week we reported that a German peddler had been murdered and robbed by some negroes at the ferry dock in West Baton Rouge. The slain man was a Jew and was given a decent burial by the Jewish Charity Organization in Baton Rouge. The culprits were unable to enjoy their booty for long; already the next morning four negroes were seized on suspicion; after a brief examina-*

*tion one of them was set at liberty; but the other three, still in posses-
sion of their booty, were hanged on the nearest tree without loss of
time, by the outraged citizens. Such a procedure, to be sure, goes far
beyond the limits of the law; but if one ponders that convicted mur-
derers get off with one day in the penitentiary, a bit of lynch procedure like this is always to be preferred in the interest of personal
security."*

*To this we add that the murdered man's name was Jacob Kriss and
that he was supposed to have emigrated from Germany to New Orleans three months ago. Through the efforts of Mr. A. Kowalski it was
possible to give the murdered man a decent burial in the local Jewish
cemetery, but no further particulars about the unfortunate man could
be learned. Mr. Kowalski is the elder of the local Jewish congregation
and was very active in the matter; but in the execution of the negroes
neither he nor any other Jew took part.*

Newly formed Jewish communities were advertising for religious
functionaries in the German Jewish press. In 1848 Dr. Max Lilienthal,
a rabbi first in New York and later in Cincinnati, issued a warning in
the *Allgemeine Zeitung* about the precariousness of positions in
American synagogues:

*. . . I entreat the cantors and teachers to give heed . . . in order
that, on the one hand, they might not be quick with their decisions to
emigrate, and on the other hand, if they read of a position in America
sent out as an advertisement, they might well bethink themselves that
they have to exchange a permanent position in their fatherland for a
precarious, annual appointment here. It is extremely painful to me to
hear accomplished men complain in my house that they have nothing
more left but to take the pack onto the back.*

Many rabbis, cantors, and teachers did come to America, filling the
needs of the New World. Some pursued their old professions; others
turned to new pursuits. One who came and encouraged others to follow was Dr. Rothenheim, a Reform rabbi in Cincinnati, who wrote of
the "great country" in a poem published in the 1855–56 *Die
Deborah*:

THE JEWISH EMIGRANT

. . . Far, far toward the West,
There is a great country,
Far across the sea it holds out
To us its brotherly hand.
    Thither shall we cross over,
    There shall be the home
    Where we can find rest
    From suffering, ignominy and agony.

The Occident, a monthly edited by Isaac Leeser and published in Philadelphia, described the variety of Jewish pursuits in its 1857–58 issues:

The clothing, shoe, dry goods, and liquor, together with jewelry and rarely the grocery trade, are nearly everywhere their sole pursuit; only a few are actually engaged in shoemaking, tailoring, watchmaking, cabinetwork, upholstery, and similar branches and still wherever they seriously apply themselves for labor, they meet with average success. We do not mean, however, to assert that the above-enumerated are the only means of support of the Jews in America; for we know well enough that we have lawyers, medical doctors, bankers, some politicians and place-men, a few teachers, authors and ministers, some shipping-merchants and auctioneers, and a very few farmers, and here and there a butcher, a baker, a distiller, a brewer, a tavern-keeper, a manufacturer, a miner, a billiard-table-maker, an apothecary, a smith, a produce and cattle-dealer, a painter and glazier, and perhaps other craftsmen. But in the main we may assert that commerce is the chief means of support for Israelites, all over the country.

Peddling, though widespread, was looked down upon by some:

Many may perhaps be assisted as hitherto, by making up for them a small pack of any sort of valuable goods and sending them into the country to try their luck at peddling among the farmers, and in the small towns; and of these, we acknowledge, up to the present time many have done well and become at length merchants of higher pre-

tensions. Nevertheless this system must come to an end; it is nearly overdone now; besides which, it is illegal in several states; for even could a license for peddling be secured, it will be at such a high rate, and clogged with so many restrictions, as either to be unattainable by the poor, or worthless for all practical purposes if they would strictly comply with the terms of law, often arbitrary and vexatious in the restrictions they contain. The very nature, moreover, of seeking a livelihood by means of small trading of this sort, has a debasing influence on the mind.

Regardless of all the difficulties, immigration and immigrant life in the quarter century prior to the Civil War evoked enthusiasm in some quarters, as seen in this 1860 report printed in *Die Deborah:* *

How wonderfully, how very beneficially conditions have changed since 1837! In those days, when a Europe-weary Jewish journeyman used to tie up his valise and say: "I am emigrating to America," it meant that he, too, was a black sheep that was good for nothing at home and who was no loss. If a stout-hearted youth, tired of dealing in second-hand goods and snail-paced commerce, came to his parents and said: "I feel within me the power for something more substantial; let me go across the sea," the parents wept and resisted, as if their son were going to the other world, from which they could hope for neither reunion nor return. If an educated Jew, because of discriminatory laws had no prospect of either a good position or a good future, expressed his determination to go to live in the land of freedom, the father used to bewail the money he had spent in vain on his education, and the aristocracy could not comprehend at all how an educated man could so lower himself that he could prefer the distant America, the land of the

---

* Because the longer prose excerpts quoted in this book are set in text (non-italic) type, an ornament is placed at the beginning and a hairline rule at the end of these selections so that the reader can easily tell where quoted material ends and the text resumes.

uneducated, the land of the blacks and Indians, to beautiful Europe.

How conditions have changed! These unnoticed artisans, these youthful adventurers have since then become the supporters of their kinfolk in the old fatherland, the founders of unhoped-for happiness of their people, have become men of consequence and influence in the commercial Old and New World!

Many, very many of these beggarly-poor emigrants are nowadays at the head of business concerns that own enormous property, command unlimited credit and amass every single year an independent fortune in pure profit. And these gigantic fortunes have been honestly and uprightly acquired, no stain, no shadow, no blame clings to them. . . .

To be sure, not all of them have reached such heights; particularly those who came over accompanied by families or those, who in the old fatherland had never learned to look out beyond the old fence in Wolfenkukuksheim, have never succeeded as they might have dreamed during the voyage across the ocean. Yet we can count hundreds of the former group. The signs of their enterprises blaze in all the big commercial cities of the Union, such as New York, Philadelphia, Cincinnati, St. Louis, New Orleans. . . .

The economic boom in post–Civil War America made for a resurgence of immigration. In anticipation of an ever swelling wave of immigrants, *Die Deborah* (1866–67) offered a warning and plea to parents in Europe to see to it that ". . . their children should first learn English before they study any foreign language whatever. Thereby they open to them an opportunity to migrate to the United States and to adjust themselves easily."

Despite the fresh winds of freedom promised after the illiberality and bigotry of the post-Napoleonic world, some Jewish leaders felt that inbred prejudice made the situation of the Jew in Europe intolerable; the only solution was a new life in the free New World. In the *Oesterreichisches Central Organ,* May 6, 1848, a call for emigration was written by Leopold Kompert, a gifted writer living in Vienna, who had already attained a literary reputation for his tales of Jewish life. A proponent of the Revolution of 1848, and deeply distressed by anti-Jewish disturbances in Prague and Bohemia, he concluded that a mass movement to America was the appropriate and prudent Jewish response:

ON TO AMERICA
Leopold Kompert

> The harvest is past,
> the summer is ended,
> and we are not saved.
> —JEREMIAH 8:20

No help has come to us! The sun of freedom has risen for the Fatherland; for us it is merely a bloody northern light. The larks of salvation are caroling in the free atmosphere; for us they are merely screeching, stormy petrels. The glow of shame and quivering wrath overwhelm us when we think of the terrible hair-raising experiences that these last weeks have brought us! Because slavish hordes and shopkeeper-like scamps did not and still do not understand the spirit of freedom, *we* must pay for it. God forbid that we hold our head ready for every blow of the club, that our eye tremble before every flash of our great and small tyrants! It has gone so far that at any hour which has brought freedom into the land, there is no other desire in us save to get out of the way of *this* freedom!

They don't want it any other way and so let it be! This is not the first time that we bow to their will. For centuries our history has been nothing but mute assent to every affliction imposed, to every torture and coercion! But always to yield, always to bow our head? Once, with the permission of the "sovereign people," we want to lose our patience; for once we want to refuse—and then to get out of the way!

That is to say to America! You who do not understand the essence of history, recognize its hint in this—that four centuries ago, exactly when the Jews were persecuted most fiercely, a Genoese had to hatch out in his hot brain the creative idea of a new world, that it gave him no rest until a Spanish queen, whose general conjured up the dark form of a Torquemada and his Dominican monks bespattered with the blood of thousands of our brethren, until, we say, Isabella of Spain allowed her admiral to discover America. Our yearning now goes out to that same America, thither should you depart! "Up and to America!" We know all of your objections, but only those of little faith and the faint-hearted will listen to them. The brave, the man of resolution will not! And can you give us no other counsel, ask the others, than to take up the wanderer's staff, and with wife and child to seek the far-off, strange land? Shall we abandon the soil that has begat us, and nourished us and in which we bury our dead? Methinks I hear already something about the fleshpots of Egypt, breathe in the exhalation of golden broth and beef a la mode—but I also see the people who are poking the fire and, from the flames of hatred, prejudice and narrowmindedness fetch its daily mess; by God, whoever has a palate for it, let him stay and gorge himself!

Two verses there are which at this time can serve as starting points for us. Moses spoke one: "Stand firm and still"; and Jeremiah the other: "The harvest is past, the summer is ended, and we are not saved."

To which verse do I give preference? To stand still and wait, bide patiently until all clashing interests are propitiated and expiated, until the spirit of humaneness has come out victor? Or since "no help has come to us"—to find it and leave for America?

It seems to me these two verses can well be combined! May those in our fatherland who wish "to stand firm and still" base that viewpoint in the sand of the future! We do not wish to hinder them from so doing, we wish to supply them with building stones for it ourselves, but to the other oppressed and downtrodden, the expelled and impoverished and plundered in the notorious communities, to all of whom "liberty" has brought calamity, to all those whom their heart tells: "For a long time to come we shall be unable to enjoy tranquility in the fatherland, we cannot forthwith change ourselves, nor them either, decades are necessary in order to introduce the first preparations for peace''—to all these we say: "For us no help has come. Seek it out in far-off America.'' . . .

Following Kompert's article, a committee was organized to aid emigration. Isidor Busch, editor of the *Central Organ*, saw its work as not only raising funds but also being ready "to serve our brethren with word and deed both *here* and *on the other side*.''

Kompert's eloquent plea and Busch's zealous organizational work struck fertile ground. Emigration was placed on the agenda of Jewish concern and enterprise, with committees established in Bohemia and Austria. The Vienna committee drafted an actual "Program of the Society for Jewish Emigration to the United States of America,'' which appeared in a later issue of the *Central Organ:*

ON TO AMERICA!
Isidor Busch

What have you here
and whom have you here,
that you wish to dig
your grave here?

With these words of the prophet we associate ourselves with the view, which is so zealously advocated by this journal, in regard to emigration to America. Yes, [on] to America! Become human beings, become free. Then you can be Jews according to the word and will of God. . . .

"In order to direct the emigration to America there has been organized by the emigrating Israelites in Pest a temporary committee, which

"(a) Gathers all necessary data and information about the ways and

means of overseas migration and settlement. For this purpose the committee is in touch with men at home and abroad who are in a position
to provide the most necessary and most accurate information regarding
this subject. At the earliest possible date it will also dispatch a commission, consisting of the most conscientious persons, equipped with
all the necessary qualifications and knowledge, to North America in
order there to work out the immediate measures concerning the purchase of property in that land;

"(b) The committee will conduct an accurate enrollment of all prospective emigrants possessing the necessary qualifications and
resources;

"(c) It will extend its operations to the procurement of means for
poor but qualified emigrants.

"(d) From time to time the committee will issue useful communications about the ways and means and progress of its
activity. . . ."

A suggestion for the establishment of a stock company to finance
emigration and colonization came from Brody, Galicia, with specific
suggestions for the sales of shares, amortization, and the like. The letter was signed "The Eternal Jew":

. . . We do not know whether a similar idea lay at the basis of Sir
Moses Montefiore's erstwhile project; either this is the case or, in any
event, the honorable Baronet should make it his own as a result of our
proposal! In reality nothing could be more serviceable to the inten-
tions of this noble friend of humanity, inasmuch as otherwise the Russian Israelites, accustomed to bondage and darkness, would hardly
make up their minds to step into entirely new surroundings, whereas a
Jewish colony from Galicia might entice them as a new home! Besides, the financial part would be well-nigh taken care of, and there
would remain nothing but to work out the plan in detail and to issue
the necessary programs in German and Hebrew. . . .

But voices opposing immigration were also aired:

AN OPEN LETTER TO ALL
PROSPECTIVE EMIGRANTS,
PARTICULARLY TO MR. LEOPOLD
KOMPERT
David Mendl

. . . Tell me you, who possibly know it better, what great calamity has befallen Israel that you wish to break the ties that bind you to the fatherland? Have they wanted to deprive us of our nationality, of our faith, somewhat as in the time of Antiochus? Have they stacked funeral piles for us as for heretics? Have they consigned our suckling babes to death in the waters? Nothing of the kind (we give thanks for that). The great giant Austria that had long lain asleep in chains has awakened; it has shaken its mighty arms and flung far away the easily-broken chains; several links of these chains hit some of our coreligionists.

The press has become free, and squibs against the Jews and Jewish emancipation have issued from the rabble and come into the hands of the rabble; does that mean anything more than that street loafers have this time begun systematically the old cry of Hep! Hep!? The bureaucracy, formerly the only legitimate power in the land, has been overthrown; its plunder-thirsty mob utilized the momentary, apparent weakness of the government to pillage Jewish residences and shops. Where it came to excesses, the narrowminded bourgeois magistrates decreed the expulsion of the Jews from those places. However, everywhere the better elements, the intellectuals, have warmly stood up for us. Writers have disavowed those squibs. The authorities, the army and the National Guard, even Christian clergymen have made sacrifices to protect the lives and property of the Jews; indeed, among Germans, Czechs, and Magyars influential voices have been heard in behalf of our rights and our freedom. Yes, while the tree of freedom showed hideous excrescences in many a place, it has borne precious fruits elsewhere; in many places the fraternization of Christian and Jewish residents was speedily and completely restored. . . .

If peril indeed does threaten the Jews, it is your sacred duty to stand beside your brethren, to battle and to wrestle, to triumph or to fall with them. Consider well before you take the step for a voyage to America; think how you would feel if a storm on the open sea were to remind you that at the same moment perhaps a still more hazardous storm is breaking over those that stayed behind, and that you have withdrawn your strongest arms from helping them. . . .

And, to consider the subject from another point of view, I ask: "Do you really believe that you will find in America the yearned-for Jerusalem?" Where *slavery* is still tolerated as a right there is no guarantee for the equality rights of the free; there rude force can turn at any moment against the weaker. Here, however, the conditions are better; old prejudices disappearing, law and justice are unfurling their banners in the land; the spirit is free of every fetter and will forcibly smash all other oppressive bonds to smithereens. The Jew also will be given back his human dignity. And even if some time is still to elapse until our salvation is realized and even if many struggles and suffering still await us, we want to hold fast and loyally to our fatherland. There will always be time to emigrate should we again see ourselves disappointed, in spite of all human precaution, in spite of all reason.

David Mendl's call for patience and faith in the regeneration of Europe was roundly rejected by the editor of the *Central Organ*. By the end of 1848, Isidor Busch and his family were on their way; they arrived in New York in January 1849, and that same year Busch began the publication of the German-language *Israels Herold*. Although short-lived, it had the distinction of being the first Jewish weekly in America. Busch went on to St. Louis, where he became a vintner, a leading abolitionist, and a political figure of some influence.

Young Adolf Brandeis was another who heeded the "On to America" call. Departing his native Prague in August 1848, he was a vanguard emissary of the prominent Wehle and Brandeis families who came, twenty-six strong, eight months later. Adolph eventually became the father of Louis D. Brandeis, who in turn became Supreme Court justice and a Zionist leader.

Many others who answered that same call continued traveling after they reached the shores of the promised land. With packs on backs, they set out on the backroads of rural America, peddling their wares and notions, and formed a mercantile network supplying the farmers with their needs. As they sold their goods they also provided their isolated and often lonely customers with news, gossip, and strands of culture. The peddler's arrival was a special event, breaking up the monotony of the long days of drudgery that farming required; he became an instrument of communication, culture, and consolidation in mid–nineteenth-century rural America.

Our knowledge of American life in the mid-nineteenth century is vastly enriched by diaries and memoirs of those Jews who took to peddling. The three accounts that follow are excerpted from *Memoirs of American Jews, 1775–1865,* edited by Jacob Rader Marcus:

PILGRIM FATHER OF PITTSBURGH JEWRY
William Frank

William Frank was one of the three or four men who founded the Jewish community of Pittsburgh in the fall of 1846. . . . He became a peddler in eastern Pennsylvania and thence went farther west. Probably because he lacked capital, he bypassed Pittsburgh and continued his trade in eastern Ohio.——J.R.M.

. . . The ship, "The Great Eagle," a large sailing vessel sailed at [the] end of thirty days. I was on the ship only one hour when I became violently seasick, which lasted three days, during which I wished many times that I had remained in Havre. I was quite well during the remainder of the journey, which was forty-nine days, landing in New York on May 1st, 1840.

Here again I had a cousin living by the name of Frank. I hunted him up and remained with him overnight. He loaned me $3 with which to reach Philadelphia, where my stepbrother, Phillip Frank, lived. He was a shoemaker and had several journeymen working for him. He had a nice business but was a poor manager, and his wife could spend more than three men could earn. He had made his start by peddling merchandise and had about four dollars' worth of odds and ends in a handkerchief, which he gave me to sell. I remained in Philadelphia seven weeks and purchased additional goods each day. [I] paid my lodging, $3 per week, to my sister-in-law. . . .

During these weeks I made the acquaintance [of] and purchased goods from Blum & Simpson, who gave me credit for goods to the extent of $100, to go peddling out of the city. I peddled in Lancaster County [Pennsylvania] one year and sent my parents $700, for them and my sister Babet and brother Moses to come to America with. They came, but my sainted mother lived only six months after arrival.

Before the family came, I had gone in partnership with David Strasburger in Kilgore, Carroll County, O., where we kept store and "batchelor hall" for a time, when Strasburger married, and we moved to Franklin, Harrison County [Ohio?].

🌿

PEDDLER IN MISSISSIPPI
Henry Seessel

Henry Seessel (1822–1911) migrated to New Orleans [ca. 1843], via Paris and Havre. . . .

He went north to Natchez, and, before he finally settled down for life in Memphis in 1857, he had worked and done business also in Vicksburg, in Cincinnati, in Lexington, Kentucky, in New Orleans, and in Richmond and Milliken's Bend, in the state of Louisiana. In between he had fought for a year in the Mexican War as a member of Cassius M. Clay's company in the Third Regiment of Kentucky Mounted Volunteers (1846–47). . . .

Seessel was in many respects the typical Jewish émigré from central Europe. . . . For years he was an itinerant merchant, peddling clothes and jewelry; he quarreled with his family; he was a trunk-

*maker, a storekeeper, a stock raiser, a saloonkeeper, and a butcher. . . .——*J.R.M.

Now, towards the end of the fourth year [in Paris], I received a letter from my brother, who at that time was living in Natchez, Miss., asking me if I wanted to come over to this country; if so, that he would send me the money to come with, provided I had none myself. I answered and asked him to send the money and I would come. . . .

Finally I made up my mind to go. Then I got everything ready and told all of my friends farewell, and, with a heavy heart, left for Havre by steamer as far as Rouen and from thence to Havre by rail. The reason I went by steamer to Rouen was I bought my ticket all the way through to New Orleans from an agent in Paris, and all the emigrants were shipped that way. . . .

The vessel's name was *Laffitte à Geyer.* We had 300 steerage passengers and a few cabin passengers. The captain and the other officers and crew were all French. We left in time, had a good voyage, and crossed the ocean in thirty days, which was a fast trip, and we had fine weather all the way.

On landing at New Orleans I was met by a young man who was looking for me, who was in the employ of a large wholesale clothing house by the name of Jonas Brothers, with whom my brother was dealing, and whom he had instructed to look out for me. They asked me many questions of how I was provided with clothes. Of course, I told them that I had to sell the best I had, to raise money enough to buy provisions at Havre. They also had instructions to furnish me with what I needed, which they did. I arrived at New Orleans early one morning, and the same evening the old steamer *Missouri* left for Natchez. I was shipped on deck for $2. . . .

After I had remained in Natchez about one week my brother and myself started on our first trip together. We had a horse loaded down with three large packages of dry goods and clothing. Both of us walked, and I had to lead the horse. This was an entirely new business to me. I had to learn a good deal. I knew nothing whatever about handling goods, nor did I know how to handle a horse. I had to learn how to curry a horse, which I had to do morning and evening. Instead of my brother making the negro, where we stopped overnight, clean our horse, he made a negro out of me and made me do the dirty work. Of course, I thought then, as green as I was, that it was my duty to do it, but I soon found out different.

I did not relish the work of peddling at all. Every time we stopped at a farm to sell goods I had to pack the heavy packages in and out of the houses, and while my brother was selling goods, I stood and watched on the outside, so no one would steal anything.

It was very easy in those days to sell goods. There were no stores at every crossroad. There were stores only in the towns. The eating did not suit me, as I was not used to eating American dishes, such as hot bread, turnip greens, and pork. The walking of from ten to twenty miles per day I did not relish, either. In fact, I would have rather worked at my trade, which I learned in Paris, for twelve hours every day for all the time than to peddle for only one day. We made our first trip and sold out in two weeks. I suppose we had no less than five hundred dollars' worth of goods; besides, my brother carried a jewelry box, out of which he sold a good deal.

After resting a few days and replenishing our goods, we started on our second trip. This time it went a little easier with me. I saw that there was no other chance, and by degrees I got used to it, but I never fancied it. This time we went farther than the first time and stayed out four weeks, and again my brother must have made a paying trip. He always got good prices for his goods. We made a third trip of four weeks and sold out again.

Now, for those three trips that I made, during which time I had to do the work like a slave, I received no pay. My brother said I had to do the work to pay him back the money he sent me to Paris, and for the clothing he had to buy for me on my arrival; but that from that time on he would give me one-third profit; that is, of the net profits, after paying expenses, when we were out together, or half profit when I went out alone, but I would have to pay board when at home. We made two more trips, and my share out of same amounted to about $50. . . .

Every time I came to Natchez after being out from two to four weeks, a dozen or so of the peddlers met and generally had a little fun together, but my brother did not like for me to have any pleasure. He, in the first place, was not on good terms with the Adlers, who kept the boardinghouse where all the other peddlers stopped, although we hailed from the same place in Europe. He thought himself above the others, he always being very proud, and, furthermore, he wanted me to help his wife in her housework at home, but to all this I seriously objected. . . .

I had some money of my own. I bought myself a cheap horse, and with the rest of my money bought a small stock of goods and commenced to peddle on my own account, but made up my mind that it would be better for me to try some other section of the country. I therefore took all my belongings and traveled as far as Vicksburg, selling goods all the way there. It took me about two weeks to make the trip, and I sold nearly all I had by the time I reached there. I found several old acquaintances there from Speyer, and many young men from our section of the country, who were mostly peddlers. Among them were the firm of Schulz & Sartorius, who had a large wholesale dry goods and clothing store, where the peddlers laid in their supplies.

After remaining a few days to rest, I also bought my goods and started out alone. I soon got acquainted among the people in the country. I also made rapid progress with the language. I learned it much sooner than many others. The reason was because I spoke French fluently. . . .

REFLECTIONS OF A NEW ENGLAND
PEDDLER
Abraham Kohn

Kohn's journal is one of the few we possess which recounts in detail the day-to-day experiences of a peddler struggling to make a living. It thus becomes a valuable historic source for a knowledge of the economic life of the ante-bellum, Jewish itinerant merchant.

There is ample evidence in his daily entries to prove that peddling was a hard way to make a living, that its difficulties embittered many a

*young man, and that it left its victims resentful, and broken in body
and in spirit.*——J.R.M.

This week I went, together with my brother Juda, from Boston to
Worcester [Massachusetts]. We were both delighted, for the trip was a
welcome change from our daily, heavy work. Together we sat in the
grass for hours, recalling the wonderful years of our youth. And in
bed, too, we spent many hours in talking.

Today, the thirtieth of October, we are here in Northborough, and I
feel happier than I have for a fortnight. Moses is in New York, and we
will meet him, God willing, at Worcester on Tuesday. . . .

I regret that the people here are so cold to immigrants and that their
watchword seems to be "Help yourself; that's the best help." I cannot
believe that a man who adapts himself to the language, customs, and
character of America can ever quite forget his home in the European
countries. Having been here so short a time, I should be very arrogant
if I were to set down at this time my judgments on America. The
whole country, however, with its extensive domestic and foreign
trade, its railroads, canals, and factories, looks to me like an adoles-
cent youth. He is a part of society, talking like a man and pretending
to be a man. Yet he is truly only a boy. That is America! Although she
appears to know everything, her knowledge of religion, history, and
human nature is, in truth, very elementary. . . . American history is
composed of Independence and Washington; that is all! On Sunday the
American dresses up and goes to church, but he thinks of God no
more than does the horse that carries him there. . . .

Thursday was a day of rest owing to twelve inches of snow. On
Friday and Saturday business was very poor, and we did not take in $2
during the two days.

On Sunday we stayed with Mr. Brown, a blacksmith, two miles
from Lunenburg. Both of us were in a bitter mood, for during the
whole week of driving about in the bitter cold we had earned no
money. I long for the beautiful days in my beloved homeland. Will
they ever return? Yes, a secret voice tells me that all of us will again
find happiness and, although there are many obstacles to be overcome,
the old maxim will guide me! . . .

Last week in the vicinity of Plymouth I met two peddlers, Lehman and Marx. Marx knew me from Fürth, and that night we stayed together at a farmer's house. After supper we started singing while I felt melancholy and depressed. O, how I thought of my dear mother while I sang! . . .

Today, Sunday, October 16th, we are here in North Bridgewater [Massachusetts], and I am not so downcast as I was two weeks ago. The devil has settled 20,000 [2,000?] shoemakers here, who do not have a cent of money. Suppose, after all, I were a soldier in Bavaria; that would have been a bad lot. I will accept three years in America instead. But I could not stand it any longer.

As far as the language is concerned, I am getting along pretty well. But I don't like to be alone. . . .

On Monday the 12th to Lyndeborough; Tuesday to Wilton; Wednesday to Mason Village; Thursday, New Ipswich; Friday, Ashburnham. On Saturday we came to Westminster, where we stayed over Sunday, the eighteenth of December. It was extremely cold this week, and there was more snow than we had ever seen in our lives. At some places the snow was three to four feet deep, and we could hardly get through with the sleigh. How often we thanked the good God that we did not have to carry our wares on our backs in this cold! To tramp with a heavy pack from house to house in this weather would be terrible. . . .

Dear, good mother, how often I recall your letters, your advice against going to America: "Stay at home; you can win success as well in Germany." But I would not listen; I had to come to America. I was drawn by fate and here I am, living a life that is wandering and uncertain. . . .

How will we find our beloved Moses, who must stamp through the snow with his pack on his back, without a brother, without a companion with whom to exchange a word? What he feels must be new to him. I know what it is like to wander alone and am anxious to hear what he has to say on the subject. . . .

On Tuesday morning at ten I left Worcester, it being my turn to travel alone for seven weeks. A thousand thanks to God, I felt far stronger than when I first left my brothers in Boston. Now I have become more accustomed to the language, the business, and the American way of life. . . .

It is hard, very hard indeed, to make a living this way. Sweat runs down my body in great drops and my back seems to be breaking, but I cannot stop; I must go on and on, however far my way lies. . . .

Here in the land of the free, where every child, every human being, preaches and enjoys liberty, it is I who am compelled to follow such a trade, to devote myself to so heavy and difficult a life. Each day I must ask and importune some farmer's wife to buy my wares, a few pennies' worth. Accursed desire for money, it is you that has driven the Bavarian immigrants to this wretched kind of trade! No, I must stop this business, the sooner the better. . . .

Not all the young Jewish immigrants took to the road. Most remained in the cities as laborers, artisans, or petty traders. A few aspired to the pulpit.

Abraham Rice, the first ordained rabbi to come to America, arrived in 1840. He became a spokesman for Orthodoxy and served congregations in Baltimore. Dr. Leo Merzbacher came soon after to occupy the pulpit of the newly established Reform congregation, Temple Emanuel in New York.

In 1846, a twenty-six-year-old former teacher and rabbinic functionary in a small Bohemian town, Isaac Mayer Wise, arrived to seek a career and future in the New World. More than any of his colleagues, he was suited by temperament and ability to succeed in this land of opportunity.

He quickly became a spokesman for progressive Judaism, championing its cause against opponents, rabbinic and lay. In 1854, he was called to serve as rabbi of Bene Yeshurun in Cincinnati. To further his cause he founded and edited the English language weekly *The Israelite* and the German *Die Deborah*. At first he attempted to form an American Judaism, moderately reform in its program. The prayerbook which he edited with two colleagues (but soon called his own) was titled *Minhag America* (The American Rite). But American Jewry did not ac-

cept religious uniformity, and he was opposed by both the traditionalists and the radical reformers. A practical man of good sense, he
realized that Reform was the wave of the future and made accommo-
dation with its radical element. Wise permitted others to shape the
movement's ideology, while he set about to found and control its institutions. He formed the Hebrew Union College, the Union of American
Hebrew Congregations, and the Central Conference of American
Rabbis—and thus earned the right to be called "The Father of Reform
Judaism in America." He embodied the youthful, ebullient spirit of
America which he found on his arrival. He was possessed of an indomitable optimism, vast energy, prudence, practicality, and an un-
flagging certainty in the truth of his way and its ultimate triumph.

Wise's memoirs tell of his first impressions of New York's religious
life, which are of considerable interest:

REMINISCENCES
Isaac M. Wise

In 1846 there were seven Jewish congregations in New York, two
communal schools, a number of Jewish mutual benefit associations,
and two charitable societies—one German, the other English. The Portuguese congregation was the oldest, and the oldest Portuguese was a
Polish Jew. Since my landlord, Friedman, was a member of this congregation, I went with him to the synagogue on Sabbath *Nach'mu;* but
I found the Portuguese ritual just as antiquated and tedious as the German and the Polish, although more decorous, dignified, and classical.
The next oldest congregation was the English-Polish, that had a hand-
some synagogue on Elm Street, and used the Polish ritual as it obtained in London.

On the very first morning I visited this synagogue, I longed for the
sight of a Hebrew book, and asked the *Shamash* whether I could obtain a volume of the *Mishnah*. That individual laughed so mockingly,
that I readily perceived what a sign of "greenness" it was on my part

to ask for an ancient Hebrew book in the New World, and that too in an orthodox synagogue. It was certainly not my fault, for I discovered only later the crass ignorance which ruled there.

On Center Street, in the second story, was the Polish synagogue. I went there the next evening, and heard some individual sniffle through a bit of *Rashi* in so pitiably ignorant a manner between *Minchah* and *Maarib,* that I never went there again.

Of the German congregations three were ultra orthodox. One of them worshiped on Henry, the other two on Attorney Street. Dr. Lilienthal had been chief rabbi of these three congregations for six months, and preached every Saturday in a different synagogue. On the first Sabbath (it was Sabbath *Hazzan*) I went to the synagogue on Henry Street to hear Dr. Lilienthal. The attendance was very large, the service according to the old German ritual. The congregation was orthodox, and just as ill-behaved as in Germany. The cantor had on a Christian gown, trilled like a mock nightingale, and leaped about like a hooked fish. After the selling of the so-called *mitzvot,* I lost all patience with the intolerable sing-song with which the reader intoned the portion and read from the *Torah* and with the innumerable *mi-shebe-rakh.* "Why is this nuisance tolerated in a metropolis?" I asked my neighbor. "I do not know," he answered; "but it takes place in all the synagogues of New York." At last the longed-for event took place. Dr. Lilienthal preached toward the close of the service. He pleased me very much, for he was an excellent and popular pulpit orator, used a glowing diction, and had a dignified carriage; but what he said about the season of mourning had long since lost all significance for me, and I was really and truly moved to mournful feelings, not for the destruction of Jerusalem, but for the disappearance of Judaism in the Polish-cabbalistical rabbinism and supernaturalism.

The youngest congregation was the Emanuel congregation. But very little was known of it in New York. On Sunday, the 10th of Ab (postponed *Tisha B'ab*), an acquaintance took me to the place where the beginnings of the temple were laid. We entered a small hall, a flight of stairs above the ground. There we found about fifty men and thirty women, the latter in a section partitioned off. A boys' choir, reenforced by a few men's voices, and a cantor with a weak tenor voice, sang some compositions of Sulzer as poorly as in a village synagogue; but dignity and decorum ruled—the beginning of a better future—and I breathed easier. Dr. Merzbacher, of blessed memory, preached. There was nothing in his delivery to attract a stranger; but he spoke of the end of the *Galut,* of the morning that was dawning also for the house of Israel. His words made me feel at home, although he did not treat the *Tisha B'ab* as drastically as I should have wished. . . .

He soon became impatient with the noise and bustle of the city, however, and seized the opportunity to apply for a rabbinic post in Albany, New York, where he first served a congregation; he writes of his terrible sense of failure following his initial sermon in which he attempted to direct the congregation from Orthodox to Reform Judaism.

Upon the landing of the steamer at Albany, drivers, dealers, landlords, railroad agents, peddlers, newsboys crowded about and pulled the "green" passengers hither and thither. All this brought me back to earth from the heights of poesy. Opposite the landing I saw my evening "star" inviting me to rest. Stern's (Star's) hotel, as they had informed me in New York, was situated opposite the landing, and thither I betook myself immediately.

Stern sees standing before him a lean, pale young man, with long hair, clad in black, and quite embarrassed. He calls his wife. She comes, receives me in a most friendly manner, and takes me into a room that was supposedly a parlor. She would, of course, have liked to know all about me at once; but I, as usual, spoke very little. My short answers embarrassed the woman, and she sent for Moses Schloss, the Aristotle of Albany Jewry. He came, accompanied by Henry Blattner, the second in the high council. "You are, I presume, the newly-arrived rabbi, and have a letter addressed to me by my brother-in-law Walter," said Schloss. I concluded from this that Walter must have written to him. I delivered my letter, which they both read. After a brief conversation, I was invited to preach on Saturday. It is self-understood that I accepted the invitation. The two gentlemen impressed me favorably. They seemed to be intelligent, cordial, open, and frank. Schloss informed me later that he took me to be quite a *Shlemihl.* Excepting these two gentlemen and the peddler whom I had met in New Haven, no one concerned himself about me. On Friday I saw the sights of the city, and in the evening I read undisturbed.

Saturday morning Moses Schloss took me to the synagogue on Herkimer Street. It was an old wooden building, with the entrance from the north. The ark was on the east, the *Bimah* in front of the ark, and the benches in four squares on the two sides, so that one-half of the congregation looked northward, and the other half southward. A Mr. Traub sang the old tunes, and the sexton, Levy, sold the *mitzvoth,* and attended to all the business. There was order and decorum as far as these were possible under existing circumstances. I preached on a text taken from the Scriptural portion of the day; but made no marked impression on the congregation.

In the afternoon Schloss said to me: "You preach very well; but you will not do for these people; they did not understand you. Still, if you wish to come to us for the holidays, I promise you a fee of one hundred dollars." I promised to write to him from Syracuse about it, because I had determined to spend the holidays in Cincinnati. I had met a Cincinnatian in New York, who praised Cincinnati to the skies. Although Schloss paid me a respectable sum of money on Sunday, and invited me once again to return for the holidays, which Blattner, Sporberg, and others also did, it was perfectly clear to me that I had failed in Albany. This aggravated and humiliated me. I left the city as early as possible Monday morning, and boarded for the first time an American railroad train in order to travel to Syracuse.

To wage their battle for a new life, immigrant Jews from Germany brought an arsenal of assets—daring, energy, ability, optimism, faith. Some also carried with them a spiritual heritage, a way of life informed by ideals and disciplined by a code of values.

One such arrival was Herman Kahn, who reached America in 1846 at the age of seventeen. Joining his relatives in Richmond, he changed his name to Cone and set out to peddle. From peddling, he graduated to the wholesale grocery business; later, his sons founded the Cone textile empire. The *American Jewish Archives* (vol. 15, April 1963, no. 1) contain a letter that Herman Kahn brought with him. It was written in the tradition of Jewish ethical wills by his brother-in-law, Joseph Rosengart, to direct the young man's conduct in the New World:

A LETTER OF ETHICAL ADMONITION
Joseph Rosengart

Place your full trust and confidence in God who will send his angels to guard you. So, do not be discouraged, and do not be afraid of leaving or of the voyage, but consider your fate a good fortune, designed for you by God.

You may shed tears, because you are leaving your parents' house, your father, brothers and sisters, relatives, friends and your native land; but dry your tears, because you may have the sweet hope of finding a second home abroad and a new country where you will not be deprived of all political and civil rights and where the Jew is not excluded from the society of all other men and subject to the severest restriction, but you will find a real homeland where you as a human being may claim all human rights and human dignity.

Be careful of your voyage and pay attention to your health as well as your belongings. Avoid the company of all but respectable and educated people. Be modest and polite to everybody. Thus you may surely expect good treatment for yourself.

Every evening and every morning turn to God with sincere prayers; do not be afraid of anybody and do not let anybody disturb your devotions. Even if some people should make fun of you at first, they will understand later and show their respect.

I recommend to you the faith of your fathers as the most sacred and the most noble. Try to follow all the Commandments most painstakingly and thereby attain actual happiness. Do not sacrifice your faith for worldly goods. They will disappear like dust and must be left behind in due time.

Remember particularly the Sabbath day, to keep it holy, for it is one of the most important pillars on which our Faith is established. Do not disregard this day and do not let gold or silver make you blind, and do not let any business however tempting induce you to violate the Sabbath, but at least on this day think seriously about your existence and your work.

It is not man's destiny to accumulate worldly goods just to be wealthy, but to acquire them to be used as means for the attainment of eternal happiness. I am, therefore, giving you as a keepsake an excellent religious book for your instruction. Make it your sacred duty to read one chapter on each Sabbath and holy day with serious devotion and meditation. Do not lay it aside when you have read it through, but keep it and read it again from time to time. You will thereby learn your religion thoroughly, act accordingly, and thus be honored by God and men. It will be your counsel in good times and bad, and will preserve you from all evil.

Honor your father and your mother, that your days may be prolonged. Even in that distant country you can show your respect and love toward your father by always remembering his good advice and by frequently writing him loving letters, thus giving expression to your devotion to him and your brothers and sisters.

Although your sainted mother is now in Heaven and although you never knew her, you can show her your greatest respect and love by following the Faith as she did. You will thus be able to know her and be with her in heaven.

Your sister and brother-in-law in America will surely receive you in their home with loving care. Consider their home as your father's house and be respectful and modest toward them, show them your filial devotion and be attached and faithful to them, as you have always been toward us. Follow their advice and their suggestions and, whatever you may undertake, first ask them for their counsel. They will always give you the best advice and you will derive benefit therefrom, I am sure.

If you should be lucky enough to become wealthy in that distant land, do not let it make you proud and overbearing. Do not think that your energy and knowledge accumulated that wealth, but that God gave it to you to use it for the best purpose and for charity. Do not forget that you are also under obligation to assist your relatives and to help them to get ahead.

However, if you should not become wealthy, be satisfied with what you do have and try to be as comfortable and happy as if you had the greatest treasures.

Follow the middle way between avarice and waste. Do not be stingy, but live according to your position and your finances and be particularly liberal toward the poor, and charitable to the needy. Be glad to help and give part of your bread and give assistance to the distressed.

Do not let anybody call you a miser, but be known as a philanthropist. On the other hand, do not be extravagant or a spendthrift. Even if the necessity should occasionally arise to spend more than usual, never feel obliged to squander. It is of utmost importance that you keep account of your expenditures and live within your income.

I am closing with the quotation:

"Do right, trust in God, and fear no man."

Buttenhausen, April 16th, 1846. [Signed] Joseph Rosengart

3. Tidal Waves from Eastern Europe: 1870–1924

I n 1881, the number of Jews reaching the shores of the United States from eastern Europe was 5,692. Five years later the number swelled to 19,936. Of these, 14,029 came from Russia, 5,326 from the Austro-Hungarian Empire, 518 from Romania. Further figures for east European immigration appear below: *

YEAR	RUSSIA	AUSTRIA-HUNGARY	ROMANIA	TOTAL
1891	43,457	5,890	854	50,201
1898	20,168	9,831	744	30,743
1901	37,660	13,006	6,827	57,818
1906	125,234	14,884	3,872	152,491
1911	65,472	12,757	2,188	90,257
1914	102,638	20,454	2,646	136,645

There was a sharp decline in immigration during World War I and the postwar years with the exception of 1921, when 119,036 immigrants arrived. In the following two years 53,524 (1922) and 49,989 (1923) newcomers were admitted, but the number fell to 10,292 in 1924 and remained at about that rate through 1930. It then fell to 5,692 in 1931 and 2,755 in 1932; it reached its nadir in 1933, which saw only 2,372 arrivals. Hitler's persecution caused a significant rise in immigrants, with 43,450 being admitted in 1939 alone. But the

* Discrepancy in numbers after 1901 is due to the transmigration of east European Jews through countries of western Europe, the Americas, and the Turkish Empire.

"tidal wave" of immigrants came during the first two decades of the century.

The number of east European immigrants in New York City in 1910, by place of origin and sex, were as follows:

ORIGIN	MALE	FEMALE	TOTAL
Russia	257,418	222,771	480,189
Austria (Galicia)	95,941	94,296	190,237
Hungary	35,224	41,401	76,625
Romania	16,461	17,123	33,584

Despite the increase in immigration in the first years of the 1880s, the really large-scale movement from eastern Europe took place in the early years of the twentieth century. Immigrants who were settled laid the base for the arrival of others. While some of the settlers were not eager to receive new immigrants who might enter into competition for jobs, the majority who came were anxious to bring over relatives who had remained behind.

Proof of their readiness to help was to be found in the immigrant community's organizations for receiving and aiding the newcomers. Sweatshop owners also awaited new "hands" to exploit; small merchants looked for new customers.

Unlike the immigration experience of other groups where the male population far outnumbered the female, there was little disparity in the Jewish community. Jews arrived in family units, and came to stay. If a man emigrated alone, for the most part he sought the first opportunity to bring over his sweetheart, or wife and children.

The immigrant experience was captured in the work of Abraham Cahan, a dominant figure of the immigrant community of New York for more than half a century. As editor of the leading Yiddish daily Der Forverts, he wielded vast powers of persuasion, directing the sentiments, tastes, loyalties, even the political preferences, of the Jewish community. He arrived in New York in 1882, escaping czarist police. He became a successful police reporter on the Commercial Advertiser, then turned to Yiddish journalism. His The Rise of David Levinsky (1917) is the classic immigrant novel, and his multivolume autobiography a rich source of immigrant history. His first impressions of

America were doubtlessly shared by many immigrants; one of his early vignettes appeared in the *Advertiser*, August 6, 1898:

IMAGINARY AMERICA
Abraham Cahan

[1882] I set foot on American soil on a scorching day in July, and the first American I saw was an old customs officer, with a white beard and in the blue uniform of his office. The headless men in gray vanished as if at the stroke of a magic wand, but then, gleaming green, fresh and beautiful, not many hundred yards off, was the shore of Staten Island, and, while I was uttering exclamations of enchantment in chorus with my fellow passengers, I asked myself whether my dreams of a meadow had not come true.

Still, pretty as America was, it somehow did not seem to be genuine, and much as I admired the shore I had a lurking impression that it was not the same sort of grass, trees, flowers, sod as in Europe, that it was more or less artificial, flimsy, ephemeral, as if a good European rainstorm could wipe it all off as a wet sponge would a colored picture made with colored chalk on blackboard.

I remember joking of the seeming unreality of things in my new home. "The ice here is not cold," I would say, "The sugar is not sweet and the water is not wet." And a homesick German thereupon added in the words of a famous poet of his that America was a country where "the birds had no sing, the flowers no fragrance and the men no hearts." Why I should have doubted the actuality of things in the New World I do not know. Now that I try to account for that vague, hidden suspicion which the sky and clouds of New York arouse in me, it occurs to me that it may have been due to my deep-rooted notion of America as something so far removed from my world that it must look entirely different from it. If Staten Island had the appearance which its reflections had in the water, if the trees and the cliffs were all upside down, I should have been surprised but satisfied. . . .

When I found myself on the street and my eye fell on an old rickety building, I expressed a feeling akin to surprise. I could only conceive of America as a brand-new country, and everything in it, everything made by man, at least, was to be spick and span, while here was an old house, weatherbeaten and somewhat misshapen with age. How did it get time to get old?

The emotional wrench suffered by the travelers as they departed is caught in a poem written by Joseph Bovshover, a Yiddish poet. Soon after his arrival on these shores in the early 1890s, he began to write poetry in English under the pseudonym of Basil Dahl. In his early days in New York, Bovshover worked as a furrier, but later abandoned his craft to devote his full time to a literary career. A political radical and anarchist, he was devoted to the furtherance of the proletarian masses, whose sufferings touched him deeply. A manuscript copy of the poem is to be found in the American Jewish Archives (January 1955):

THE DEPARTURE
Basil Dahl

It was in March. The sun stood low;
Beneath its crimson, warmer glow
The snow hath long begun to thaw
From roofs of shingles, tile, and straw.
The pendant circles melted fast,
And winter seemed to breathe his last.
But though the winter's gloom and blast
Were almost vanished in the past.
Which made all bosoms white and glad,
Mine was depressed and chilled and sad.
For I was soon to leave my home
Resolved to distant shores to roam
In search of that which to possess
I thought was bliss and happiness.

No more to walk the scented wood
Not far from which my cradle stood,
No more to measure with fond looks
The well-beloved familiar nooks
Of house and garden, yard and street,
The friends of youth no more to meet,
To see no more the faces near
Of parents well-beloved and dear:
Alas, this thought was hard to bear.
And yet, though hard, I could not tear
My heart away from its desire
Which was to 'scape, as from a fire,
The czar's oppressed and knouted lands
And seek the happier, freer strands.

My mother wept, my sire grew pale,
And, like a leaflet in the gale,
I shook in all my limbs with fear,
Yet checked the course of many a tear,
Partly because I would not swell
The sad news of their last farewell,
And partly, too, because I wept
Full oft before, and waking kept
Long hours at night beside their beds,
Kissing in thought their hoary heads.

At last this parting hour drew nigh.
The sun was set, and on the sky
Where the horizon's bound expands
Red streaks of clouds like blood-tugged bands
Gleamed with an awful, ominous light
And filled my bosom with affright.
Like lumps of lead were both my feet;
I clenched my fists, rose from my seat,
Grasped with one hand my coat and trunk,
And with the other, like one drunk,
Embraced both parents in the gloom,

Ran to the door, and left the room.
But when the open street I'd gained,
I stopped and turned and then remained
Some moments rooted on the spot.
For by the door of our poor cot,
All heedless of the evening's chill,
I saw my mother standing still,

Surrounded by some female friends
With drooping head and wilted hands,
But pale and trembling like a reed.
Alas, alas, my heart did bleed
To see her there, so lone and lorn,
Away from her, her youngest torn.
Mine eyes grew dim, my spirits sunk.
A while I thought to dash the trunk
Against the pavement, to return
To her whose heart I knew would yearn
For me with pure, maternal love.
But strong, resistless forces drove
Me suddenly from where I stood.
I left her. Was it right and good?

Many accounts of the journey to America exist. The memoirs of the physician Benjamin L. Gordon run the gamut of immigrant experiences, beginning with the need to steal across the border in Europe—which is described in his book.

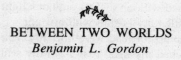

BETWEEN TWO WORLDS
Benjamin L. Gordon

I remained home for two weeks following the Passover holidays waiting for my steamship ticket to arrive. During this time I made the necessary preparations for the long journey to America. I made arrangements with Hirsh, the son of Naphtali, to convey me secretly to Germany. Owing to the fact that I was of military age, I could not pass through the regular customs gate, and I was compelled to cross the boundary line at night in order not to be detected by the sentinels guarding the frontier against smugglers and persons who did not possess proper passports.

It was two o'clock in the morning when my guide, whose business it was to smuggle out travelers without passports to Germany, called for me. I was glad that my sisters and brothers were asleep. I had arranged for my parents to see me off by entering Germany through the regular gate on the next day. After walking silently in the dark for about an hour, we reached a forest near the frontier about three miles north of the regular gate. From behind trees we could see and hear the guards marching to and fro. In a few moments we heard the shots of revolvers from a distance; this usually meant that contraband runners were being fired upon. "Let us go now!" said my guide. "The soldiers are now busy with the contraband runner and we can safely pass the boundary line." I crossed the boundary line without the slightest mishap. . . .

We got off the train at Königsberg where we had to wait for a train to Hamburg scheduled for the following morning. This gave me an opportunity to take a good look at this historic city. Incidentally, it was at this railroad station that I first observed the miracle of electric lights. Königsberg is celebrated as the birthplace of the great philosopher Kant, and it was distinguished for its culture and great personalities. Among the disciples of Kant were many prominent Jews, such as David Friedlander, Isaac Eichel, Marcus Herz, and Aaron Joel. Eichel published his Hebrew journal, *Hameaseph* (The Gatherer) in Königsberg.

The Jewish population of Königsberg at that time was about 4,000, which number included many Russian and Lithuanian Jewish merchants who had previously settled there. There were also a number of Russian Jewish immigrants who had tarried there because of lack of funds to continue their journey to America. These persons were waiting for the "German Society" to assist them. . . .

The next day I took the train to Hamburg, the port of embarkation, where we met representatives of the *Hilfverein* who took the immigrants to the Jewish immigration house. Upon our arrival there, we were all treated to rolls and coffee. The immigration house consisted of a large room with benches extending all around the four walls. At the center of the room was a desk, fenced in by railing, where a clerk registered our names and examined our steamship tickets. I was told that the *Bohemia* of the Hamburg-America Line, on which I was to travel, was under repair and would not be ready for ten days.

When I told the clerk that my funds would not permit me to stay in Hamburg that long, he suggested that I help him in the office, do odd jobs around the building, and in return he would see to it that I would get my food and lodging during that period. My main job was to assist mothers with their children and to furnish information to new immigrants. I received the necessary data from a circular printed in German. I had two hours free from my duties each day, which I utilized in taking long walks through the city. I visited the ancient Jewish synagogue and other institutions. I walked on the banks of the river Elbe, and I passed my time watching the tugs, the ferries, and the tall-gabled medieval edifices leading to the park and the public square.

I was greatly impressed with the many institutions maintained by the Western Jews for the relief of their harassed and distressed brethren of the East. Every capital in Europe at that period had its benevolent association: The French had their *Alliance Israélite Universelle;* the English had their *Anglo-Jewish Association* and the Germans, as noted, had their *Hilfverein der deutschen Juden.* These organizations worked individually and collectively to facilitate the passage of the Jewish refugees of Eastern Europe to the various countries of refuge. They had their agents at all frontier stations, ports, and railroad stations. The *Hilfverein* had thirty-two such bureaus in all parts of Germany. This organization obtained reduced rates from railroad and shipping lines, provided the refugees with food while passing through Germany, and, in many instances, even paid the cost of transportation. . . .

After wandering around the streets of Hamburg for a period of ten days, I was more than glad to see an announcement in the papers that the *Bohemia,* on which I was to sail, would leave Hamburg on the next day. I was ready at the dock so early on the morning of the departure that I was the first passenger to walk up the gangplank and board the vessel. The weather was ideal; the sun was bright and the sea calm; but my heart and mind were not so peaceful.

I knew that I was going to the Land of the Free, but I also was cognizant of the fact that no one expected or awaited me there. I did not have the slightest idea as to how I was going to make a living: I had no trade and was physically unfit for hard manual labor. Then, too, the fact that I was leaving the continent where my ancestors had lived for so many centuries weighed heavily on my mind.

Of course, I was happy to go to America, but to one who has no funds, no trade, and no relations, one of the freedoms in the New World could be freedom to starve. I was rudely awakened out of my reverie by loud blasts of the boat's whistle, signaling the last call for all to get on board. . . .

Castle Garden—A Gehenna

Of the actual arrival in New York, George M. Price gave a detailed and somewhat bitter account. During 1890–91 a series of his articles about his early days in America appeared in *Voskhod,* a Russian-Jewish periodical published in St. Petersburg. These articles appeared in book form in 1893 (*The Russian Jew in America*); as an appendix to his book, he had added a memoir of his experiences and those of fellow immigrants on their arrival in New York. This brief excerpt from the appendix, translated by Leo Shpall, is taken from *Publications of the American Jewish Historical Society* (vol. 47):

Castle Garden is a large building, a Gehenna, through which all Jewish arrivals must pass to be cleansed before they are considered worthy of breathing freely the air of the land of the almighty dollar. In the spacious courtyard of this institution, which is surrounded by high

*walls so that no one can enter or leave except through the gate, at
which are stationed half a dozen guards, those immigrants who have
not as yet been admitted [to the United States] have to find a place for
themselves. . . . About the conveniences of the immigrants, the Americans of Castle Garden worry very little. The Europeans, they say, are
anyway unaccustomed to luxury; they can be satisfied with the soiled
courtyard of the "Gates of Freedom," as the Yankees call this prelim-
inary prison. The courtyard of Castle Garden accommodates no more
than several hundred. You can just visualize a sight when they confine
in it more than a thousand Jews, recently liberated from the terrors of
the trip, who had hoped to be welcomed with music. . . . For about a
week, they kept us in this Hades where we had to sleep on the floor
under the open skies, which is not comfortable at any time, particularly when it rains. Little by little, they finally found accommodations
for those who came on our boat. Some of us they placed in houses;
others were sent to Greenpoint; and the rest, among whom was I, they
simply expelled from the Gates of Freedom. "Go [they said], our land
is big and fruitful, go ahead and live in it by begging." . . .*

The Morning Was Glorious

Unlike George Price, young Mary Antin epitomizes the immigrant in
love with America and everything about it. It was a love expressed in
agitation for complete assimilation of the immigrant. She called for a
shedding of all Jewish customs, traits, beliefs. Her faith in being accepted into Anglo-Saxon society was strengthened by her marriage to
Prof. Amadeus V. Grabau. In time, however, the professor left Mary
to settle in China, and as she grew older she had cause to rethink her
girlish optimism about America and "true" Americans. Her autobiography, *The Promised Land,* became a minor classic of immigrant literature.

For the youthful Mary Antin, everything was glorious: departure,
trip, arrival—which she describes in an earlier memoir, written in
1898, when she was eighteen years old:

PLOTSK TO BOSTON
Mary Antin

The morning was glorious. It was the eighth of May, the seventeenth day after we left Hamburg. The sky was clear and blue, the sun shone brightly, as if to congratulate us that we had safely crossed the stormy sea, and to apologize for having kept away from us so long. The sea had lost its fury; it was almost as quiet as it had been at Hamburg before we started, and its color was a beautiful greenish blue. Birds were all the time in the air, and it was worth while to live merely to hear their songs. And soon, oh joyful sight! we saw the tops of two trees!

What a shout there rose! Everyone pointed out the welcome sight to everybody else, as if they did not see it. All eyes were fixed on it as if they saw a miracle. And this was only the beginning of the joys of the day!

What confusion there was! Some were flying up the stairs to the upper deck, some were tearing down to the lower one, others were running in and out of the cabins, some were in all parts of the ship in one minute, and all were talking and laughing and getting in somebody's way. Such excitement, such joy! We had seen two trees!

Then steamers and boats of all kinds passed by, in all directions. We shouted, and the men stood up on the boats and returned the greeting, waving their hats. We were as glad to see them as if they were old friends of ours.

Oh, what a beautiful scene! No corner of the earth is half so fair as the lovely picture before us. It came to view suddenly—a green field, a real field with grass on it, and large houses, and the dearest hens and little chickens in all the world, and trees, and birds, and people at work. The young green things put new life into us, and are so dear to our eyes that we dare not speak a word now, lest the magic should vanish away and we should be left to the stormy scenes we know.

But nothing disturbed the fairy sight. Instead, new scenes appeared,

beautiful as the first. The sky becomes bluer all the time, the sun warmer; the sea is too quiet for its name, and the most beautiful blue
imaginable.

What are the feelings these sights awaken! They can not be described. To know how great was our happiness, how complete, how
free from even the shadow of a sadness, you must make a journey of
sixteen days on a stormy ocean. Is it possible that we will ever again
be so happy?

It was about three hours since we saw the first landmarks, when a
number of men came on board, from a little steamer, and examined
the passengers to see if they were properly vaccinated (we had been
vaccinated on the *Polynesia*), and pronounced everyone all right. Then
they went away, except one man who remained. An hour later we saw
the wharves.

Before the ship had fully stopped, the climax of our joy was
reached. One of us espied the figure and face we had longed to see for
three long years. In a moment five passengers on the *Polynesia* were
crying, "Papa," and gesticulating, and laughing, and hugging one
another, and going wild altogether. All the rest were roused by our excitement, and came to see our father. He recognized us as soon as we
him, and stood apart on the wharf not knowing what to do, I thought.

What followed was slow torture. Like mad things we ran about
where there was room, unable to stand still as long as we were on the
ship and he on shore. To have crossed the ocean only to come within a
few yards of him, unable to get nearer till all the fuss was over, was
dreadful enough. But to hear other passengers called who had no
reason for hurry, while we were left among the last, was unendurable.

Oh, dear! Why can't we get off the hateful ship? Why can't papa
come to us? Why so many ceremonies at the landing?

We said goodbye to our friends as their turn came, wishing we were
in their luck. To give us something else to think of, papa succeeded in
passing us some fruit; and we wondered to find it anything but a great
wonder, for we expected to find everything marvellous in the strange
country.

Still the ceremonies went on. Each person was asked a hundred or
so stupid questions, and all their answers were written down by a very

slow man. The baggage had to be examined, the tickets, and a hundred other things done before anyone was allowed to step ashore, all to keep us back as long as possible.

Now imagine yourself parting with all you love, believing it to be a parting for life; breaking up your home, selling the things that years have made dear to you; starting on a journey without the least experience in traveling, in the face of many inconveniences on account of the want of sufficient money; being met with disappointment where it was not to be expected; with rough treatment everywhere, till you are forced to go and make friends for yourself among strangers; being obliged to sell some of your most necessary things to pay bills you did not willingly incur; being mistrusted and searched, then half starved, and lodged in common with a multitude of strangers; suffering the miseries of seasickness, the disturbances and alarms of a stormy sea for sixteen days; and then stand within a few yards of him for whom you did all this, unable to even speak to him easily. How do you feel?

Oh, it's our turn at last! We are questioned, examined, and dismissed! A rush over the planks on one side, over the ground on the other, six wild beings cling to each other, bound by a common bond of tender joy, and the long parting is at an END.

Where Was the Freedom, Where the Human Equality?

For Israel Kasovich, on the other hand, nothing was glorious. The dream, to be sure, was grand and noble: to come to the new world, to establish an agricultural colony, and to live a brotherly cooperative life. This was the goal of the *Am Olam* (Eternal People) movement, named from an essay by Peretz Smolenskin at its founding in Odessa in 1881. Its program was derived from movements for agrarian socialist life then current in Russia—in returning to the soil a man returns to himself, strikes roots in the cosmos.

Groups of *Am Olam* enthusiasts did found colonies in Louisiana, North Dakota, and Oregon, but they were all short-lived. By 1890 the

movement had perished; only the dream remained. Kasovich describes
how that dream began to vanish.

THE DAYS OF OUR YEARS
Israel Kasovich

At last New York hove into sight. The ship drew near to Castle Garden. The members of the *Am Olam* party were dressed in holiday at-
tire. We were lined up on the deck in expectation of a warm welcome.
Thus we stood in a festive frame of mind, and our leaders unfurled our
large flag, so that the world might see and know who was coming
here. But no sooner had the flag begun to wave triumphantly in the
air, displaying conspicuously the large golden words "Am Olam,"
than a man ran over to us and ordered us to lower the flag. We told
him with an air of self-assurance that this was a free country, whereupon he became furious, snatched up the flag and hurled it straight into
the sea. We felt as though our faces had been slapped.

We disembarked at Castle Garden. The circular building was
jammed with immigrants who had arrived before us. There was no
place to sit down, but who cared to sit there, when we felt sure we
were being awaited outside?

They took down our names and records. Unlike today, they made
very little fuss over it in those days, and presently we walked into the
small Battery Park just outside Castle Garden, and halted. There was
no one there to meet us, and we did not know where to go. Our
leaders hurried away to obtain information, and we waited. Tired and
weary, the women and the children sat down upon the grass, whereupon a policeman rushed up and ordered them to get off the grass.

A couple of hours later our leaders returned, accompanied by a representative of the Immigrant Aid Committee, and told us to go back to
Castle Garden, where we would have to pass the night. As the building was filled with other immigrants, we stayed in the courtyard. Here
there were no seats; you either stood or sat upon the cold pavement.

A representative of the aforesaid committee brought us bread and sausages, and began to pass them around among us. Many refused to take the victuals, preferring to go out and buy their own food; but they were no longer able to leave the premises, all gates having been locked for the night.

Night fell. Many of the women sat crying softly. The men were despondent. Each asked the other, "What is going on here?" and there was no one to answer. We waited for the morrow. The night happened to be a chilly one, and a cold wind was blowing from the ocean. Our belongings were still in the ship's baggage room, and we had to sleep on the bare and cold ground. But who slept? We took off our upper garments and wrapped them around the children, who fell asleep on the cold pavement, while their mothers sat on the ground nearby, sighing and groaning and choking with tears.

When it grew light, we presented a sorry spectacle. We all looked exhausted and dismal as though we had just emerged from a long illness, and in addition we were covered with dust. A little later some one brought us again bread and sausages and cold coffee. There was fresh wailing among our womenfolk, who did not want to eat the bread of charity.

A couple of hours later Castle Garden became deserted. The other immigrants, the Gentiles, had no one to wait for, so they went each his way, and meanwhile we were advised to seize the vacant seats in the deserted building.

We spent a couple of days in Castle Garden, sleeping on the bare benches, then a representative of the Immigrant Aid Committee came to take our womenfolk away to houses of shelter on certain islands. Again there was wailing. Our women refused to go alone, but our leaders succeeded in calming them, and finally they went.

We men walked aimlessly around, while our leaders hurried hither and thither and spoke in whispers. Finally, after a couple of days more of uncertainty, we were called together and informed that as regards our becoming farmers, that was now entirely out of the question, and that each of us had better try to find something to do. We divided up the money still remaining in the treasury, and every one felt beaten. We were ashamed of ourselves. To think that we had allowed ourselves to be thus led astray! For who would have gone to America if not to become a tiller of the soil?

Our *Am Olam* group was now disbanded and scattered. The students had rented a vacant shop, purchased a few mattresses and made their home there, living together on a semicommunistic basis. Most of them went to work; one technical student from St. Petersburg, who was too weak to work, peddled lemonade.

I set out for the office of the Immigrant Aid Committee in order to ask for advice. When I came near the place I saw a line of people, men and women, with tickets in their hands. At the door stood a policeman, who behaved anything but gently. Near him stood a Russian Jew employed by the committee, and he behaved even worse than the policeman. It was impossible to get inside. If one needed help, he had first to procure a ticket, and then stand in line and wait for his turn. I knew, however, that the chairman of the committee was Michael Halperin, of whom I had read that he was a great man and had a fine command of the Hebrew language. Accordingly, I wrote him a letter in Hebrew asking him for advice. When I handed the letter to an attendant, I was admitted at once. Halperin told me that the committee had as yet no funds to establish agricultural colonies, and that even if it had the money, it would not do so, because the colony established the year before for the refugees from Yelizavetgrad had proven a failure. The latter had deserted the colony and were now back in New York. He therefore advised me to find some kind of occupation, and for my two young brothers-in-law he gave me his personal cards addressed to two manufacturers, who were sure to give them employment.

After this interview, I proceeded to Essex Street and rented a flat consisting of a tiny kitchen and two small rooms. Here I installed the women and the children, purchased all that was necessary for the house, and rented out one room to two lodgers. And now commenced a terrible battle with the bedbugs, which did not let us sleep a wink all night.

My brothers-in-law found work with the aid of Halperin's cards. The younger one stripped tobacco leaves for three dollars a week; he would come home from work all wan and waxen, and keep on vomiting. The older one was employed at turning a heavy wheel; he would return home all dirty like a chimney sweep, and too weak to eat. My mother-in-law would meet them with bitter laments, and I had a guilty feeling. On Saturday, when the children had to go to work, the house would be filled with wailing; so I used to rise before the rest and go away in order to avoid the scene. Nobody said anything to me, but I was ashamed to look them in the face.

I myself scanned the newspapers to find out where "hands" were wanted; I ran all over the city, but could find no work, employers rejecting me on account of my delicate hands. My neighbors, who had long been in this country, advised me to become a peddler. A fine occupation, forsooth! I had come to America to be a tiller of the soil, and now I was to become a peddler! Another couple of weeks passed, and I was still idle. I softened somewhat and agreed to become a peddler; in America, it was said, such an occupation was not looked upon as degrading, but as good as any other business. A neighbor kindly took me to a wholesaler of his acquaintance, and asked him to treat me well. The wholesaler told me that he, too, had once been a peddler, and that all the Jewish millionaires here had started out as peddlers, that being the best way to become Americanized and to work one's self up. He ordered a clerk to fetch a basket and they began to fill it with all kinds of notions: stockings, socks, combs, buttons, handkerchiefs, towels, scissors, pocket knives, etc. The proprietor himself made out my bill. And how cheap everything was! Whoever heard in Russia of a pair of scissors selling for ten cents, or of a pair of women's stockings, ditto? I paid twelve dollars for the goods, and received by way of premium a strap for the basket. The wholesaler himself adjusted the strap on my shoulder, and showed me how to hold the basket; he told me not to be shy but to knock at every door, and wished me success, whereupon I set out to try my fortune as a peddler.

My portable shop was pulling me down to the ground, and it seemed as if my shoulder blade would break any minute. Rivers of perspiration were streaming down my face and body, my feet were staggering under the heavy weight, and I was ashamed to look people in the face. I had now been walking for a long time, yet had not knocked at a single door. How could I get myself to knock at a door and to intrude uninvited? Presently a gang of Gentile street urchins began to pelt me with stones and lumps of coal. I ran into a house more dead than alive, climbed to the sixth floor, and made a sale amounting to ten cents.

I returned home with shooting pains in my side and a swollen shoulder. My wife sat by my side and wept softly, while my mother-in-law wailed and complained bitterly, "A fine pass we have come to, woe is me!"

The next day I made up my mind to knock at every door. I went and knocked, but many refused to open the door, shouting that they did not need anything. Some did buy a couple of cents' worth of goods, but with the air of one giving alms, as though they took pity on a poor immigrant. My face burned with shame, but I dragged myself along and, as I did so, thought of our sweet dreams about a well-ordered agricultural colony and the nice and quiet life we were going to live as farmers. Thus lost in reverie, I noticed an open door, forgot that here one must knock first, and walked right in. The house wife, who happened to be cleaning the stove, seized one of the stove lids and hurled it at me, at the same time shouting: "Get out of here!" Fortunately, the lid missed me. I at once bounded out of the flat, closed the door behind me, and began to run wildly, nearly breaking my neck. I proceeded straight home, where I threw down my peddler's basket and declared I would not go peddling any more.

My father-in-law, who had not yet found employment, decided to try his hand at peddling. He shouldered my basket and began to walk toward the door. We attempted to dissuade him, but he laughed and said to me: "If you have tried, I may try as well." A couple of hours later he returned and told us that all he had taken in was blows, and plenty of them. He had been assailed by loafers, who ran after him, pulled his beard, kicked him, and showered him with refuse from the garbage cans.

The upshot of the matter was that we sold the basket with the contents thereof to a peddler for six dollars. And now I was idle again. Our little capital was steadily diminishing, and our disappointment was great indeed. We had uprooted our home and traveled to a distant land overseas in order to lead a quiet, honest, independent life as tillers of the soil, as Jews and as free citizens, and instead of this we had to live amid noise and dirt, and to eke out a livelihood by engaging in a contemptible business that smacked of begging, or else by hiring ourselves out as wage slaves and toiling like horses for our daily bread. For the class struggle was more bitter here than in Russia. Nor was there any evidence of a particular love for us here; we were stoned in the streets, and many refused to rent their houses to Jews. Again, it was impossible to observe the Jewish religion here, many being compelled to work on the Jewish Sabbath and holidays. Where, then, was the freedom, where the human equality? And so we were filled with longing for our old home and our old life.

Meanwhile letters arrived from friends in Russia, who already knew the whole truth from my letters, and they wrote me that there was a new Minister of the Interior in Russia, one who was a liberal man, and that better times were expected. Accordingly, they advised me to return home.

My father-in-law pleaded that we go back to Russia. My mother-in-law wailed and begged to be taken back to the old country; here, she said, we would lose both this world and the next. And my wife argued that since we failed to realize the main object of our voyage to America—namely, to engage in farming—we ought to return to Russia.

As the number of immigrants peaked, the problems grew. One man "concerned about the welfare of his people" wrote a "Letter to the Editor" of *Ha-Magid* on May 3, 1882:

As a kindness to our oppressed brethren in Russia and for the good of all, I beg of you . . . have mercy on the unfortunates and warn them with all your power of persuasion not to leave their native land to come to America. I see the pain of the afflicted when they come here. My hair stands on end, and I find myself incapable of describing the fate of the poor unfortunates. The "benefactors" who send their poor brethren to America will need to render an account before the Almighty because of the tragedy they inflict upon them. The number of newcomers grows daily at an alarming rate, and our brethren here can care for only a portion of them. The rest suffer hunger and pain, and there is no one here to open their homes to them . . . therefore, every Jew who can must make it his sacred task to warn the unfortunates that they should not rush like cattle into the valley, where they literally put their lives in danger. . . . Only the young, healthy, unmarried men with a trade may be able, after years of hard labor, to make a living. The others will simply languish. They are already a burden and an embarrassment to those already settled here . . .

Der Yiddisher Emigrant, a Yiddish newspaper published in St. Petersburg, reported regularly on immigrant hardships. The following selections are translated by the editor:

AN UNUSUAL DAY ON ELLIS ISLAND
(vol. 5, no. 1, 1911)

The American newspapers report that since Ellis Island exists, there has not been such a commotion as on 24 December of the past year [1910]. When the officials arrived in the morning they found no fewer than 2,159 immigrants. Some had already been excluded and some had still to be examined by the "Special Inquiry." The newspapers are full of descriptions of a horrible night which these people had to endure. There was not sufficient space for all. People had to lie on the floor in freezing weather. Some became sick because of the cold.

Most of the detained were Jews from Russia, Galicia, and Romania. The heartrending cries of those denied the privilege to step upon American soil, and [the cries] of their relations who besieged the island, are indescribable. We record here but a few instances.

Two children, a boy of fifteen and a girl of fourteen, came from Switzerland. Their father, an American citizen, had died there recently during a visit to his old country. They have a wealthy uncle in America who wants to take them in. The mother had given them a letter in which she states that she entrusts them to their uncle. Despite all of this, the children are being sent back.

Bessie and Clara Binstack, two sisters, lovely children, came to their brother. The brother is wealthy, but they are both being sent back because one is fifteen years and eight months, and the law states that children under the age of sixteen will not be admitted unless they are accompanied by a parent.

ARRIVING IN NEW YORK
(vol. 5, no. 5, 1911)

Many immigrants arriving in New York often have great difficulty in finding their relatives because the addresses have been incorrectly written. Not knowing the names of the thousands of streets of New York, many mistakes are made in copying the address, and many immigrants wander about for days until they can locate their relatives through the newspapers.

If one is going to a relative or friend who is a businessman or manufacturer, he should take care to have the home address as well as that of the business. Ships often dock on days when business establishments and factories are closed, and he will not be able to locate his relative without the home address.

Some immigrants, on disembarking, think that it is wisest to hire a "carriage." To do this is [a] simple waste of money in a city like New York, where public transportation to the farthest point costs ten kopeks. A carriage will cost five to ten dollars, and if the address is wrong, the immigrant will have the extra expense of a night's lodging in a hotel. The immigrant who is not met by a relative is advised to consult a representative of the Jewish Immigration Association, who is always present at the docks, and who offers help without any charge.

IMMIGRANTS WITH "PREPAIDS"
(vol. 5, no. 5, 1911)

We have already reported a number of times that lately the American immigration officials have been dealing most strictly with immigrants whose ship tickets had been sent to them, i.e., "prepaid." They consider the fact that the ticket had been bought for the immigrant sufficient evidence that he is a pauper and will, therefore, become a burden to society (sufficient cause for his deportation).

The American newspapers tell of such an incident, which occurred in Philadelphia, where, incidentally, the treatment of a newly arrived immigrant is better than in New York.

On October 30 of the previous year, the immigrant Asher Weinblatt arrived from Kovno. He was detained because it was determined that he had received his ticket from a friend in Chicago. The immigration court—the Board of Special Inquiry—ordered his deportation because his passage had been paid by another and this was sufficient indication that he would likely become a public charge. Weinblatt presented an appeal which was rejected. His cause was then taken up by the Society for Protection of Jewish Immigrants, which took the matter to court. At a special hearing, it was determined that Mr. Weinblatt was an expert bookbinder and that he has friends in Chicago who were ready to support him. The judge ordered the immigration court to reconsider its decision. The Board of Special Inquiry turned to Washington for instruction. Word came back that Mr. Weinblatt be permitted to enter.

IMMIGRATION TO THE UNITED STATES
(vol. 5, no. 5, 1911)

In the month of January, 36,361 immigrants arrived in the United States. Among the newcomers were:

Jews	6,054
Italians	6,842
Poles	2,412
Germans	2,637
English	2,464

Indications are that there will be an increase in Jewish immigrants to the United States this year [June 31, 1910–July 1, 1911]. During the previous year the total of Jewish immigrants was 84,260. During the first seven months of this year [July 1, 1910–February 1, 1911] 61,490 arrived. Even if there will be no increase during the next five months, the total will be in excess of 90,000 for the year.

QUARANTINES
(*vol. 5, no. 15, 1911*)

The hearing on the quarantine isles of New York harbor—Hoffman and Swinburne—has been going on for a few weeks now. The isles are the ones to which immigrants smitten with a communicable disease are taken.

Last year, a number of letters by immigrant women were published in some New York newspapers. The letters described the sad plight of those unfortunate enough to be placed in the quarantine hospitals. Accusations of beating the sick, of violating women patients, forcing the confined to do the most menial labor which attendants were being paid to do, caused quite a stir when made. But a considerable time passed before an inquiry was ordered. Now witnesses are appearing before the Commission. Almost all state that the isles were ruled like a private preserve. The doctor in charge treated the confined like animals. The attendants beat adults and children alike, the food was inedible, the sanitary conditions scandalous, etc., etc.

Lawyers representing Jewish inmates who suffered through the quarantine confinement are present at the hearings, which will continue for some time yet.

REPORT OF THE
NATIONAL COUNCIL OF JEWISH WOMEN
TO THE IMMIGRATION CONFERENCE
AT LIBEAV
(*vol. 5, no. 16, 1911*)

In the United States there are no national laws concerning the husband's obligations to his wife and children. No law of the nation makes it a criminal offence to abandon or not to support one's family.

There are state laws, however, which make abandonment a criminal offence. . . .

If it can be demonstrated that the husband abandoned his wife, he will not only be subject to criminal prosecution, but will also be forced to provide for her needs. If he does not do so, the wife has a right to charge to him the costs of rent, food, clothing, and medical expenses. She is also entitled to demand a divorce. According to the law she may demand a divorce if he had abandoned her without justifiable cause or refuses to live with her. . . .

The divorce we speak of is a civil divorce. As for a religious divorce, the government will not become involved.

We received the following letter from the Sheltering Aid Society of New York, which throws light on the practical aspects of this problem:

The strongest laws on abandonment are those of the state of New York. There a husband may be jailed for abandoning his wife. The charity organizations have attempted to bring about the enactment of a natural law which would be in force in all the states, but, unfortunately, this has not been accomplished.

From a practical standpoint, even the strict laws of the state of New York are difficult to enforce. According to American judicial procedure, the abandoned wife must appear before the judge in person. Thus, if the abandoned wife is in Europe and the husband is in New York and has even married again, nothing can be done. In bigamy cases, the wife must appear in person before the court to press charges. We often receive requests from Russia to "save" the poor unfortunate *agunah* (abandoned wife). When we have succeeded in being of help, it was only through moral suasion and not legal action that we were able to do so.

YOUNG LADY EMIGRANTS
(*vol. 5, no. 18, 1911*)

From European harbor cities we have been receiving reports that lately a large number of young lady emigrants have been traveling alone.

They thus are in danger of being accosted by persons who would take advantage of their loneliness and innocence. It is, therefore, important to warn such young ladies against such persons who would press them into white slavery. If such girls turn to representatives of the immigration societies, the agents should inform their colleagues in the port cities of their arrival so that they can be protected.

In line with the problem alluded to in the foregoing news item, the Council of Jewish Women printed the following warning in English as well as in German and Yiddish:

WARNING

BEWARE OF ANY PERSON WHO GIVES ADDRESSES, OFFERS YOU EASY WELL PAID WORK, OR EVEN MARRIAGE. THERE ARE MANY EVIL MEN AND WOMEN WHO HAVE IN THIS WAY LED GIRLS TO DESTRUCTION. ALWAYS INQUIRE FOR THE PERSONS WHOSE NAMES ARE GIVEN ON THE OTHER SIDE OF THIS CARD, WHO WILL FIND OUT THE TRUTH FOR YOU, WHO WILL ADVISE YOU AND GIVE YOU ALL NECESSARY INFORMATION OR AID.

4. From Open to Restricted Immigration

Thirteen colonies lodged on the Atlantic seaboard joined together toward the end of the eighteenth century to form the United States of America. The young nation began almost immediate expansion, and by the middle of the nineteenth century reached across the continent to the Pacific. Vast stretches of land were opened for inhabitants. Europe, in the throes of a population explosion, was ready to offer up its excess people.

When the Napoleonic Wars came to an end, immigrants began to come in greater waves—first from the western lands, by mid-century from Germany and middle Europe, and by the end of the century and into the twentieth in increasing numbers from eastern and southern Europe, the eastern provinces of the Austro-Hungarian Empire, and Russia.

In the decade 1820–1830, the number was 128,393; three decades later, 1850–1860, it had grown to 2,799,423. In the ten years 1880–1890, the number of immigrants to the United States leaped to 5,246,613. During the latter two decades mentioned above, Jews came in large and increasing numbers.

Initially no laws encouraged or impeded immigration to the United States. But a serious decrease in the number of immigrants during the Civil War years impelled Congress to enact the first national immigration law in July 1864, the purpose of which was to encourage immigrants to come. That law was repealed in 1868, but it had had its effect: waves of immigrants came in record numbers, giving muscle and sinews to a rapidly emerging industrial giant of a nation. The numbers increased to such an extent that legislation to control immigration and to permit selectivity was soon enacted.

A debate was joined as to whether immigration should be open or selective, and, if selective, to what degree. As the numbers of immigrants increased, the issues were sharpened; debate turned into argument, propaganda, and lobbying. Those favoring restricted immigration began to win the victories, at first minor, then of consequence. In 1885 the Alien Contract Labor Law was passed to prohibit the importation of contract labor from abroad. It was a measure to keep paupers away, and to offer some degree of protection to American labor.

The first effective law restricting immigration was enacted on March 3, 1891:

"Be it enacted by the Senate and House of Representatives of the United States of America in Congress assembled, That the following classes of aliens shall be excluded from admission into the United States, in accordance with the existing acts regulating immigration, other than those concerning Chinese laborers: All idiots, insane persons, paupers or persons likely to become a public charge, persons suffering from a loathsome or a dangerous contagious disease, persons who have been convicted of a felony or other infamous crime or misdemeanor involving moral turpitude, polygamists, and also any person whose ticket or passage is paid for with the money of another or who is assisted by others to come, unless it is affirmatively and satisfactorily shown on special inquiry that such person does not belong to one of the foregoing excluded classes, or to the class of contract laborers excluded by the act of February twenty-sixth, eighteen hundred and eighty-five, but this section shall not be held to exclude persons living in the United States from sending for a relative or friend who is not of the excluded classes under such regulations as the Secretary of the Treasury may prescribe."

Immediately upon passage of this act, four national Jewish bodies joined in protest: the Independent Order B'nai B'rith, the Jewish Alliance of America, the Baron de Hirsch Trustees, and the Union of American Hebrew Congregations. Their spokesman, Simon Wolf, wrote on July 27, 1891, to the Secretary of the Treasury, calling attention to the question of immigration of Russian Hebrews to the United States. The organizations pledged their combined efforts to educate all newcomers in the responsibilities and duties of American citizenship. Their joint appeal closed with the following statement:

To close the avenues of this free and liberty-loving country, that has always opened its gates to the down-trodden and unjustly persecuted, would be against the underlying genius and theory of our glorious and beloved Constitution.

Neither the letter nor spirit of the laws of our country require us to "close the gates of mercy on mankind." . . .

It is apposite to mention that about ten years since, in consequence of enforcement of the cruel edicts recently being again carried out, a very large number of Russian Hebrews sought this land of liberty as a haven of rest. They have been assimilated in the mass of citizenship, and, so far as can be ascertained, not a single one has become a public burthen.

To refuse asylum to such people by reason of misfortune would give the right to deny rescue of a shipwrecked crew cast on our shores by dire disaster. No law, human or divine, requires such technical interpretation.

The Russian Hebrews are wrecked on their voyage of life; cast out on tempestuous oceans by inhuman machinations. National and international law should not interfere when humanity throws them life-preservers to save them from being engulfed by the waves, even of a sea of despair.

Mr. Wolf received an immediate reply to his letter of appeal from the Treasury Department. The issue seemed to revolve around whether Jewish organizations actively encouraged Jewish immigration or merely assisted those who arrived on their own:

AUGUST 1, 1891

TREASURY DEPARTMENT OFFICE OF THE SECRETARY

You call attention to the bitter hardships suffered by many thousands of Hebrews by reason of their forcible expulsion from their homes in the Russian Empire, and you state among other things that there is no organization in the United States which assists or encourages destitute Hebrew refugees to come to this country; that you deplore this form of immigration; that the efforts of the several Hebrew societies represented by you are confined to ameliorating the condition of these unhappy people after their arrival at American ports by relieving those in distress and aiding all to avoid massing in the seaboard cities and to distribute themselves to widely separated localities where they may as soon as possible become self-sustaining. You state that you have no complaint to make in connection with the official treatment of refugees who have already arrived, and that you do not apprehend any future cause for complaint in this regard; but you urge the consideration that practically enforced immigration of this nature cannot properly be classed as "assisted" immigration within the meaning of our laws, and finally you declare the readiness of the people and associations for whom you speak to give to the Government in all cases a satisfactory bond guaranteeing that none of these refugee immigrants shall become a public charge.

Be assured, gentlemen, that I fully concur in your estimate of the magnitude of the present calamity which has befallen so many of your race, as well as in your hope that an early mitigation or cessation of the current measures of expulsion may render unnecessary any general migration of Russian Hebrews to America or elsewhere. Unquestionably a great or sudden influx of expatriated and destitute aliens of any race would be a grave misfortune to any country, and American Hebrews act both patriotically and humanely when they advise Jewish refugees against coming hither, but at the same time endeavor to render self-supporting those who finally come. Obviously the support of great numbers of dependent persons is a tax upon the resources of the country, even though paid from private funds, and, quite as plainly, industrial conditions here might be seriously disturbed by the sudden arrival and the enforced competition of a multitude of needy people. Hence it is important to the last degree that the volume of this expected refugee immigration be not excessive or threatening, and that with entire certainty it be promptly and widely distributed, so as to supply a real want in scattered communities, and interfere as little as possible with existing and normal industrial conditions. The apparent scope and thoroughness of your plans for securing this immediate and wide distribution of the expected refugees are most gratifying, and upon the success of your associations in carrying out these plans will largely depend the possibility of the Government meeting your views in other respects.

While the immigration laws of the United States must, and will, be enforced, I agree with you that those laws were never enacted in derogation of the plainest requirements of humanity, and no worthy immigrant, who, in all other respects, meets the demands of our statutes, should be excluded from the country because, through the action of others, he is for the time being homeless and without property.

I shall rely upon your voluntary assurance that you will actively urge upon your brethren in Europe the attitude of our laws toward assisted immigration. I also beg to remind you that any tendency abroad to deflect toward this country the movement of destitute refugees, or to stimulate their migration hither, would be distinctly hostile to the spirit manifested in your letter and to the spirit in which the Government of the United States desires to treat this difficult and delicate problem.

Thanking you for your expressions of confidence that this Department, while executing the immigration laws efficiently, will also execute them humanely, I am,

Respectfully yours,

[Signed] *Charles Foster,*
Secretary.

During the same period, on July 3, 1891, an article in *Ha-Magid* warned against the rising anti-immigration sentiment:

The United States of America is not what once it was: a land of fullest freedom, freedom of commerce, labor, residence, a land of one law for the native-born and the stranger. The laws against the Chinese and the pauper immigrants, tariffs on foreign products, the prohibition against imported labor—all show that even the Americans have learned to make a distinction between the native-born and the stranger. They want to go even further in this matter. A law to raise further the tariff on foreign goods is now being discussed. Its purpose is not to increase revenue, of which there is now a surfeit, but simply to close the door to products of foreign manufacture. . . . When a nation begins to think in such terms, terms of we–they, it is not long before it proceeds from goods to people. It begins with foreign products, but it will end up with immigrants. It should, therefore, be no surprise that the hundreds and thousands of immigrants who come to America's shores are no longer welcomed with open arms. There is particular discrimination against the newcomers who settle in the big cities, where competition for jobs is very keen. . . . The day is near when the gates of the United States will be closed to immigrants, and not a vestige will remain of freedom of movement. The American legislature is already studying the question of immigration, examining the newcomers and their ways, to determine what kind of immigrant America should accept. As soon as they finish with the Chinese, they will turn to the Jews and Italians and find all kinds of reasons for their exclusion. . . . The Jew is always the first to be sacrificed, the first thrown stone falls on his head. The agitation against Jewish immigration has already taken on serious proportion. Who knows where it will end?

That same summer, the prestigious *North American Review* (August 1891) published an article by the equally esteemed Goldwin Smith arguing that Russian persecution of the Jew had been vastly exaggerated, and if indeed it existed, one should look to the Jew as its cause.

A native of England, professor of modern history at Oxford, Smith had championed the cause of the North in the Civil War. He was welcomed to the United States in 1868 and used his not inconsiderable gifts and influence in the service of a variety of causes, among them the advocacy of having Canada merge with the United States.

Smith's article, excerpts of which follow, aroused a storm of opposition. His argument was clear: the Jew will be neither a useful nor loyal citizen. He will only exploit, divide, and attempt to dominate. Be wise and prudent—shut the door to him. But in spite of many rejoinders, the article made its contribution to the cause of restrictive immigration.

NEW LIGHT ON THE JEWISH QUESTION
Goldwin Smith

The rising of the native populations of northern and eastern Europe against the Jews continues to increase in extent and in horror. From Germany, Russia, Austria, and the Danubian principalities it has spread to the Ionian Islands. In Russia, where the government takes the lead, the movement has assumed a form which calls forth general cries of indignation and pity. There are symptoms of a sympathetic movement even in France. The anti-Semitic revolt is, in fact, one of the great features of the age. Yet most of those who talk and write about it seem to mistake its nature and its cause.

The general belief has been that the anti-Semitic movement is religious, and that the Jews are being persecuted, as they were, or are assumed to have been, in the middle ages, on account of their faith. Such was the tenor of all the manifestoes, speeches, and editorials in which British indignation against Russia found vent after the anti-Semitic disturbances of 1880. Everybody said that the dark ages had come again, and that the murderous atrocities of medieval fanaticism were being reënacted in the nineteenth century.

Now, persecution is not the tendency of the Russian or of the church to which he belongs. The Eastern Church, while it has been superstitious and torpid, has always been tolerant, and, compared with other orthodox churches, free from the stain of persecution. . . .

After the last anti-Semitic disturbances in Russia, and when the vials of British wrath had been fully poured forth upon the Czar and his people, the British consuls at the different places in Russia at which disturbances had taken place were directed to report on them to the government. Their reports are comprised in two blue books (1881), into which few probably took the trouble to look at the time, but which every one who undertakes to deal with this question and pass judgment on the conduct of the Russian Government and people ought to make a point of reading. . . .

The most important part of the evidence given in the consuls' reports, however, is that which relates to the cause of the troubles. At Warsaw, where the people are Roman Catholics, there appears to have been a certain amount of passive sympathy with the insurgents on religious grounds. But everywhere else the concurrent testimony of the consuls is that the source of the agitation was economical and social, not religious. Bitterness produced by the exactions of the Jew, envy of his wealth, jealousy of his ascendency, combined in the lowest of the mob with the love of plunder, were the motives of the people for attacking him, not hatred of his faith. Vice-Consul Wagstaff, who seems to have paid particular attention to the question and made the most careful inquiry, after paying a tribute to the sober, laborious thrifty character and the superior intelligence of the Jew, and ascribing to these his increasing monopoly of commerce, proceeds:

The peasants, the vice-consul tells us, often say, when they look at the property of a Jew, "That is my blood." In confirmation of his view he cites the list of demands formulated by the peasants and laid before a mixed committee of inquiry into the causes of the disorder. These demands are all economical or social, with the exception of the complaint that Russian girls in Jewish service forget their religion and with it lose their morals. Everything, in short, seems to bear out the statement of the Russian Minister of the Interior, in a manifesto given in the blue book, that "the movement had its main cause in circumstances purely economical," provided that to "economical" we add "social," and include all that is meant by the phrase "hatred of Jewish usurpation" used in another document. . . .

The explanation of the whole trouble, and of all the calamities and horrors attending it, past or to come, is that the Jews are, to adopt the phrase borrowed by Vice-Consul Wagstaff from natural history, a parasitic race. Detached from their own country, they insert themselves for the purpose of gain into the homes of other nations, while they retain a marked and repellent nationality of their own. They are not the only parasitic race, though they are incomparably the most important and formidable; the Armenians, the Greeks of the dispersion, ancient and modern, the Parsis, and even the humble Gypsies, being other instances, while the Lombards in the middle ages and the Italians generally when their country had fallen under foreign dominion showed something like the same tendency. There is, therefore, nothing miraculous or mysterious in their condition. . . .

The dislike of the Jew and the desire to be rid of him have received a strong impulse, as has been truly said, from that reviving spirit of nationalism which, dating from the rising of the nations against Napoleon, has been fostered by the school of history of which Augustin Thierry was a model, and is showing itself not only in Russia, Germany, Hungary, and Bohemia, but in Ireland, Scotland, and Wales. The Jew is now detested not only because he absorbs the national wealth, but because, when present in numbers, he eats out the core of nationality. It is true that all nations are more or less composed of mixed races and have in them, perhaps, some even of the cave-dwellers' blood; but then the other elements amalgamate and the result is a nation, with which the tribal Jew does not blend. This is not the place for discussing the question between the nation and humanity; but the tribe, of which Judaism is a survival, is narrower, not broader, than the nation.

The derabbinization is far advanced, but the denationalization will not be complete, or anything like complete, till the Jew gives up the tribal rite of circumcision, which must always carry with it tribal sentiment and a feeling of separation from the rest of mankind. The intense love of gain and the addiction to the money trade are ingrained, and it is probable that many generations will pass before the balance of the Hewbrew intellect and character is restored by a community of pursuits with other men. Whether any of the tribal morality, the presence of which in the Talmud cannot be denied, still lingers in the mercantile dealings of the Jew, those who are brought into commercial relations with him must decide. He is—indeed, he has always and everywhere been—a conforming citizen, and has refused none of the burdens of the state, though he has made them as light as he could. He adopts also the language of the country in which he lives, reserving that of Judea for the interior of the synagogue. But he changes his country more easily than others. When the Southern Confederacy fell, its leaders generally stood by the wreck and did their best for those whom they had led; but Judah Benjamin went off to pastures new. . . .

It is also with a certain air of exploitation, the attitude of the cosmopolitan trader, that the genuine Jew takes up any political cause or party. It is impossible that a man should be heartily loyal to two nationalities at once; and so long as a trace of Jewish nationality remains the Jew cannot be a thorough Englishman or American. In fact, when a Jewish question arises in any part of the world, we are made to feel that there is a Jewish interest apart from that of the several nations in which the Jews have their abode. England was made to feel this in her disputes with Russia, and France was made to feel it in the Tunisian expedition. Light, however, would be thrown on this part of the matter if some Jewish authority would tell us distinctly what relation Jewish nationality or the tie of Jewish race bears to the nationality of the country in which the Jew happens to dwell.

The Jew of America and western Europe has not much reason to complain of his present position. In a society of which wealth is the ruling power, his financial skill, sharpened by immemorial practice and aided by the confederacy of his kinsmen, makes him the master of wealth. In Europe patrician pride bows its head before him, and royalty itself is at his feet. The press is rapidly falling under his influence, and becoming the organ of his interests and his enmities. If any hearts still rebel against an ascendency of the stock exchange and a worship of material success in its least beneficent form, they are so few that they need not be taken into account. Here, in the West, we have no cruel and desperate problem before us. We must allow existing influences to work on, taking care, perhaps, to guard ourselves against commercial combinations, and to look now and then behind the curtain of the press.

Selection of Immigration . . . Has the Highest Ethical Sanction

Three years later, Prescott F. Hall, lawyer, author, and Boston brahmin, became the founder and leading spirit of the Immigration Restriction League, which he brought into being in 1894. A prolific writer of books on various aspects of law, he called his literary and legal talents into the service of a selective, i.e., Anglo-Saxon, Aryan immigration:

IMMIGRATION LEGISLATION: ETHICAL ASPECTS OF LEGISLATION
Prescott F. Hall

In any discussion of the immigration question, there are always many persons who, admitting the legal power, question the moral right of a country to exclude immigrants, at least such as are honest and well disposed. . . .

It must be remembered, however, that we are living in a democracy which our ancestors established here, and that a democracy is a very delicate machine, requiring for its successful operation certain political and moral ideals, and the intelligent cooperation of every citizen. Our institutions were established by a relatively homogeneous community, consisting of the best elements of population selected by the circumstances under which they came to the new world. Today, much of our immigration is an artificial selection by the transportation companies of the worst elements of European and Asiatic peoples. If the founders of the nation had been of the recent types, can we suppose for a moment this country would enjoy its present civilization? Even as it is, we have been obliged to desert the political theories of the early days, and to adopt various despotic devices in order to control the inferior elements which have come into our body politic.

The most valuable service which the American nation can render to humanity at large is to preserve and to perfect the institutions of its founders. Assuming that we are aiming at making the world as a whole a better place to live in, we must remember that we can accomplish this through the medium of the nation as well as through the medium of the individual and, bearing in mind that the birth rate in the older countries soon restores in them the precise condition which obtained before immigration took place, we find that in many cases the benefit is not to the country whence the immigrants come, but only, if at all, to the immigrants themselves. By making this "great experiment of free law and educated labor," as General Walker has called it, a triumphant success we shall help the world more than by allowing indiscriminate immigration.

We may go further, and say it is our duty toward the world, not only to preserve in this country the conditions necessary to successful democracy but to develop here the finest race of men and the highest civilization. We have in the United States a unique opportunity to try the effect of hybridizing race-stocks upon an enormous scale. In every other department, when we try such experiments, we take care to select the best specimens of each stock. The race horse, the seedless orange, and scores of valuable animals and plants, have been developed as the result of artificial selection, which would never have been brought into existence without it. The human reason is, indeed, one of the forces through which the Power of the Universe works, and it is hard to understand why the *laissez faire* advocates claim it should be excluded from the one field of immigration problems.

Natural selection cannot be trusted of itself to bring about the best results. "Survival of the fittest" means that those survive who are fittest for survival but not necessarily fittest for any other purpose. This is seen when we compare a statesman or college president, who has two children and educates them so that they take useful and important places in society, with some poor drunkard in the slums who has a dozen children and gives them no advantages at all. With modern sanitation these children do not die, as they might have once, but they start with a frightful handicap and are likely to be, to some extent, weakly, criminal and comparatively valueless to the community. Now, the second man has "survived" in his children six times as much as the first man, and yet neither he nor his children may be as fit for any purpose as the first man and his children. In other words, the mere test of reproductive power in time is not a test of qualitative or teleological value. Many who perished in the French Revolution and in the other great massacres of history were undoubtedly superior in every way to those who killed them. The tempest, the plague and the avalanche destroy equally the just and the unjust. . . .

Let us, then, continue the benefits of that selection which took place in the early days of the nation by sifting the immigration of today, so that no discordant elements shall enter to imperil the ideals and institutions of our nation, and to the end that we may produce a still finer race to help the world in its progress. Such selection of immigration surely has the highest ethical sanction.

The arguments for restricted immigration were mounting. In answer to those who pleaded that the doors of the "sweet land of liberty" remain open to those seeking freedom from persecution, Goldwin Smith and others launched a campaign to argue that the plight of the Russian Jew was nowhere as serious as American Jews claimed.

Opposition to Jewish immigration was part of opposition to a continued influx of immigrants which would change the character of the American nation. This had formed the substance of Prescott Hall's plea for a selection.

Edward Alsworth Ross was more direct. According to him, the Jews lacked morality, were addicted to crime, and were an undesirable element. One of his outspoken articles appeared in *The Old World in New York* (1914).

THE EAST EUROPEAN HEBREW
E. A. Ross

The Jewish immigrants cherish a pure, closeknit family life and the position of the woman in the home is one of dignity. More than any other immigrants they are ready to assume the support of distant needy relatives. They care for their own poor, and the spirit of cooperation among them is very noticeable. Their temper is sensitive and humane; very rarely is a Jew charged with any form of brutality. There is among them a fine elite which responds to the appeal of the ideal, and is found in every kind of ameliorative work.

Nevertheless, fair-minded observers agree that certain bad qualities crop out all too often among these eastern Europeans. A school principal remarks that his Jewish pupils are more importunate to get a mark changed than his other pupils. A settlement warden who during the summer entertains hundreds of nursing slum mothers at a country "home" says: "The Jewish mothers are always asking for something extra over the regular kit we provide each guest for her stay." "The last thing the son of Jacob wants," observes an eminent sociologist, "is a square deal." A veteran New York social worker cannot forgive the ghetto its littering and defiling of the parks. "Look at Tompkins Square," he exclaimed hotly, "and compare it with what it was twenty-five years ago amid a German population!" As for the caretakers of the parks their comment on this matter is unprintable. Genial settlement residents, who never tire of praising Italian or Greek, testify that no other immigrants are so noisy, pushing and disdainful of the rights of others as the Hebrews. That the worst exploiters of these immigrants are "sweaters," landlords, employers and "white slavers" of their own race, no one gainsays.

The authorities complain that the east European Hebrews feel no reverence for law as such and are willing to break any ordinance they find in their way. The fact that pleasure-loving Jewish business men spare Jewesses but pursue Gentile girls excites bitter comment. The insurance companies scan a Jewish fire risk more closely than any other.

Credit men say the Jewish merchant is often "slippery" and will "fail" in order to get rid of his debts. For lying, the immigrant has a very bad reputation. In the North End of Boston "the readiness of the Jews to commit perjury has passed into a proverb." Conscientious immigration officials become very sore over the incessant fire of false accusations to which they are subjected by the Jewish press and societies. United States senators complain that during the close of the struggle over the immigration bill they were overwhelmed with a torrent of crooked statistics and misrepresentations by the Hebrews fighting the literacy test.

Graver yet is the charge that these east European immigrants lower standards wherever they enter. In the boot and shoe trade some Hebrew jobbers who, after sending in an order to the manufacturer, find the market taking an unexpected downward turn, will reject a consignment on some pretext in order to evade a loss. Says Dr. Bushee: "The shame of a variety of underhanded methods in trade not easily punishable by law must be laid at the door of a certain type of Jew." It is charged that for personal gain the Jewish dealer wilfully disregards the customs of the trade and thereby throws trade ethics into confusion. Physicians and lawyers complain that their Jewish colleagues tend to break down the ethics of their professions. It is certain that Jews have commercialized the social evil, commercialized the theatre, and done much to commercialize the newspaper. . . .

Crime

The Hebrew immigrants usually commit their crimes for gain; and among gainful crimes they lean to gambling, larceny, and the receiving of stolen goods rather than to the more daring crimes of robbery and burglary. The fewness of the Hebrew in prison has been used to spread the impression that they are uncommonly law-abiding. The fact is it is harder to catch and convict criminals of cunning than criminals of violence. The chief of police of any large city will bear emphatic testimony as to the trouble Hebrew lawbreakers cause him. Most alarming is the great increase of criminality among Jewish young men and the growth of prostitution among Jewish girls. Says a Jewish ex-assistant attorney-general of the United States in an address before the

B'nai B'rith: "Suddenly we find appearing in the life of the large cities the scarlet woman of Jewish birth. . . . In the women's night court of New York City and on gilded Broadway the majority of street walkers bear Jewish names. . . . This sudden break in Jewish morality was not natural. It was a product of cold, calculating, mercenary methods, devised and handled by men of Jewish birth." Says the president of the Conference of American Rabbis: "The Jewish world has been stirred from center to circumference by the recent disclosures of the part Jews have played in the pursuance of the white slave traffic."

Enveloped in the husks of medievalism, the religion of many a Jew perishes in the American environment. The immigrant who loses his religion is worse than the religionless American because his early standards are dropped along with his faith. With his clear brain sharpened in the American school, the egoistic, conscienceless young Jew constitutes a menace. As a Jewish labor leader said to me, "the non-morality of the young Jewish business men is fearful. Socialism inspires an ethics in the heart of the Jewish workingman, but there are many without either the old religion or the new. I am aghast at the consciencelessness of the *Luft-proletariat* without feeling for place, community or nationality."

The persistence of the issue was manifest in an article appearing in the *New York Times,* January 29, 1905, excerpts of which appear below:

The grave and growing importance of the immigration problem is based upon positive assurances that upward of a million aliens will this year be added to the population of the United States—a record-breaking year. To the vast tidal wave of controversy which the existing situation has let loose over the country, the declaration of Commissioner General Sargent that the United States is swiftly approaching, or already faces one of the gravest crises of its history—a crisis which he believes can only be met and mastered by immediate remedial legislation tending to restrict immigration and also to deflect it toward the more sparsely settled sections. He foresees a gigantic western im-

migration movement by reason of the gathering revolution in Russia, and he strongly advises congressional action tending to strengthen the hands of the Immigration Bureau in coping adequately with the situation. Vast hordes of fear-driven, poverty-stricken Russians, especially of southern Russia, are pouring through every loophole of escape to this country according to information in his possession . . .

While the article deals with all immigrants, Frank P. Sargent, U.S. Commissioner General of Immigration, "probing on into the subject with savage jabs, as though it were a sore that needed a thorough amputation," is directly quoted:

"During the present month all records for deportation have been broken, over a thousand immigrants having been ineligible for admission into the country. What is the principal reason for their ineligibility? Disease and destitution. Since the outbreak of the Russo-Japanese war thousands and thousands of Russian Jews are fleeing here to escape conscription. Poor fellows, most of them are hardly more than food for powder, having been ill-fed, ill-housed, and ill-clad all their lives, and the impromptu accommodations here on the island are amazing luxuries to them. Others who are being deported today are contract laborers and decrepit men and women inveigled by steamship agents who have willfully disregarded the law."

In Defense of the Immigration

"From 1870 to 1891, when America as a whole was pro-immigrant, American Jewry was restrictionist in approach . . . From 1891 to 1924 . . . a complete reversal of attitudes prevailed . . . Acknowledged Jewish spokesmen such as Simon Wolf, Max J. Kohler, Abram Elkus and Louis Marshall . . . tried to demolish, or at best modify, every piece of restrictive legislation as it arose." So states Esther Panitz in two articles published in the *American Jewish Historical Quarterly* (vol. 53, no. 2, Dec. 1963, and vol. 55, no. 1, Sept. 1965).

Among the *Selected Papers and Addresses* of Louis Marshall, the

noted constitutional lawyer and Jewish leader, is the following letter
written to Governor Carrol S. Page of Vermont:

JANUARY 28, 1907

I am very much interested in defeating the so-called Immigration
Bill which passed the United States Senate some time ago, which was
passed in amended form by the House, and which is now in the hands
of the Conference Committee, of which Senator Dillingham is a member. . . .

The bill as it passed the Senate is subject to three objections, which
are of a most serious character and which in my judgment are contrary
to the genius of our institutions:

(1) It seeks to impose an educational qualification upon immigrants,
not only males but females.

I can see no good reason for such a qualification. An educated immigrant is not ordinarily the most beneficial. The ranks of the anarchists and of the violent socialists are recruited from the educated
classes, frequently from among those who read and write several languages. The illiterate immigrant comes here to work; to seek opportunities for educating his children, which he does not get abroad, and of
becoming a useful member of society. It is the illiterate immigrants
who are now building our railroads, and canals, and subways. The native American shrinks from such labor. The sons of our farmers are
becoming professional men, or clerks. Even the German and Irish immigrants of a quarter of a century ago do not seek employment which
involves heavy manual labor.

Personally I know a great deal concerning the immigrant, because
my parents were both of that class, and I can say as a result of an acquaintance with thousands of them, that literacy is not a proper test of
desirability. The entire wealth of my father when he landed consisted
of a five-franc piece. While he was able to read and write, I am sure
that he would not have been able to read fluently the Constitution of

the United States in German, the only language which he could read, and that he would not have understood it; and yet you are able to say whether or not he has been a good citizen. What is true of him is true of millions who have come to this country from abroad.

(2) One of the most objectionable clauses in the act is the so-called "low vitality" clause.

Under this clause, the inspectors at the port of entry are empowered arbitrarily to deport the immigrant at whose door this charge is laid. The phrase is vague, and is susceptible of all manner of interpretation. It would apply most harshly against those refugees who are coming to our shores from Russia, and who are the victims of the most inhuman persecution. These immigrants, who have been subjected to the attacks of the Black Hundreds, whose families have been massacred, come in a state of great mental depression, due to excitement, worry, and grief. They are in many instances people of deep religious convictions, who, by reason thereof, while in transit have abstained for a number of weeks from eating what they considered to be prohibited food, and in consequence become gaunt and emaciated in appearance. We all know that travel and confinement in the steerage of a trans-Atlantic liner are not conducive to the creation of robustness. Hence, to such people as these, the clause in question bears the potentiality of untold mischief.

The House Bill contains a clause which creates an exception in favor of the victims of persecution; the Senate Bill is silent on that subject.

(3) Another very objectionable clause is that which provides for an inspection of the immigrant abroad, and which empowers the inspectors to take such action as will prevent a person who does not meet with their approval from being transported to this country.

Aside from the serious doubt as to whether a foreign government would permit American inspectors to exercise their functions abroad, the serious difficulty with this provision is, that the power conferred on the inspectors, although of the most arbitrary character, is from the very nature of things, when exercised, final and conclusive. There is no way of reviewing the action of such an inspector by any superior officer, or by any American tribunal. He will soon regard himself as a Czar, and the unfortunate immigrant will of necessity be dependent on his tender mercies; the opportunities for corruption would be manifold and the scandals which would arise would seriously reflect upon the honor of our country.

You would not only place me, but many of my friends who are deeply concerned in the outcome of this legislation, under lasting obligations to you, if you would support us in this endeavor to defeat a measure which, if it becomes a law, will produce incalculable harm, not only to those who seek our hospitable shores, but also to the country in whose welfare we are all concerned.

The official statement on the American Immigration Laws issued by William Williams, Commissioner of Ellis Island, was reprinted in *Der Yiddisher Emigrant* (vol. 5, no. 10, 1911). It appears here in the editon's English translation:

1. The immigration officials will not indicate which immigrant will be admitted until he has arrived and been examined.

2. The immigration laws apply to all foreigners, even those who had previously resided in the United States, including one who had already received his "first papers."

3. The immigration laws apply to all foreigners, no matter which class (on board ship) they arrive in. All third class (steerage) passengers are examined on Ellis Island. Cabin passengers are examined on board; only those whose right to immigrate is questioned are taken to Ellis Island.

4. The law stipulates that if the examining inspector cannot determine whether to permit the immigrant to enter, the immigrant is to be detained for Special Inquiry. The Special Inquiry is conducted by three inspectors.

5. The following persons are forbidden to enter: idiots; feeble-minded, epileptics; paupers, or those who will become public charges

(see nos. 8 and 9); persons suffering from tuberculosis or loathsome and communicable diseases (including trachoma); persons who have a physical or mental handicap which will interfere with their making a living (see no. 10); anarchists, prostitutes, whiteslavers, and those who live off prostitution; laborers who came to America on contract; persons who have received their travel expenses from an organization, a society, or a foreign government; children under the age of sixteen, unless accompanied by their father or mother.

6. In determining whether an immigrant will fall under the category of pauper who will become a public charge, the immigration officials take into consideration his trade or profession, his skill (his physical and emotional ability to pursue his trade), the number of persons he will have to support in America and abroad, his prospects of finding work here, and the amount of money he brings with him.

7. Since the law does not stipulate how much money an immigrant is to bring with him, no specific amount can be indicated. But in most cases, it would be dangerous for an immigrant to arrive without a minimum of $25 and a railroad ticket to his place of destination. Often the immigrant needs more money; in any case, he should have enough to be able to support himself until he can find work.

8. The law about contract labor refers only to physical labor, skilled and unskilled. The law makes exception for actors and actresses, doctors, singers, clergymen of all persuasions, professors and teachers, members of the learned professions, household help, and for the skilled professions if there exists a shortage in these skills.

9. Children under sixteen who are not traveling with a parent may only be permitted to enter through permission of the Secretary of Commerce, granted only under unusual circumstances. The children must be physically fit, must be traveling to close relatives who are able to support them, who will send them to school till age sixteen and will not impose upon them labor beyond the youthful capacity.

10. A foreigner who has been in the country less than three years may be deported at any time if
    a) he has entered illegally,
    b) he evaded inspection,

c) he has become a public charge for causes which already existed at the time of his entry.

The forces for restriction of immigration became dominant in postwar isolationist, xenophobic America. On May 7, 1921, Congress enacted a law which limited "the number of aliens of any nationality who may be admitted . . . in any fiscal year . . . to 3 per centum of the number of foreign born persons of such nationality resident in the United States as determined by the . . . census of 1910. . . ."

In 1924 the Johnson-Reed Act provided that for the following three years the percentage was to be cut from three to two percent, and the base year of calculation moved back to 1890. After 1927, the maximum number of immigrants to the United States was set at 150,000.

This was clearly an act to do away with any sizable immigration from eastern and southern Europe. Such immigration as was permitted favored those from western and northern Europe.

Congressman John Cable of Ohio summed up the argument for selective immigration in an article in *The Outlook* on January 23, 1924.

The selection of future citizens to this United States should not depend upon the horse-power of steamships. The admission of immigrants to this country is too serious a matter to be determined by a race of ships across the ocean, the speediest vessels being able to land the more fortunate ones at Ellis Island after executing a transatlantic Marathon.

This unsatisfactory condition is the result of the present three per cent restrictive Immigration Act. Unless extended or amended, it expires June 30, 1924. Only three per cent of the number of foreign-born nationals who reside in the United States as determined by the 1910 Census may be admitted during the fiscal year, and not more than twenty per cent of these are admissible in any one month.

Therefore, because of this regulation, we have the spectacle of public health doctors and inspectors working overtime at the beginning of each month, making hurried examinations of those eagerly seeking admission to this country. At the same time, we know that nothing is more important than the proper selection of those who, as potential citizens, are to become associated with the country's future.

The new bill framed by the House Committee on Immigration, which will be submitted to Congress during its present session, provides for a radical change in this respect. The proposed new legislation will eliminate this particularly bad feature of the present Immigration Act.

I may say in connection with this proposed new legislation that about eighty-five per cent of the members of the House of Representatives favor a more restrictive measure. This fact has been shown both by their votes and by their great interest in this all-important question.

In providing for a new law, that will cope with the difficult problem of immigration, special emphasis has been placed on the so-called "certificate plan." This represents a part—the most essential part, it seems to me—of the proposed new measure.

This carefully thought out method of determining future citizenry of foreign birth at their native homes will, I believe, serve to eliminate many evils that experience has shown to exist in former immigration measures.

Not only are the American people concerned with the number who may come here, but they also reserve the right to know something about the kind of immigrant who seeks a permanent residence here. There is no good reason why this country should make of itself an asylum for the physically, mentally, or morally unfit. This question is too serious a one to be treated lightly or with the apparent laxity which certain figures show has too often been the case in the past. . . .

I have hope of great benefit resulting from this proposed certificate plan of admission to this country. In a word, this represents a system of selective immigration. Its operation begins at the home of the prospective immigrant. We learn something about the newcomer before he actually leaves his country. . . .

With this passport the immigrant, under the law, will be required to furnish essential information pertaining to himself and his family, including the family record of health; also in this manner it will be determined if the applicant has ever been arrested, and if so, the facts concerning the offense with which he was charged; his ability to read at least one language or dialect, as already prescribed by law; his occupation; and, if the custom of registering its people is in vogue in his country, then he will be asked to submit a copy of his record to the United States authorities.

With this information at hand, the American Consul will then pass on the application, and if the applicant appears to be admissible his passport will be visaed; otherwise not. Today the Consul has little latitude. All he is able to do under the circumstances, in many cases, is to warn the immigrant of the likelihood of being refused admission at our ports.

The proposed certificate to be used by the immigrant will be made out in duplicate, the immigrant retaining the one when he is admitted, the Secretary of Labor retaining the other for his files. Thus every immigrant and his native record, sworn to under oath, will become a part of what the Secretary of Labor hopes will constitute a new registration system for the handling of immigrant cases.

The final examination for admission should be made at our ports of entry by American doctors and inspectors on American soil, surrounded by American influence, where we have American hospitals and buildings for the temporary detention of those whom it may appear necessary to hold for future examination.

With the certificate plan in operation, every immigrant coming here will have the assurance that, so far as the particular quota under which he comes is concerned, he will not be turned back and be compelled to repeat the long sea voyage and at considerable expense, because of the fact that speedier ships bringing numbers of his countrymen had already exhausted the quota.

Under this new arrangement, the congestion at Ellis Island will cease, for the last of the month or the last of the year will be as safe as the first for those holding such certificates.

With the orderly flow of immigrants through Ellis Island a more thorough examination, at the same time, will be insured, and a better opportunity given for the weeding out of any chance undesirables.

The primary duty of Congress is to legislate for the American people; still there are those who press the claim that the present law is too restrictive. The records, however, refute this. Before the war, for instance, a million admitted of both immigrant and non-immigrant classes was a fair average. Let us compare this figure with the last fiscal year. North and South American and adjacent islands are not included within the quota territory. While 357,803 only may be admitted under the present quota, yet in round numbers 523,000 immigrant aliens were admitted, many coming from Mexico and Canada. The non-immigrant alien includes those who come here for business or pleasure—professional, skilled, learned classes, and the like. In addition, it is a safe guess that there were around 100,000 who came in unlawfully, seeping in over the border and from Cuba. This total of 773,000 compares very favorably with the million before the war. But, based on evidence submitted to the Committee, an additional million immigrants each year would have come to America under prewar legislation.

Under the proposed act, one objectionable feature of immigration should be removed. I refer to the numerous personal appeals made to the members of Congress in behalf of families that have been divided through the rigidity of the present quota law.

This appeal presents unlimited opportunities for fraudulent and shyster lawyers and dishonest go-betweens, of whose activities this Committee has abundant proof. These irresponsible persons often use the names of Senators and Representatives without their knowledge, and their "interest" in the immigrant is made at great cost to these uninformed, unsuspecting, and helpless strangers.

On the whole, our duty lies first with the alien now in our land. Give him the privilege of an education, teach him the history and ideals of our country, the duties and obligations of citizenship. This is the highest of duties—the making of Americans for a bigger, better America.

Congressman Albert Johnson, chairman of the Committee on Immigration, House of Representatives, who gave his name to the 1924 bill, summed up the arguments of the restrictionists in his article, "The Coming Immigration Law," which appeared in the same issue of *The Outlook:*

After years of study, including investigations in lands across the Atlantic and lands across the Pacific, the majority of the members of the House Committee on Immigration are, I believe, of the opinion that mankind is literally at the crossroads. The distresses of the peoples of the world, white, black, and yellow, are so many and the increase in the birth rate in all countries except France and Mexico is so great that the probabilities are that our own children will resent the fact that we have not been more successful in passing more stringent immigration restrictive acts. Our grandchildren will, fifty or sixty years from now, in all probability, be scratching hard for a foothold and food in the United States of America—the past land of boasted riches and untold resources.

I believe that the majority of the people of the United States, including even those of alien birth, have come to a very firm conclusion with respect to immigration. They think, and the majority of the House Committee on Immigration and Naturalization agrees, I believe, that—

1. Immigrants shall never again come to the United States as mere commodities in the labor scheme.

2. That the name melting-pot is a misnomer and that the asylum idea is played out forever.

3. That the countries of the world shall no longer dump upon the United States their criminals, their feeble, their aged, and their undesirables.

4. That if we are to clean house and provide those guarantees for every last alien now within our borders, each one of whom is included in those magnificent words which begin the first sentence of the Preamble to the Constitution, "We the people of the United States," that

we should, as far as possible, admit the husbands or wives, minor un-married children, fathers and mothers, and even grandfathers and grandmothers, of those aliens now here, but decline to admit other dependents in any number under any quota scheme from any country; as a matter of fact, eighty-five per cent of all immigrants who have come to the United States in the past ten years have come to relatives, and for the last fiscal year ninety-eight per cent of all immigrants who came from Poland came to relatives, nearly all supplied with money furnished by these relatives; and although a very large number started without money and arrived without money, they were able within three weeks to find the money to send for more relatives.

5. That in order to prevent the growth of racial hatred, with its ac-companying religious differences, it is highly desirable to keep out from the United States as many new arrivals as possible until we have thoroughly cleaned house.

6. That the United States should not continue to admit for perma-nent residence within its borders those who are, under the law, ineligi-ble to citizenship, and that sooner or later the United States must amend its Constitution so as to deny citizenship to those born here whose parents were ineligible to citizenship.

PART TWO

The American Jewish Experience:
Light and Shadow

5. *Family:*
Problems and Promise

Should I leave a land where freedom lives
in every corner? . . . Things have been
going rather badly for me. . . . Those who
know me show me little compassion.

—LETTER FROM HUSBAND IN NEW YORK
TO WIFE IN WARSAW, 1868

The mist of light and shadow that characterized the lives of new arrivals is reflected in a letter written by a husband living in New York to the wife he had left behind in Warsaw. It is doubtful whether the letter ever reached its destination, for it was intercepted by the censor in Warsaw, who had it translated into Polish. Copies of the translation were preserved in the archives of the censor and of the Warsaw Jewish community. It was published in Itzhak Schipper's *Nasz Przeglad* in 1938. The full text follows:

NEW YORK, NOV. 8, 1866

My Dear Wife Pearl Orenstein:

I am really surprised that you would even think that I am so foolish as to return home with neither money nor a livelihood, to await a handout from our parents and to become the laughing stock of all our friends.

Should I leave a land where freedom lives in every corner; a land, where the old ways are not hallowed; where there is no trace of that old nonsense; a land of freedom of thought; and above all, a land where there are things more important than good digestion? Shall I return to that accursed and foolish environment which I left? And what kind of society can I be part of there? Of one thing you may be certain: the long *kapote* [coat worn by the *Chasidim*] which I wore but could not bear, I will never again wear! Should I return home to expose myself to ridicule and have "nonbeliever" shouted at me by the stupid, who will avoid me when they really should respect me? No, this I will never do! At least not as long as I will need to live among the *Chasidim*.

I do believe that even in Warsaw one can be happy if fortune smiles on him. But as for myself, I would not want it, even if I would find great wealth there. Here my soul is free, there she would be fettered. Still, I hope some day to return home, but I will live true to my convictions, and I hope some day to carry on a business there or elsewhere, which would afford me a good living.

I have only been here a short time, but I have already learned the stratagems they are applying toward me. Someone told me that a certain carpenter is looking for me and that he brought with him a letter from you to the Rabbi of New York. What nonsense! Don't you know that New York does not have a rabbi? First of all, this is a free country. Anyone can do what he wants. No one is controlled here. And second, what can a rabbi do to me? Can he grab me by the ears and send me home? Is it wise that you send a person to find me who is not of the finest, who can hurt my business by telling all kinds of stories about me? No! That is not the right way. I swear by God that day and night I think of you and my dear children, thinking only how I can make for you a good and secure future, when we will be able to live together as we ought to.

In the meanwhile, I have not been able to do much business because I do not know the language, and that is an absolute must. I never learned a trade, and to begin now is too difficult. To go from house to house peddling as so many who have no trade do, that I couldn't do. It would be too difficult for me, for I was not trained for such work at home. So, things have been going rather badly for me. Truthfully, what can I write to you? So that some people will have pity on me, and others will see it as punishment from God? Unfortunately, I have found few friends among those I have met here because I have not been able to become part of a cultured group. Those who know me show me little compassion. So I waited until I could save some money to send to you because the money I brought with me went before I could even turn around. Now, thank God, my situation has improved a little, and I will get to some money. So I write you this letter, you shouldn't think that I have forgotten you and our dear children.

Your eternally faithful and loving husband,
Alter Orenstein

P.S. At present I cannot tell you where to write to me because I do not know where I will be. I am leaving New York now because I have no prospects here. With the greatest of efforts, I might be able to send you a hundred rubles, but I know that sending such a sum can't help you as much as it can harm me. You are with the family which will not permit that you will lack for anything. But for me, who am in a strange land looking . . .

The letter contains all the elements so frequently repeated in the immigrant drama: the religious and cultural maverick (the husband had been a *Chasid* of the Rebbe of Ger) breaking out of a constricting environment, the *luftmensch* (he who lives on air) without a trade or training, the "cultured" gentleman coming out of a milieu where physical labor was disdained and finding himself in a strange land and society where only hard work brings rewards. Here too are the abandoned wife, fearful that the husband will forget her, and her worried family trying to get her husband back to her so she should not be condemned to a living widowhood.

The tone of the letter is one of ambivalence and inner conflict: expressing nostalgia for home and its security, but love for America and its freedom; lonely for wife and children, but not ready to pay the price that rejoining them would demand; boasting about the greatness of America, but admitting that he has not been able to make his way; speaking bravely of a bright future, but suggesting that his present plight not be told to old friends who may pity and jeer.

Indeed, it contains the blend of immigrant hope and disappointment, of optimism and awareness of harsh reality, of the fear and sadness that marked the life of the Jewish immigrant in America.

A poetic version of the same admixture, with emphasis on the disappointing realities of American life as they confronted "greenhorn" families, appears in a poem by Elyakum Zunser, the most popular folk bard of the east European Jewish community. His verses recorded and commented upon the life of Russian Jewry in the second half of the nineteenth century: young Jewish boys pressed into army service; the ethical pietistic *musar* movement; *Hovevei Zion,* the "lovers of Zion," the nascent movement for the settlement and colonization of the ancient homeland; and the exodus to America. He planned to settle on the land in Palestine, but circumstance took him to a printing shop in New York. In the New World as in the Old, he continued to publish his songs, and here as there they became the popular ballads of his generation.

Zunser's poem, "For Whom Is the Gold Country?," was published in pamphlet form, with a portrait of the author and the music score, in 1894, five years after his arrival in America. It sings of anticipation and reality—of dreams of a golden land turned to dross. It asks the question that nagged at the hearts and consciences of many a newcomer. The editor has attempted to retain the doggerel form of the verse in his translation:

FOR WHOM IS THE GOLD COUNTRY?
Elyakum Zunser

1

While yet a child
Of America, I was told:
"How happy its people,
It's a Land of Gold!"

I came to the land, saw it and Lo!
Tears and suffering and tales of woe.
In its narrow streets, on square and place,

Darkness, poverty, writ on each face
   Stand from morn till night
   Huddled masses, a frightful sight.
One would sacrifice his child for a cent,
Or drive a man from his rooms for rent.
   Here a greenhorn hung'ring for bread
   Falls in the street, starved, dead!
Poverty, misery, darkness, cold—
Everywhere, in this Land of Gold!

2

Of toil and sweat, and sweat and toil
The worker has no lack
Weary when the season's "busy"
Hungry when it's "slack."
The boss is his worker's keeper
Until a machine can do it cheaper.
What a man is, and what he's been,
Is sacrificed to the machine.
And more and more the streets are filled
With wandering men whom fate has willed
   To be a brother to the horse
   Who pulls the streetcar down the course.
The machine has done its job—
See that broken, crippled mob.
One loses his sight, another his hand
To the machine, in this Golden Land.

3

The greenhorn is fair game and prey
To every gang that's seen,
The policeman turns his head away;
How helpless the man who's green!
The policeman sees the peddler's flaw
And drags him to the court of law

No justice here, who'll care and toil
For a poor frightened peddler in the law's coil?
   The lawyer comes to sell his ware,
   His fee is his only care.
Justice here is bought and sold,
In this golden land, this Land of Gold.

4

What value human life
All is bloodshed, all is strife.
A train leaves its road and rails,
A river of blood and widow's wails.
A coal mine explodes without warning
Hundreds of families sit in mourning.
   See a tenement burning bright.
   See it every day and night.
He jumped from the window—neck broke,
All who remained choked with smoke.
   A child's in the fire escape! (So frail, so sweet)
   Too late! She falls charred to the street.
Oh, how many times has the death knell tolled
In this golden land, this Land of Gold!

5

See here the woman, once lovely and mild,
Where's her complexion of flowers?
Enslaved in the factory while yet a child
She grows old not with years, but in hours.
The wedding bells a warning relate:
Marriage is a snare, an opiate.
All your toil till now is as naught
Compared to the slavery your marriage has bought.
Oh, how the flower does fade and wither
As the wife scurries hither and thither,
   Driven about by the baby's yell
   Caring for three boarders as well.

Never ending toil makes the body grow weary,
Care and worry and the eyes grow bleary.
A woman's lot (too dread to be told)
In this golden land, this Land of Gold!

6

Look with me at New York's Downtown
The air is heavy and vile
In filthy tenements, they press down
People, in herring-barrel style.
The food they sell to those in need
Is not fit for cattle to feed,
And many a man has taken to bed
Laid low by the food he's been fed.
The newspaper boy's life is hard and grim,
He has papers to sell—so many!
On New York's streets he risks life and limb,
Oh, how hard to earn a penny!
    The child leaves school, gives up education,
    To keep his family from the throes of starvation.
Oh, how harsh is Life's demand,
In the land of gold, this Golden Land!

7

But happy the life of him who has money
His years are full of laughter, his day's always sunny
Power and pleasure his wealth does bring,
The millionaire is America's king!
Gold and silver to the rich flow,
As the rivers flow to the ocean,
No favor to friend, no mercy to foe
God Mammon has all his devotion.
His power is great, his will none can thwart,
His word is law in every court.
Newspapers proclaim his fame,

They sing his deeds, they shout his name.
　　Mines are his, and trains as well,
　　So much! None can count or tell.
America is his to have and hold,
　His golden land. *His* Land of Gold!

Though much nostalgic literature has appeared about "the good old days in the ghetto," the facts of life were grim. The squalid tenements, into which so many newcomers were crowded, made family living exceedingly difficult. The conditions are graphically described in this report from the collection *The Russian Jew in the United States,* in an essay by M. Fishberg on:

"THE TENEMENT APARTMENT"

A "double-decker" is usually a building six to seven stories high, about twenty-five feet wide, and built upon a lot of the same width and about 100 feet deep. Each floor is usually divided into four sets of apartments, there being seven rooms on each side. The front apartments generally consist of four rooms each, and the rear of three rooms each, making altogether fourteen rooms upon each floor, only four of which receive direct light and air from the street or from the small yard at the back of the building. Of these four rooms only two are large enough to deserve the name of rooms. The front one is generally about 10 feet 6 inches wide by 11 feet 3 inches long; this is used as a parlor. The next room is a kitchen, generally of the same size as the parlor, which receives its air and light from a window opening into the narrow "air-shaft" or such a supply which may come to it through the door opening into the front room. This room contains a range, a sink, and one or two glass-door closets for dishes. Behind these two rooms are two bed-rooms in the four-room apartments or only one in the three-room apartments. The name of bed-room is applied to these holes by the landlords who charge rent for them, but in reality they are hardly more than closets, being each about 7 feet wide and 8 feet 6 inches long. When a fair-sized bed is in position, there is hardly left sufficient space for one to pass through the room. These rooms get no air or light whatever save such as comes from the window opening into the air-shaft, and with the exception of the highest stories are generally almost totally dark. Water-closets are provided in the hall-way, one for two apartments or for two families. The vast majority of these "dumb-bells" contain no bath-rooms, though some of the latest models do contain a bath-tub in each apartment or one for the entire building—for about twenty-five families.

The ventilation in these houses is obtained through the so-called air-shafts, which have been called by some witness before the Tenement House Commission "foul air shafts," "culture tubes on a gigantic scale." Owing to its narrowness and its height, evidently the air-shaft cannot afford light to the rooms, particularly the bed-rooms, but only semi-darkness. The air that it does supply is foul, because it contains the air coming from the windows of the other apartments (there are as many as sixty windows opening in some of these air-shafts). Moreover, the air-shaft is used by some as a convenient receptacle for garbage and all sorts of refuse and indescribable filth thrown out of the windows, and this filth is often allowed to remain rotting at the bottom of the shaft for weeks without being cleaned out. In many houses this air-shaft is also used for the clothes lines, and on washing days the air and light are obstructed by the linens hung on these lines to dry. . . .

The number of persons to an apartment depends on the size of the family inhabiting it, on the financial and social condition of its members and on their personal habits. The better class live in three or four rooms. Considering that a family of the Ghetto consists on an average of six persons the better class require three or four rooms for every six persons. But the large majority of the East Side Jews are very poor, and cannot afford to pay ten to eighteen dollars rent per month; they therefore resort to lodgers to obtain part of their rent. In the four-room apartments, one bed-room is usually sublet to one or more, frequently to two men or women, and in many houses the front room is also sublet to two or more lodgers for sleeping purposes. The writer on many occasions while calling professionally at night at some of these houses, beheld a condition of affairs like this: A family consisting of husband, wife, and six to eight children whose ages range from less than one to twenty-five years each. The parents occupy the small bed-room together with two, three or even four of the younger children. In the kitchen, on cots and on the floor, are the older children; in the front room two or more (in rare cases as many as five) lodgers sleep on the lounge, on the floor and on cots, and in the fourth bed-room two lodgers who do not care for the price charged, but who desire to have a "separate room" to themselves.

Tragic Aspects of Ghetto Life

Those dark tenements, the lack of money, the daily struggle to keep body and soul alive inevitably took its toll. The very stability of the family—the traditional pillar of Jewish life—came under heavy threat.

One of the keenest early analysts of this aspect of East Side life was Lincoln Steffens, a non-Jew and a leading journalist and "muckraking" reformer at the turn of the century. In his *Autobiography,* a rich mine of information and evaluation of America's growing to maturity, he spoke of his infatuation with the East Side; but as a sensitive observer, he also saw the dark clouds hanging over New York's poor Jews:

I had become as infatuated with the Ghetto as eastern boys were with the wild west, and nailed a mazuza on my office door. I went to the synagogue on all the great Jewish holy days; on Yom Kippur I spent the whole twenty-four hours fasting and going from one synagogue to another. The music moved me most, but I knew and could follow with the awful feelings of a Jew the beautiful old ceremonies of the ancient orthodox services. . . .

The tales of the New York Ghetto were heart-breaking comedies of the tragic conflict between the old and the new, the very old and the very new; in many matters, all at once: religion, class, clothes, manners, customs, language, culture. We all know the difference between youth and age, but our experience is between two generations. Among the Russian and other eastern Jewish families in New York it was an abyss of many generations; it was between parents out of the Middle Ages, sometimes out of the Old Testament days hundreds of years B.C., and the children of the streets of New York today. We saw it everywhere all the time. Responding to a reported suicide, we would pass a synagogue where a score or more of boys were sitting hatless in their old clothes, smoking cigarettes on the steps outside, and their fathers, all dressed in black, with their high hats, uncut beards, and temple curls, were going into the synagogues, tearing their hair and rending their garments. The reporters stopped to laugh; and it was comic; the old men, in their thrift, tore the lapels of their coats very carefully, a very little, but they wept tears, real tears. It was a revolution. Their sons were rebels against the law of Moses; they were lost souls, lost to God, the family, and to Israel of old. The police did not understand or sympathize. If there was a fight—and sometimes the fathers did lay hands on their sons, and the tough boys did biff their fathers in the eye; which brought out all the horrified elders of the whole neighborhood and all the sullen youth—when there was a "riot call," the police would rush in and club now the boys, now the parents, and now, in their Irish exasperation, both sides, bloodily and in vain. I used to feel that the blood did not hurt, but the tears did, the weeping and gnashing of teeth of the old Jews who were doomed and knew it. Two, three thousand years of continuous devotion, courage, and suffering for a cause lost in a generation. . . .

"Oh, Meester Report!" an old woman wailed one evening. "Come into my house and see my childer, my little girls." She seized and pulled me in (me and, I think, Max) up the stairs, weeping, into her clean, dark room, one room, where her three little girls were huddled at the one rear window, from which they—and we—could see a prostitute serving a customer. *"Da, se'en Sie,* there they are watching, always they watch." As the children rose at sight of us and ran away, the old woman told us how her children had always to see that beastly sight. "They count the men who come of a night," she said. "Ninety-three one night." (I shall never forget that number.) "My oldest girl says she will go into that business when she grows up; she says it's a good business, easy, and you can dress and eat and live."

"Why don't you pull down your curtain?" I asked.

"We have no curtain," she wept. "I hang up my dress across, but the childer when I sleep or go out, they crowd under it to see."

"Ask the woman to pull her blind."

"I have," she shrieked. "Oh, I have begged her on my knees, and she won't."

I went over and asked the girl to draw her curtain.

"I won't," she cried in a sudden rage. "That old woman had me raided, and the police—you know it—you know how they hound us now for Parkhurst. They drove me from where I was and I hid in here. That old woman, she sent for the police, and now I have to pay— big—to stay here."

"All right, all right," I shouted to down her mad shrieks of rage. "But her children look—"

"I don't care," the girl yelled back. "It serves her right, that old devil. I will get even. I will ruin her nasty children, as she says."

I threatened to "make" the police close her up, and down she came, all in tears.

"Don't, please don't, Mr. Reporter," she cried. "They'll run me out, the cops will, for you; I know; and I'll have a hell of a time to get found again by my customers. I'm doing well here now again; I can soon open a house maybe and get some girls and be respectable myself if—"

So we compromised. She pinned up a blanket on her window, and I promised not to have her driven out. When I came out into the street there was a patrolman at the door.

"What's the kick?" he asked.

I told him briefly all about it; he knew, nodded. "What's to be done?" he asked.

"Nothing," I answered hastily. "I have fixed it. Don't do anything. It's all all right now."

It wasn't, of course. Nothing was all right. Neither in this case, nor in prostitution generally, nor in the strikes—is there any right—or wrong; not that the police could do, nor I, nor the *Post,* nor Dr.

Parkhurst. It was, it is, all a struggle between conflicting interests, between two blind opposite sides, neither of which is right or wrong.

The problem of crime and prostitution in the overcrowded tenements was a frequent subject in the press, as seen in the following report from the *New York Tribune,* November 25, 1900:

LANDLORDS PERMIT WICKEDNESS TO FLOURISH

The squalor, the poverty, the hopeless drudgery, and the queer features of this foreign district are evident to the visitor, no matter how hurriedly he goes over the ground, but the crime with which that part of the city is infested has been concealed from the general public until it gained such proportions that men like Bishop Potter were compelled to step in and call a halt. The police say, and the records show, that there is less drunkenness there than in other parts of the East Side tenement-house district, that there are not many cases of assault, and that street fights are of rare occurrence. But the big tenement houses in Chrystie, Allen, Stanton, and Forsyth Streets shelter crime in its worst form, and the inmates of these apartments contaminate their neighbors and create an atmosphere in which good morals cannot exist. For years these places have been known by the red lamps which shone in the windows or hallways. These lamps increased in number to such an extent that the district became known as the "red light district," and the degraded men who lived on the vice of the inmates of the houses were known in that section as "lighthouses." The police, the landlord, and the "lighthouse" formed a combination against which the respectable element could make no headway.

A peculiar feature of the situation is the lack of interest displayed on the part of what is known as "the decent" class in the crusade against the dive and red-lamp proprietors. Nearly all the red-lamp places are on the first floors of tenement houses, and the buildings with high, old-fashioned stoops are most in favor. For that reason the places are often referred to by the police as "stoops." When an objectionable tenant moves into a "stoop," puts up lace curtains and other decorations too expensive for and not in harmony with the surroundings, a tenant or possibly several tenants usually make objection and protest. But the "stoop" pays at least twice as much rent when occupied by the objectionable people as it would if only respectable people lived there, and the objectors are told to move out if they don't like their neighbors. In a comparatively short time the children in the house, possibly those of the original objectors, become the friends of the degraded inmates, and in return for candy, cast-off clothes, "show" tickets, and other bribes they become the spies, the watchers, and agents of the people in the "stoop" apartment, and are finally engulfed in the sea of vice.

All this has been known to the police for years as well as it has been known to the people who seek the betterment of the district, but the district was too good a source of revenue for some people to be purified. The law which requires the posting of the name of the owner of a tenement house has been evaded, and although owners are responsible, they have not hesitated to let their apartments to any person who would pay a high rental, regardless of the use made of them. The owners of these houses know that it is difficult to procure evidence against tenants, and until the question of purification was brought forward because of the insolence of the police to the rector of the Pro-Cathedral, the Tammany motto, "What are you going to do about it?" stared the good people in the face.

The landlords are for the most part people who made their money in the district. There are some houses whose owners have moved uptown, but the greater number live in the houses which shelter the objectionable tenants. The "housekeeper" is an institution of the district. In other parts of the city he is known as the agent, janitor or superintendent. He usually fixes the rate of rent and collects it, and with him complaints are lodged. He must know the police in order to be a good "housekeeper," and his word "goes" with many tenants as to where coal, wood, groceries, and other necessary articles should be purchased. The "housekeeper" does not hesitate to charge $30 a month for a $15 apartment when the tenant is of a certain character, but his receipt, when he gives one at all, never shows such figures. He has a wholesome fear of documentary evidence, and where he gives a receipt it is for the legitimate amount, and the signature is not often one by which the real owner may be identified. The extra rent, the blackmail which he extorts from the tenants, may be given to the owner, or he may keep it for himself or share it with the owner and others. There is no fixed rule or regulation about that point, and it makes little difference to the "stoop" tenant where the money goes or how it is divided—he or she knows that so long as it is paid promptly the red lamp may burn and the police will not see it or, seeing it, will not know what it means.

James B. Reynolds of the University Settlement said that he had endeavored for a long time to have red-light places in Rivington Street suppressed, but without success. He said, "It is hard to get sufficient evidence against the landlord, because the very power which should aid us has been on the other side. The law is deficient, and should be amended so that the landlord would become responsible for the tenant. He should be placed on a level with a common carrier; then no bad people could remain in his house, except by the consent or the connivance of the owner or his agent, and, the name of the owner being posted, as it should be, it would be an easy matter to put an end to the nuisance."

Fathers in the tenements rarely saw their children because of long hours in the sweatshop. The bitterness of this deprivation was captured by Morris Rosenfeld, himself an immigrant from Poland and a sweatshop laborer, who ultimately became "poet laureate of the ghetto."

The poem *Mein Yingele* ("My Little Boy") appears in his collection, *Songs of Labor;* set to music, it became one of the most popular songs of the immigrant generation:

MY LITTLE BOY
Morris Rosenfeld

I have a little boy at home,
A pretty little son;
I think sometimes the world is mine
In him, my only one.

But seldom, seldom do I see
My child in heaven's light;
I find him always fast asleep . . .
I see him but at night.

Ere dawn my labor drives me forth;
'Tis night when I am free;
A stranger am I to my child;
And strange my child to me.

I come in darkness to my home,
With weariness and—pay;
My pallid wife, she waits to tell
The things he learned to say.

How plain and prettily he asked:
"Dear mamma, when's 'Tonight'?
O when will come my dear papa
And bring a penny bright?"

I hear her words—I hasten out—
This moment must it be!—
The father-love flames in my breast:
My child must look at me!

I stand beside the tiny cot,
And look, and list, and—ah!
A dream-thought moves the baby-lips:
"O, where is my papa!"

I kiss and kiss the shut blue eyes;
I kiss them not in vain.

They open,—O they see me then!
And straightway close again.

"Here's your papa, my precious one;—
A penny for you!"—ah!
A dream still moves the baby-lips:
"O, where is my papa!"

And I—I think in bitterness
And disappointment sore;
"Some day you will awake, my child,
To find me nevermore."

Women—Old and New

Hard as life as the breadwinner was for men, the social impact of
America upon the immigrant woman was even harsher and more dislo-
cating. It was she who had to cope with not only a strange environment but also a radical change of role expectation and status. The
conflict between the generations affected her intimately and per-
vasively. Because the home was her province, she felt more "responsible" than did her husband for the ways of the children. The "modern" daughter was not only a source of bewilderment to her, but an
affront as well.

Hutchins Hapgood (like Steffens, a gentile infatuated with the East
Side) wrote what has become a classic on the subject, *The Spirit of the
Ghetto*. Here he described two distinct types of Jewish women:

THE ORTHODOX JEWESS

The first of the two well-marked classes of women in the Ghetto is that
of the ignorant orthodox Russian Jewess. She has no language but
Yiddish, no learning but the Talmudic law, no practical authority but

that of her husband and her rabbi. She is even more of a Hausfrau than the German wife. She can own no property, and the precepts of the Talmud as applied to her conduct are largely limited to the relations with her husband. Her life is absorbed in observing the religious law and in taking care of her numerous children. She is drab and plain in appearance, with a thick waist, a wig, and as far as is possible for a woman a contempt for ornament. She is, however, with the noticeable assimilative sensitiveness of the Jew, beginning to pick up some of the ways of the American woman. If she is young when she comes to America, she soon lays aside her wig, and sometimes assumes the rakish American hat, prides herself on her bad English, and grows slack in the observance of Jewish holidays and the dietary regulations of the Talmud. Altho it is against the law of this religion to go to the theatre, large audiences, mainly drawn from the ignorant workers of the sweatshops and the fishwives and pedlars of the push-cart markets, flock to the Bowery houses. It is this class which forms the large background of the community, the masses from which more cultivated types are developing.

Many a literary sketch in the newspapers of the quarter portrays these ignorant, simple, devout, housewifely creatures in comic or pathetic, more often, after the satiric manner of the Jewish writers, in serio-comic vein. The authors, altho they are much more educated, yet write of these women, even when they write in comic fashion, with fundamental sympathy. They picture them working devotedly in the shop or at home for their husbands and families, they represent the sorrow and simple jealousy of the wife whose husband's imagination, perhaps, is carried away by the piquant manner and dress of a Jewess who is beginning to ape American ways; they tell of the comic adventures in America of the newly arrived Jewess: how she goes to the theatre, perhaps, and enacts the part of Partridge at the play. More fundamentally, they relate how the poor woman is deeply shocked, at her arrival, by the change which a few years have made in the character of her husband, who had come to America before her in order to make a fortune. She finds his beard shaved off, and his manners in regard to religious holidays very slack. She is sometimes so deeply affected that she does not recover. More often she grows to feel the reason and eloquence of the change and becomes partly accustomed to the situation; but all through her life she continues to be dismayed by the precocity, irreligion and Americanism of her children. Many sketches and many scenes in the Ghetto plays present her as a pathetic "greenhorn" who, while she is loved by her children, is yet rather patronized and pitied by them. . . .

THE MODERN TYPE

The other, the educated class of Ghetto women, is, of course, in a great minority; and this division includes the women even the most slightly affected by modern ideas as well as those who from an intellectual point of view are highly cultivated. Among the least educated are a large number of women who would be entirely ignorant were it not for the ideas which they have received through the Socialistic propaganda of the quarter. Like the men who are otherwise ignorant, they are trained to a certain familiarity with economic ideas, read and think a good deal about labor and capital, and take an active part in speaking, in "house to house" distribution of Socialistic literature and in strike agitation. Many of these women, so long as they are unmarried, lead lives thoroughly devoted to "the cause," and afterwards become good wives and fruitful mothers, and urge on their husbands and sons to active work in the "movement." They have in personal character many virtues called masculine, are simple and straightforward and intensely serious, and do not "bank" in any way on the fact that they are women! Such a woman would feel insulted if her escort were to pick up her handkerchief or in any way suggest a politeness growing out of the difference in sex. It is from this class of women, from those who are merely tinged, so to speak, with ideas, and who consequently are apt to throw the whole strength of their primitive natures into the narrow intellectual channels that are open to them, that a number of Ghetto heroines come who are willing to lay down their lives for an idea, or to live for one. It was only recently that the thinking Socialists were stirred by the suicide of a young girl for which several causes were given. Some say it was for love, but what seems a partial cause at least for the tragedy was the girl's devotion to anarchistic ideas. She had worked for some time in the quarter and was filled with enthusiastic Tolstoian convictions about freedom and non-resistance to evil, and all the other idealistic doctrines for which these Anarchists are remarkable. Some of the people of the quarter believe that it was temporary despair of any satisfactory outcome to her work that brought about her death. But since the splits in the Socialistic party and the rise among them of many insincere agitators, the enthusiasm for the cause has diminished, and particularly among the women, who demand perfect integrity or nothing; tho there is still a large class of poor sweat-shop women who carry on active propaganda work, make speeches, distribute literature, and go from house to house in a social effort to make converts.

As we ascend in the scale of education in the Ghetto we find women who derive their culture and ideas from a double source—from Socialism and from advanced Russian ideals of literature and life. They have lost faith completely in the orthodox religion, have substituted no other, know Russian better than Yiddish, read Tolstoi, Turgenef and Chekhov, and often put into practice the most radical theories of the "new woman," particularly those which say that woman should be economically independent of man. There are successful female dentists, physicians, writers, and even lawyers by the score in East Broadway who have attained financial independence through industry and intelligence. They are ambitious to a degree and often direct the careers of their husbands or force their lovers to become doctors or lawyers—the great social desiderata in the matchmaking of the ghetto. There is more than one case on record where a girl has compelled her recalcitrant lover to learn law, medicine or dentistry, or submit to being jilted by her. An actor devoted to the stage is now on the point of leaving it to become a dentist at the command of his ambitious wife. "I always do what she tells me," he said pathetically. . . .

But the charm of sincere feeling they have; and, in an intellectual race, that feeling shapes itself into definite criticism of society. Emotionally strong and attached by Russian tradition to a rebellious doc-

trine, they are deeply unconventional in theory and sometimes in practice; altho the national morality of the Jewish race very definitely
limits the extent to which they realize some of their ideas. The passionate feeling at the bottom of most of their "tendency" beliefs is
that woman should stand on the same social basis as man, and should
be weighed in the same scales. This ruling creed is held by all classes
of the educated women of the Ghetto, from the poor sweat-shop
worker, who has recently felt the influence of Socialism, to the
thoroughly trained "new woman" with her developed literary taste;
and all its variations find expression in the literature of the quarter.

Another, lighter version of the life of women and the recreational
needs of the young people is that of Abraham H. Fromenson, Zionist
leader and publicist, and editor of the English pages of the *Tageblatt*.
The following selection is from the collection *The Russian Jew in the
United States:*

The ladies of the Ghetto are never "at home," but the welcome visitor
is always sure of his glass of tea, his dish of preserves, and some fruit.
There are no "Kaffee Klatches" here; nor progressive euchres, or
bridge-whists. Hospitality is simple, homely, genuine. There are no
social circles, "social life" as that term is understood does not exist.
"Parties" are given; not "coming out" parties, but "engagement parties," "graduation parties," "bar-mitzvah parties." The wedding, of
course, is the big function. Hundreds of societies give dances and
"receptions" (the latter being a more pretentious name for the former)
during the winter, to which anyone may come if he can pay the price
of a ticket and "hat check." Some societies couple entertainments
with these receptions. The great social events are the "entertainment
and ball" of the Beth Israel Hospital, the Hebrew Sheltering House
and Home for the Aged, the Daughters of Jacob, the Young Men's
Benevolent League, and the New Era Club. It is at these functions that
the East Side makes its most gorgeous sartorial display, and it is by no

means either a crude or cheap display. The women for the most part are as exquisitely clad as their sisters who visit the Horse-Show, and the diamonds worn at these affairs can be outblinked only by the collection on the grand tier at the Metropolitan Opera House. Strange as it may sound to many, the East Side is not all poverty and suffering.

The Harlem contingent has acquired some "society" manners, but like newly acquired things, these manners do not fit very snugly, and their wearing is very amusing. Perhaps, with much effort some of the social aspirants will become accustomed to the new burden. The "climbing" is confined, for the most part, to the wives of physicians and lawyers and manufacturers. The great mass regards it all with quiet derision, and will have nothing to do with "visiting lists" and the rest of what they call "blowing from themselves." With the mass, relatives and friends are to be visited when time allows, or when occasion demands.

Owing to home-conditions on the East Side there is only such social life for the young folks as is made possible by organization membership, and as may express itself in the dances mentioned above, or in "open-meetings," indulged in by the "literary" societies, the Zionist societies, and the clubs in the settlements. In the summer time there are the picnics, which are dances in an open pavilion, with a few patches of grass surrounding it, all enclosed with a high fence. Much has been said against these "picnics" and it must be admitted that many of them are not very desirable. There is great need for healthy, wholesome recreation, for expression of the buoyancy of youth; and it is greatly to be regretted that the facilities for the things that help to make boys and girls better, purer men and women are so very few.

Generations in Conflict

Given all the conditions so far described, intergenerational conflicts were inevitable. In a family where the Yiddish-speaking parents sent their children to American schools but who themselves could scarcely speak English, familial ties were loosened by tensions, and the old values began to shatter. The children began to look down on their parents and on their Jewish life-styles, as Hutchins Hapgood points out in *The Spirit of the Ghetto:*

In America, even before he begins to go to our public schools, the little Jewish boy finds himself in contact with a new world which stands in violent contrast with the orthodox environment of his first few years. Insensibly—at the beginning—from his playmates in the streets, from his older brother or sister, he picks up a little English, a little American slang, hears older boys boast of prize-fighter Bernstein, and learns vaguely to feel that there is a strange and fascinating life on the street. At this tender age he may even begin to black boots, gamble in pennies, and be filled with a ''wild surmise'' about American dollars.

With his entrance into the public school the little fellow runs plump against a system of education and a set of influences which are at total variance with those traditional to his race and with his home life. The religious element is entirely lacking. The educational system of the public schools is heterogeneous and worldly. The boy becomes acquainted in the school reader with fragments of writings on all subjects, with a little mathematics, a little history. His instruction, in the interests of a liberal non-sectarianism, is entirely secular. English becomes his most familiar language. He achieves a growing comprehension and sympathy with the independent, free, rather sceptical spirit of the American boy; he rapidly imbibes ideas about social equality and contempt for authority, and tends to prefer Sherlock Holmes to Abraham as a hero.

The orthodox Jewish influences, still at work upon him, are rapidly weakened. He grows to look upon the ceremonial life at home as rather ridiculous. His old parents, who speak no English, he regards as ''greenhorns.'' English becomes his habitual tongue, even at home, and Yiddish he begins to forget. He still goes to *heder* but under conditions exceedingly different from those obtaining in Russia, where there are no public schools, and where the boy is consequently shut up within the confines of Hebraic education. In America, the *heder* assumes a position entirely subordinate. . . .

The orthodox parents begin to see that the boy, in order to "get along" in the New World, must receive a Gentile training. Instead of hoping to make a rabbi of him, they reluctantly consent to his becoming an American business man, or, still better, an American doctor or lawyer. . . .

The growing sense of superiority on the part of the boy to the Hebraic part of his environment extends itself soon to the home. He learns to feel that his parents, too, are "greenhorns." In the struggle between the two sets of influences that of the home becomes less and less effective. He runs away from the supper table to join his gang on the Bowery, where he is quick to pick up the very latest slang; where his talent for caricature is developed often at the expense of his parents, his race, and all "foreigners"; for he is an American, he is "the people," and like his glorious countrymen in general, he is quick to ridicule the stranger. He laughs at the foreign Jew with as much heartiness as at the "dago"; for he feels that he himself is almost as remote from the one as from the other.

"Why don't you say your evening prayer, my son?" asks his mother in Yiddish.

"Ah, what yer givin' us!" replies, in English, the little American-Israelite as he makes a beeline for the street.

The boys not only talk together of picnics, of the crimes of which they read in the English newspapers, of prize-fights, of budding business propositions, but they gradually quit going to synagogue, give up *heder* promptly when they are thirteen years old, avoid the Yiddish theatres, seek the up-town places of amusement, dress in the latest American fashion, and have a keen eye for the right thing in neckties. They even refuse sometimes to be present at supper on Friday evenings. Then, indeed, the sway of the old people is broken.

"Amerikane Kinder, Amerikane Kinder!" wails the old father, shaking his head. The trend of things is indeed too strong for the old man of the eternal Talmud and ceremony.

Bintel Brief: Letters to the Editor

In the Old World, where one lived with relatives and friends, there had always been a receptive ear for troubles. Who did not have a wise uncle or solicitous neighbor to whom one could go for sage advice? In the New World, the editor of the "Letters" column came to serve a similar function.

The letters were enormously popular with the readership. Others' troubles eased their own. The foolishness of a neighbor made one feel wiser. And what topics for juicy discussion!

The editor welcomed them because they helped sell papers. The most popular letters column was *A Bintel Brief* (A Sheaf of Letters) in the *Forverts,* the Yiddish daily, and they represented a veritable potpourri of human problems that beset immigrant Jewish families. The selections that follow were written in 1906, when the column first began. It continued for sixty years, and an excellent collection, *A Bintel Brief,* was published in 1971:

MARCH 6, 1906

Dear Mr. Editor:

I am a greenhorn. I have only been five weeks in the country. I am a jewelry maker. I left a blind father and a stepmother in Russia. Before my departure my father begged me not to forget him. I promised that I would send him the first money I should earn. I walked around two weeks and looked for work. But at the end of the third week I succeeded in getting a job. I worked a week and received eight dollars for the week. I am working the third week now. I paid for my board and bought certain necessities, such as a hat, shoes, and some small items, and I have a few dollars, too. Now, Mr. Editor, I want to ask you to give me some advice, as to what to do. Should I send my father a few dollars for Passover, or should I keep them for myself? Because the work at our place is at an end, and I may have to be without work. So that I do not know what to do. I hope that you will give me some advice, and I shall obey you just as you tell me.

Youah Mednikoff

MARCH 13, 1906

Dear Mr. Editor:

My married life consists of the following: We are living in a room and bedroom on the top floor on Allen Street. We cannot pay more than eleven dollars a month. I have two children so they are pale, without a drop of blood. More than once the doctor told me I should move, because the children haven't enough air. Lately, however, I realized that many of my acquaintances, who are not better off than we, live nevertheless in nice, comfortable rooms and in a better neighborhood. They have each several boarders, and in this way the rent does not come to much. I began to reason with my husband that we ought to do the same, so he does not want to listen. He does not want to have any boarders, because he fears, that on account of them there would be quarreling between us. He is simply afraid that I would become jealous, if we were to take in a female boarder, and that he would become jealous if a male boarder is taken in. "Who can tell what may happen!" he says. I laughed at it, but he is like steel and iron and does not want to hear of it. He is in the shop the whole day and when he comes home, he eats and goes somewhere or goes to bed. But I want to work hard, wait on boarders so that I may have comfortable rooms for my children, and for myself too. Mr. Editor, which of us is right?

Rose Eisenberg

MARCH 27, 1906

Dear Mr. Editor:

My wife is one of those types who loves when passing someone to rub her shoulder, so that one may feel that she is present. She is a great preacher of women's rights. Women, she says, stand on a much higher plane than men, and the woman who cannot control her husband is an animal. Wherever she puts her foot, there you find accidents. She is very nervous. She has a big mouth, cries easily, and hates to listen to anyone. Such is my wife. I myself am a peace-loving, quiet man. I conduct a small business, a two-by-four grocery store. My wife is the business lady in the family. This is how she talks to me: "What can I do when I have a dummy for a husband, such a *shlemiel*." And so, she is the head of the business, and I am the arm. Work for me, says she, she has plenty, a steady job for day and night. If there is no work for me in the store, says she, then do the housework. For me, home is a prison. I am out in the open just once a year: on *Yom Kippur* when the store is closed and my old woman is in the synagogue. During the entire year, when there is any time, she is the first to go out. And when she goes out she sees to it that I have so much work that I cannot go out even. There is always quarreling in the house. . . .

How can one stand for so much? I have children whom I love, and their fate frightens me. A divorce can be of little use to me. I see no way out.

Do not publish my name; also pardon me for writing so much. This is not even a tenth of my heavy heart.

The Woman's Husband

MARCH 15, 1906

Dear Mr. Editor:

The story I want to tell you is this. I have two little girls, one 10 years and the other 13. Both go to school. A few months ago a friend of mine told me, that he saw one of my girls walking about arm-in-arm with a little boy, who probably goes to the same school with her. I happen to be a busy man, I have a stationery store and am always occupied, I cannot even get away for a minute. Of course my wife is busy with a new one, and she too cannot leave the house. So with tears in my eyes I begged my friend to stop working for a few days at my expense and watch my two girls. . . . And he saw something horrible. As soon as my daughters walked out of school, they walked up to the corner of the street and stood waiting. . . . About fifteen minutes later two boys from the same school met them. My friend followed them, and he saw how the boys took candy, chocolates and peanuts from their pockets and treated my daughters. The girls would take the presents and for this would drag around for many hours through tens of streets. It would not have grieved me, because they walked around, but my friend saw such wicked behavior on the part of the boys, who are very much like the "gang" of the great bandits. At each street corner they would go into a hallway. My daughters would laugh out loud, and my friend heard both times how they agreed to meet in the evening at a certain spot in Hester Street Park. My friend watched them in the park too, and his face burned for shame at what he saw the little bandits do and at the indifference of the two girls. Walking home from the park, they several times walked into other hallways. What they did there, this my friend did not see, because I told him, not to show himself to my daughters since they know him.

I cannot keep them in the house: And so I can find no way out. I am afraid to turn to the police, lest they be given over to the Gerry Society and even there, I think, they do not turn into nuns.

What is to be done, dear Editor?

The Unhappy Father

FEBRUARY 26, 1906

Dear Mr. Editor:

I have been a servant girl these two years. I came to America six years ago. For four years I worked in a shop and I got sick, but I was still strong enough to be employed as a servant. . . . This is my story. I contracted consumption while working in the shop and had to go to Denver, Colorado. There are no shops here, so I have become a servant. My first job was in the household of an upstart real estate operator and a Gentile to boot. And here is what happened: Not an evening passed, when the house was not full of guests. The tables were set with all good things, and I, tired out, broken, sat in the kitchen at the table with the dog and cat. If the son or the mistress wanted to spit they found no other place to spit but the kitchen and exactly at the time when I was eating. In short, I quit and I am now with rich German Jews. So I tell you that I feel even more depressed and more unhappy than when I was with the spitting Gentiles. I am writing you this letter, in order that servants the world over might understand their plight, as I do, and might understand, as I do, to who it was that humiliated them and brought them to such a horrible position. And then if they only knew it, they would have united and our position would then have been greatly bettered.

With socialist greetings
Trilby

FEBRUARY 20, 1906

Dear Mr. Editor:

Working for a very long time with a Gentile woman in the shop, I came to know her very intimately, and we began to go out together very often. In the end, we fell in love with each other. Naturally, we decided that I should not be a Gentile nor she a Jewess. But in the course of a year I realized that we were not compatible. Whenever an acquaintance, a friend, comes home, I note a great dissatisfaction on her face. When she sees me reading a Jewish paper, her face changes color. She does not tell me anything, but I see that the woman is wasting away like a candle. I feel that she is very unhappy with me although I am certain she loves me. On top of that, she is to become a mother soon. Her tie to me becomes stronger. Only a few weeks ago Christ awoke within her. Every Sunday she rises at dawn, hurries to church and comes back with eyes swollen from crying. Whenever I go out with her and it happens that we pass a church, tremors seize her.

Give me, dear Mr. Editor, some advice as to what I should do. To convert to Christianity is out of the question. She will not stop going to church. What can be done, that there may not be so much trouble in our home?

Hyman Frumkin

6. Work: Onward and Upward

The first task facing the new immigrant was to find work. The German Jews who had come in the mid-nineteenth century became pioneers in peddling, and dispersed throughout the country; many advanced to the position of large-scale merchants and traders, opening department stores and amassing family fortunes.

But several decades later, when the larger waves of Jews arrived from eastern Europe, the country's economy was less expansionist and offered fewer opportunities. Elias Tcherikower points this out in his definitive work on *The Early Jewish Labor Movement in the United States:*

Like other immigrants, Jews were constrained to adjust to the forces they found at work in the American economy. The masses of Jews had little alternative but to flock to the metropolises of America, and to join the ranks of the industrial proletariat. Inevitably, many of them remained in New York . . . the center of those industries, particularly the garment industry, in which Jews could . . . become integrated. But whether they stayed in New York or moved on, driven by inexorable economic necessity, these petty tradesmen, artisans and Luftmenschen of Eastern Europe were transformed in large part into proletarians in America, with all the needs, problems, and conflicts attendant upon this class.

The majority had arrived with little in their pockets. From 1899 to 1903 only 12.9 per cent of the Jewish ("Hebrews") immigrant heads of families brought with them a capital of "$30 or over," while 17.6 per cent of all immigrants had that amount or more. The per capita average of the Jews was $20.43; that of all immigrants, $22.78. . . .

Those that did take to peddling included yeshiva students, former teachers, and preachers—generally, the more orthodox types. They met with derision and hostility:

By then, "No beggars and peddlers" signs had already made their appearance. Venturing out of the Jewish streets, the Yiddish-speaking bearded peddler would often be met by a hail of rotten fruit, the mocking of urchins, and the not infrequent assaults of the dregs of the population, neighbors in the poorest sections of the city. It is of interest to note that what had in Russia been everyday occurrences had, with the shift in expectations and environment, become unbearable. The immigrant become tailor—which, relatively speaking, meant staying within a Jewish world—seems to have gone through a psychologically less painful period than the peddler, thrust into a wholly alien world.

The most primitive form of peddler was the house-to-house salesman, whose stock-in-trade was a miscellany of pins, shoelaces, garters, combs, and a few cakes of perfumed soap. On a somewhat higher level was the customer peddler, who had steady, individual accounts. Pushcart peddlers, carrying a greater variety and quantity of goods, were also somewhat more respectable. The country peddlers, traveling from town to town, stopping at farms, generally had their regular customers. The acme of achievement in this line was reached by the owners of the stores which supplied the peddlers with their goods; most often, they were German Jews who had worked their way up in the course of time. Orchard Street, in New York, was the center of this "wholesale" trade. Becoming a fullfledged peddler required a total investment of some ten dollars: five for the license, one for a basket, and the rest for one's wares. More than a few avoided the first expense and cut down on the last.

However, the masses became workers in factories and industries:

From its inception, the East European Jewish community in America bore a proletarian character. Never had Jews entered industry in such mass, both as entrepreneurs and as workers, as they did in the four decades around the turn of the century. For the first time in Jewish history in the Diaspora Jewish entrepreneurs bought and Jewish workers sold labor power on a large scale.

This revolutionary transformation, however, while consonant with American economic development, did not mean that Jews were integrated as individuals into the American economy. Jewish capital and labor, concentrated as they were in the needle trades and, to a smaller extent, the tobacco industry, developed patterns and techniques of their own. And . . . the characteristic features of these industries— contracting, the sweatshop, and the like—though by no means "Jewish" innovations, were developed to their peak after Jewish entrepreneurs had begun to dominate the field. . . .

The sweatshop and the tenement were the cemeteries in which the dreams about the goldene medine *were laid to rest. In the light of the new experiences, new sets of ideologies, aspirations, and movements came into being. . . .*

Those who had been workers in Europe—the Bialystok weavers, the prayer-shawl workers of Kolomyja, the Vilna stocking-makers—had known the taste of industrial exploitation. The Weber and Kempster report of 1891 detailed industrial conditions of Jewish workers in Minsk, Vilna, Bialystok, and so forth. Nor was the New York sweatshop a novelty for those who had spent some time in London on their way to America. The only objective difference was in the greater degree of automatization and specialization in America. But what was of utmost psychological importance was that this was America! That life in the goldene medine *was to be as difficult as life in impoverished Russia was wholly unexpected. And as for those who had not experienced industrial conditions—the great majority of the immigrants— adjustment to the shop was even more difficult.*

In *Songs of Labor* Morris Rosenfeld—having experienced the sweatshop—writes of how it dehumanizes man. Edwin Markham in "The Man with the Hoe" sees the farm laborer become a "brother

to the ox''; Rosenfeld describes how the factory worker becomes
''a machine'':

IN THE FACTORY
Morris Rosenfeld

Oh, here in the shop the machines roar so wildly,
That oft, unaware that I am, or have been,
I sink and am lost in the terrible tumult;
And void is my soul . . . I am but a machine.
I work and I work and I work, never ceasing;
Create and create things from morning till e'en;
For what?—and for whom—Oh, I know not!
  Oh, ask not!
Who ever has heard of a conscious machine?

No, here is no feeling, no thought and no reason;
This life-crushing labor has ever supprest
The noblest and finest, the truest and richest,
The deepest, the highest and humanly best.
The seconds, the minutes, they pass out forever,
They vanish, swift fleeting like straws in a gale.
I drive the wheel madly as tho' to o'ertake them,—
Give chase without wisdom, or wit, or avail.

The clock in the workshop,—it rests not a moment;
It points on, and ticks on: Eternity—Time;
And once someone told me the clock had a meaning,—
Its pointing and ticking had reason and rhyme.
And this too he told me,—or had I been dreaming,—
The clock wakened life in one, forces unseen,
And something besides; . . . I forget what;
  Oh, ask not!
I know not, I know not, I am a machine.

At times, when I listen, I hear the clock plainly;—
The reason of old—the old meaning—is gone!
The maddening pendulum urges me forward
To labor and labor and still labor on.
The tick of the clock is the Boss in his anger!
The face of the clock has the eyes of a foe;
The clock—Oh, I shudder—dost hear how it drives me?
It calls me "Machine!"—and it cries to me "Sew!"

At noon, when about me the wild tumult ceases,
And gone is the master, and I sit apart,
And dawn in my brain is beginning to glimmer,
The wound comes agape at the core of my heart;
And tears, bitter tears flow; ay, tears that are scalding;
They moisten my dinner—my dry crust of bread;
They choke me—I cannot eat;—no, no, I cannot!
Oh, horrible toil! born of Need and of Dread.

The sweatshop at mid-day—I'll draw you the picture:
A battlefield bloody; the conflict at rest;
Around and about me the corpses are lying;
The blood cries aloud from the earth's gory breast.
A moment . . . and hark! The loud signal is sounded,
The dead rise again and renewed is the fight . . .
They struggle, these corpses; for strangers, for strangers!
They struggle, they fall, and they sink into night.

I gaze on the battle in bitterest anger,
And pain, hellish pain wakes the rebel in me!
The clock—now I hear it aright!—It is crying:
"An end to this bondage! An end there must be!"
It quickens my reason, each feeling within me;
It shows me how precious the moments that fly.
Oh, worthless my life if I longer am silent,
And lost to the world if in silence I die.

The man in me sleeping begins to awaken;
The thing that was slave into slumber has passed:
Now; up with the man in me! Up and be doing!
No misery more! Here is freedom at last!
When sudden: a whistle!—the Boss—an alarum!—
I sink in the slime of the stagnant routine;—
There's tumult, they struggle, oh, lost is my ego;—
I know not, I care not, I am a machine! . . .

The ghetto laureate was not the only one to describe the conditions in the sweatshop. Jacob Riis was another early observer, having made some exploratory visits in the late 1880s:

HOW THE OTHER HALF LIVES
Jacob Riis

Up two flights of dark stairs, three, four, with new smells of cabbage, of onions, of frying fish, on every landing, whirring sewing machines behind closed doors betraying what goes on within. . . . Five men and a woman, two young girls, not fifteen, and a boy who says unasked that he is fifteen, and lies in saying it, are at the machines sewing knickerbockers, "kneepants" in the Ludlow Street dialect. The floor is littered ankle-deep with half-sewn garments. In the alcove, on a couch of many dozens of "pants" ready for the finisher, a bare-legged baby with pinched face is asleep. A fence of piled-up clothing keeps him from rolling off on the floor. The faces, hands, and arms to the elbows of everyone in the room are black with the color of the cloth on which they are working. . . .
They are "learners," all of them, says the woman, who proves to be the wife of the boss, and have "come over" only a few weeks ago. . . . The learners work for week's wages, she says. How much do they earn? "From two to five dollars."

They turn out one hundred and twenty dozen "kneepants" a week, for which the manufacturer pays seventy cents a dozen. Five cents a dozen is the clear profit, but her own and her husband's work brings the family earnings up to twenty-five dollars a week, when they have work all the time. But often half the time is put in looking for it. They work no longer than to nine o'clock at night, from daybreak. There are ten machines in the room; six are hired at two dollars a month. For the two shabby, smoke-begrimed rooms, one somewhat larger than ordinary, they pay twenty dollars a month. She does not complain, though "times are not what they were, and it costs a good deal to live."

Eight dollars a week for the family of six and two boarders. How do they do it? She laughs, as she goes over the bill of fare, at the silly question: Bread, fifteen cents a day, of milk two quarts a day at four cents a quart, one pound of meat for dinner at twelve cents, butter one pound a week at "eight cents a quarter of a pound." Coffee, potatoes, and pickles complete the list. At the least calculation, probably, this sweater's family hoards up thirty dollars a month, and in a few years will own a tenement somewhere and profit by the example set by their landlord in rent-collecting. It is the way the savings of Jewtown are universally invested, and with the natural talent of its people for commercial speculation the investment is enormously profitable. . . .

Turning the corner into Hester Street, we stumble upon a nest of cloak-makers in their busy season. Six months of the year the cloak-maker is idle, or nearly so. Now is his harvest. Seventy-five cents a cloak, all complete, is the price in this shop. The cloak is of cheap plush, and might sell for eight or nine dollars over the store-counter. Seven dollars is the weekly wage of this man with wife and two children, and nine dollars and a half rent to pay per month. A boarder pays about a third of it. There was a time when he made ten dollars a week and thought himself rich. But wages have come down fearfully in the last two years. Think of it: "come down" to this. The other cloak-makers aver that they can make as much as twelve dollars a week, when they are employed, by taking their work home and sewing till midnight. One exhibits his account-book with a Ludlow Street sweater. It shows that he and his partner, working on first-class garments for a Broadway house in the four busiest weeks of the season, made together from $15.15 to $19.20 a week by striving from 6 A.M. to 11 P.M., that is to say, from $7.58 to $9.60 each. The sweater on this work probably made as much as fifty per cent, at least on their labor. Not far away is a factory in a rear yard where the factory inspector reports teams of tailors making men's coats at an average of twenty-seven cents a coat, all complete except buttons and button-holes. . . .

We have reached Broome Street. The hum of industry in this six-story tenement on the corner leaves no doubt of the aspect Sunday wears within it. One flight up, we knock at the nearest door. The grocer, who keeps the store, lives on the "stoop," the first floor in East Side parlance. In this room a suspender-maker sleeps and works with his family of wife and four children. For a wonder there are no boarders. His wife and eighteen-year-old daughter share in the work, but the girl's eyes are giving out from the strain. Three months in the year, when work is very brisk, the family makes by united efforts as high as fourteen and fifteen dollars a week. The other nine months it averages from three to four dollars. The oldest boy, a young man, earns from four to six dollars in an Orchard Street factory, when he has work. The rent is ten dollars a month for the room and a miserable little coop of a bedroom where the old folks sleep. The girl makes her bed on the lounge in the front room; the big boys and the children sleep on the floor. Coal at ten cents a small pail, meat at twelve cents a pound, one and a half pounds of butter a week at thirty-six cents, and a quarter of a pound of tea in the same space of time, are items of their house-keeping account as given by the daughter. Milk at four and five cents a quart, "according to quality." The sanitary authorities know what that means, know how miserably inadequate is the fine of fifty or a hundred dollars for the murder done in cold blood by the wretches who poison the babes of these tenements with the stuff that is half water, or swill. Their defense is that the demand is for "cheap milk." Scarcely a wonder that this suspender-maker will hardly be able to save up the *dot* for his daughter, without which she stands no chance of marrying in Jewtown, even with her face that would be pretty had it a healthier tinge.

Up under the roof three men are making boys' jackets at twenty cents a piece, of which the sewer takes eight, the ironer three, and the finisher five cents, and the buttonhole-maker two and a quarter, leaving a cent and three-quarters to pay for the drumming up, the fetching and bringing back of the goods. They bunk together in a room for which they pay eight dollars a month. All three are single here, that is: their wives are on the other side yet, waiting for them to earn enough to send for them.

Edwin Markham, who was moved by the plight of the farm laborer to write his classic poem, described the plight of boys and girls in the sweatshops of the ghetto no less poignantly. His article appeared in *Cosmopolitan Magazine,* January 1907:

✿✿✿

60,000 CHILDREN IN SWEATSHOPS

Long before Hannah made a coat for little Samuel, women sat in the home at garmentmaking. The sweated sewing in the tenement home today is only a belated following of this custom of the ages. But the leisurely sewing of the old times was far away from the nerve-racking work of our hurried age. The slow ways are gone. In unaired rooms, mothers and fathers sew by day and by night. Those in the home sweatshop must work cheaper than those in the factory sweatshops if they would drain work from the factory, which has already skinned the wage down to a miserable pittance. And the children are called in from play to drive and drudge beside their elders. The load falls upon the ones least able to bear it—upon the backs of the little children at the base of the labor pyramid.

All the year in New York and in other cities you may watch children radiating to and from such pitiful homes. Nearly any hour on the East Side of New York City you can see them—pallid boy or spindling girl—their faces dulled, their backs bent under a heavy load of garments piled on head and shoulders, the muscles of the whole frame in a long strain. The boy always has bowlegs and walks with feet wide apart and wobbling. Here, obviously, is a hoe man in the making. Once at home with the sewing, the little worker sits close to the inadequate window, struggling with the snarls of thread or shoving the needle through unwielding cloth. Even if by happy chance the small worker goes to school, the sewing which he puts down at the last moment in the morning waits for his return.

Never again should one complain of buttons hanging by a thread, for tiny, tortured fingers have doubtless done their little ineffectual best. And for his lifting of burdens, this giving of youth and strength, this sacrifice of all that should make childhood radiant, a child may add to the family purse from 50 cents to $1.50 a week. In the rush times of the year, preparing for the changes of seasons or for the great "white sales," there are no idle fingers in the sweatshops. A little child of "seven times one" can be very useful in threading needles, in cutting the loose threads at the ends of seams, and in pulling out bastings. To be sure, the sewer is docked for any threads left on or for any stitch broken by the little bungling fingers. The light is not good, but baby eyes must "look sharp."

Besides work at sewing, there is another industry for little girls in the grim tenements. The mother must be busy at her sewing, or, perhaps, she is away from dark to dark at office cleaning. A little daughter, therefore, must assume the work and care of the family. She becomes the "little mother," washing, scrubbing, cooking. In New York City alone, 60,000 children are shut up in the home sweatshops. This is a conservative estimate, based upon a recent investigation of the Lower East Side of Manhattan Island, south of 14th Street and east of the Bowery. Many of this immense host will never sit on a school bench. Is it not a cruel civilization that allows little hearts and little shoulders to strain under these grown-up responsibilities, while in the same city a pet cur is jeweled and pampered and aired on a fine lady's velvet lap on the beautiful boulevards?

Newspaper stories recorded many facets of immigrant working conditions. Strikes were endemic to the system:

13,000 TAILORS ON STRIKE
(*New York Times,* July 29, 1895)

The great strike threatened by the Brotherhood of Tailors and said to involve nearly 13,000 men, women, and girls began yesterday. It is the largest strike in this branch of the trade that has taken place, and the members of the brotherhood responded to the order to strike with unanimity. There are some 630 shops represented in the brotherhood, and of these, 610 immediately obeyed the order to strike. By ten o'clock yesterday morning about 10,000 workers had left their employment, and two hours later 3,000 more joined the ranks of the strikers.

The order to strike was issued very early in the day, and read as follows: "To all members of the United Brotherhood of Tailors. Stop Working at Once. By order of all locals." Then followed the signatures of the members of the general executive board of the brotherhood. Before sunrise over 100 tailors had assembled in Walhalla Hall. These were hurriedly sent out as committees of two and three to the shops in Suffolk Street and Rutgers Place and vicinity to call out the tailors. Meyer Schoenfeld, who is regarded as the manager of the brotherhood, formed a kind of central committee of some of the first comers, and this committee organized the other committees with orders to the shops to strike. These committees began their work in Attorney Street and, after dividing the territory among themselves, worked their way westward to the Bowery visiting every shop. The working people who had been prepared for the strike quit work as soon as the committee appeared. These were principally operators, basters, finishers, and pressers. . . .

The principal cause of the strike was the refusal of the Contractors' Association to sign an agreement prepared by the brotherhood to date from September 15. This agreement provides that the contractors are to employ only union members in good standing and that the brotherhood shall give the contractors all the hands they need. Fifty-nine hours shall constitute a week's work, ten hours a day for the first

five working days, from 7:00 A.M. to 6:00 P.M., with one hour for dinner, and nine hours on the sixth day, from 7:00 A.M. to 5:00 P.M.,
with one hour for dinner. No overtime is to be permitted. The minimum rates of wages demanded in the agreement are: basters $13 per
week and upward, finishers $9 per week. The tenement-house sweating system is to be abolished.

POLICE CLUB STRIKERS
(*New York Tribune,* August 10, 1905)

Strikers or their sympathizers wrecked the bakeshop of Philip Federman at No. 183 Orchard Street early last night amid scenes of the most
tumultuous excitement. Policemen smashed heads right and left with
their nightsticks after two of their number had been roughly dealt with
by the mob. Two men were arrested and charged with inciting to riot,
assault, and disorderly conduct. Bricks and bottles were thrown down
on the heads of the policemen from houses in the neighborhood. The
reserves of the Eldridge Street station had their hands more than full
coping with the maddened crowd.

Word was passed to the headquarters of the strikers in Great Central
Palace at No. 90 Clinton Street shortly after seven o'clock that there
was a "roughhouse" in Federman's bakery in Orchard Street between
Rivington and Stanton Streets, one of the most densely populated sections of the East Side. It had been rumored that Federman, who
usually had eight bakers in his employ, had set three men to work in
the places of the strikers. Shouting "scabs," accompanied with unintelligible maledictions on them, the crowd in the Central Palace rushed
pellmell to Federman's. There they found the street filled with a howling mob which swayed back and forth from sidewalk to sidewalk
shouting and beating each other. Half a hundred of the first of the new
arrivals piled on top of Isidor Bernstein of No. 11 King Street, a
watchman for Federman, and bore down his burly form in spite of the
vigorous way he played on their heads and shoulders with his club.

Four of the crowd forced their way to the basement bakery where Federman and his three assistants cowered in one corner. Dough filled the great mixing troughs and furnished fine ammunition for the insurgent quartet. They threw it at the boss and his three men and, when tired of that, splashed it about the floor and walls of the rooms. They tried to destroy every implement they could lay hands on, and by the time their energy was somewhat exhausted there was not a pane of glass in the windows or any value left in the material in the place. . . .

So great was the press of the crowd that the patrol wagon bearing the reserves could not force a way through the densely packed bodies. The horses' bridles were grabbed in spite of their rearing and plunging, and forward progress was stopped. Detectives Landers and Galligan, sitting with their feet hanging out of the tail of the wagon, were pulled out into the street by their heels. Then the other policemen in the wagon leaped out and charged the crowd, striking right and left, forward and back with their nightsticks.

Howls of pain rose higher than the shouts against the police. The police tore the crowd apart and plunged into the basement of the bakery where the trouble originated. They pulled out two men, Louis Mandesiever of No. 249 Broome Street and Max Siegel of No. 55 Norfolk Street, both almost unrecognizable from the dough that smeared their clothes and faces and both bleeding from gashes in their heads.

It was impossible to get the patrol wagon started when the two prisoners had been bundled into it. Then the bricks and bottles began to descend from the windows. Patrolmen Hart and Sweeney forced their way into the houses and searched for the throwers high and low, but in vain. The mob finally gave way under repeated charges by the police and permitted the patrol wagon to pass. Patrolman Finley was bruised and cut and his uniform ruined from his being rolled in the mud. Bernstein was so badly beaten that he was sent home in care of a physician. The mob gave way only bit by bit under the repeated charges of the police to clear the street; it then retreated into the nearest doorways from which it hooted and jeered police and bosses alike. . . .

Meantime, the *kosher* bread famine had become acute. Lunchrooms lay idle, and the Hebrew grocers could not get any bread to sell, as it was unsafe to receive any. The strike leaders' evident intention was to starve out the people in the hope of bringing matters to a climax. The bread famine was principally confined to the district between Hester and Houston Streets as far as Avenue C. Rye bread, which was selling before the strike at two and one-half cents a pound, was eight cents a pound and hard to get at the money. At Pyocken Polski's union restaurant at No. 87 Attorney Street, there was no bread, and there was no business done all day. Groceries were in the same plight, and biscuits which were on the shelves for months went off like hot cakes. The most serious riot of the afternoon took place at the bakery of Joseph Bock, No. 138 Orchard Street. Bock, who is treasurer of the boss bakers' association, was away at the time, and his assistants barricaded the place. Forty strikers tried to storm the cellars in order to get the employees on strike, but Patrolman Sofsky of the Eldridge Street station came along on a run and captured a ringleader, using his club freely. . . .

There was a disposition on the part of the strikers to get women into the mobs, with the object of working public sentiment if women were clubbed. The police, seeing this, were careful not to make too indiscriminate a use of their sticks. Five women upset a pushcart loaded with bread at Orchard and Stanton Streets, trampling the loaves into the mud. A number of women also snatched a basket from a man who was delivering bread at Stanton and Ridge Streets.

The strikers sent committees around on every pretext. One committee was sent to Philadelphia to prevent *kosher* bread from being sent from that city to New York. Another committee was sent to Jersey City and Hoboken with the same object. A meeting of the Hebrew boss bakers' association, which has been formed since the strike began, was held yesterday afternoon at No. 252 Broome Street, and the boss bakers had a noisy time. The meeting was behind closed doors, but the wrangling could be heard outside. A schedule of demands from the strikers had been submitted, based on recognition of the union. After the meeting the following statement was made:

"We are ready to pay the wages demanded, but will on no account recognize the union or sign any agreement. Further, we can consider no negotiations with walking delegates or the strike leader, Samuel Kurtz. Our bakeries are closed. We can get men, but they are afraid to go to work, and we are not asking our men who did not strike to work for fear of provoking riots.''

The sweatshot was replaced by the factory, as one journalist reports. Manufacturers preferred the new system because it permitted greater use of machinery which made for lower unit costs. For labor it was a mixed blessing. Working conditions were better, but work was more monotonous and more tiring. Its greatest boon was that it permitted industry-wide unionization, thus laying the groundwork for the great clothing unions, the Amalgamated Men's Clothing Workers and the International Ladies Garment Workers Union:

TASK WORK BOWING TO FACTORY SYSTEM
(*The Outlook*, November 21, 1903)

Go tonight at nine or even ten o'clock down through the ghetto. You will find scores of small coat shops still lighted. These are nonunion shops, and a glimpse into one of them reveals the task system running at full speed. The room is low and crowded. The air is close, impure, and alive with the ceaseless whir of machines. The operator bends close over his machine—his foot on the treadle in swift, ceaseless motion; the baster stands just behind, at the table; the finisher works close between them. On the table is a pile of twenty coats. This is their "task"—the day's work, which most teams never accomplish. Of the three teams here, the swiftest can finish their task in fourteen hours' labor. The other two seem forever behind and striving to catch up. Five tasks a week is their average. They need no overseer, no rules, no regular hours. They drive themselves. This is the secret of the system, for three men seldom feel sick or dull or exhausted at the same moment. If the operator slackens his pace, the baster calls for more coats. If at six o'clock the baster gives out, the finisher spurs him on through the evening.

The positions are tense, their eyes strained, their movements quick and nervous. Most of them smoke cigarettes while they work; beer and cheap whisky are brought in several times a day by a peddler. Some sing Yiddish songs—while they race. The women chat and laugh sometimes—while they race. For these are not yet dumb slaves, but intensely human beings—young, and straining every ounce of youth's vitality. Among operators twenty years is an active lifetime. Forty-five is old age. They make but half a living.

This is but the rough underside of the system. Widen the focus, include employers, then employers of employers, and the whole is a live human picture of cutthroat competition. At the top the great New York manufacturers of clothing compete fiercely for half the country's trade—a trade of sudden changes, new styles, rush seasons. When, three years back, the raglan overcoat came suddenly into favor, at once this chance was seized by a score of rivals, each striving to make the coat cheapest and place it first on the market. Each summoned his contractors and set them in turn competing for orders. He knew them all and knew how desperately dependent they were upon his trade. Slowly the prices were hammered down and down until the lowest possible bids had been forced. Then enormous rush orders were given.

This system is now hard pushed by a swifter rival, and is falling behind in the race. In these days of machine invention, a process to live must not only be swift and cheap; it must be able, by saving labor, to grow forever swifter and cheaper. This the task system can no longer do. The factory system, so long delayed by the desperate driving of the task, began in 1896. In New York today, 70 per cent of the coats are made by the factory. The small shops—on task or week wages—are mere survivals of the past.

Endless saving, dividing, narrowing labor—this is the factory. Down either side of the long factory table forty operators bend over machines, and each one sews the twentieth part of a coat.

And the human cost—is it, too, reduced? Is the worker better off here than he was in the sweatshop? To consider this fairly we must compare the nonunion factory with the nonunion sweatshop. Wages by the week for the most skilled workers are slightly higher in the factory than they were in the sweatshop. They are lower for the unskilled majority. This majority must slowly increase, for the factory system progresses by transferring skill to machinery. Hours are shorter; work is less irregular; the shop is sanitary; the air is more wholesome—but the pocketmaker is often as exhausted at 6:00 P.M. as the coatmaker was at 10:00 P.M., for his work is more minute, more intense, more monotonous. This concentration, too, is growing.

Still, the workers have gained most decidedly. The factory is a help to the union. Through the past twenty years labor unions were formed again and again, only to be broken by new waves of ignorant immigrants. In the system of small scattered shops the unions had no chance. The free American workman bargained alone, with a contractor who said, "I have no power," and a manufacturer who said, "I have no workmen." All this is ended. Contractor and manufacturer are slowly becoming one. The bargain is direct, and the workmen are learning to strike it together.

The factory system made wide-scale unionization possible; a tragic fire at the Triangle Waist Company of New York in March 1911, which took the lives of 146 workers, gave it urgency and a rallying cry. It became obvious soon after the fire that many lives would not have been lost had there been greater concern shown for the safety of the workers. The Triangle Fire dramatized the plight of laborers who worked incredibly long hours in unsanitary and unsafe shops, who could be fired at will, and who were forced to seek employment in an area on Essex Street near Hester which everyone called the *Chazer Mark* or "Pig Market."

The "appalling horror" of the fire is described in a contemporary newspaper article:

THE TRIANGLE FIRE
(*New York World*, March 26, 1911)

At 4:35 o'clock yesterday afternoon, fire, springing from a source that
may never be positively identified, was discovered in the rear of the
eighth floor of the ten-story building at the northwest corner of Washington Place and Greene Street, the first of three floors occupied as a
factory by the Triangle Waist Company. At two o'clock this morning
Chief Croker estimated the total dead as 154. More than a third of
those who lost their lives did so in jumping from windows. The firemen who answered the first of the four alarms turned in found thirty
bodies on the pavements of Washington Place and Greene Street.

It was the most appalling horror since the Slocum disaster and the
Iroquois Theater fire in Chicago. Every available ambulance in Manhattan was called upon to cart the dead to the morgue—bodies charred
to unrecognizable blackness or reddened to a sickly hue—as was to be
seen by shoulders or limbs protruding through flame-eaten clothing.
Men and women, boys and girls were of the dead that littered the
street; that is actually the condition—the streets were littered.

The fire began in the eighth story. The flames licked and shot their
way up through the other two stories. All three floors were occupied
by the Triangle Waist Company. The estimate of the number of employees at work is made by Chief Croker at about 1,000. The proprietors of the company say 700 men and girls were in their place. Before
smoke or flame gave signs from the windows, the loss of life was fully
under way. The first signs that persons in the street knew that these
three top stories had turned into red furnaces in which human creatures
were being caught and incinerated was when screaming men and
women and boys and girls crowded out on the many window ledges
and threw themselves into the streets far below. They jumped with
their clothing ablaze. The hair of some of the girls streamed up aflame
as they leaped. Thud after thud sounded on the pavements. It is a
ghastly fact that on both the Greene Street and Washington Place sides

of the building there grew mounds of the dead and dying. And the worst horror of all was that in this heap of the dead now and then there stirred a limb or sounded a moan.

Within the three flaming floors it was as frightful. There flames enveloped many so that they died instantly. When Fire Chief Croker could make his way into these three floors, he found sights that utterly staggered him, that sent him, a man used to viewing horrors, back and down into the street with quivering lips. The floors were black with smoke. And then he saw as the smoke drifted away bodies burned to bare bones. There were skeletons bending over sewing machines.

The elevator boys saved hundreds. They each made twenty trips from the time of the alarm until twenty minutes later when they could do no more. Fire was streaming into the shaft, flames biting at the cables. They fled for their own lives. Some, about seventy, chose a successful avenue of escape. They clambered up a ladder to the roof. A few remembered the fire escape. Many may have thought of it but only as they uttered cries of dismay.

Wretchedly inadequate was this fire escape—a lone ladder running down to a rear narrow court, which was smoke filled as the fire raged, one narrow door giving access to the ladder. By the score they fought and struggled and breathed fire and died trying to make that needle-eye road to self-preservation.

Shivering at the chasm below them, scorched by the fire behind, there were some that still held positions on the window sills when the first squad of firemen arrived. The nets were spread below with all promptness. Citizens were commandeered into service, as the firemen necessarily gave their attention to the one engine and hose of the force that first arrived. The catapult force that the bodies gathered in the long plunges made the nets utterly without avail. Screaming girls and men, as they fell, tore the nets from the grasp of the holders, and the bodies struck the sidewalks and lay just as they fell. Some of the bodies ripped big holes through the life nets.

Concentrated, the fire burned within. The flames caught all the flimsy lace stuff and linens that go into the making of spring and summer shirtwaists and fed eagerly upon the rolls of silk. The cutting room was laden with the stuff on long tables. The employees were toiling over such material at the rows and rows of machines. Sinisterly the spring day gave aid to the fire. Many of the window panes facing south and east were drawn down. Draughts had full play. The experts say that the three floors must each have become a whirlpool of fire. Whichever way the entrapped creatures fled they met a curving sweep of flame. Many swooned and died. Others fought their way to the windows or the elevator or fell fighting for a chance at the fire escape, the single fire escape leading into the blind court that was to be reached from the upper floors by clambering over a window sill! On all of the three floors, at a narrow window, a crowd met death trying to get out to that one slender fire escape ladder.

It was a fireproof building in which this enormous tragedy occurred. Save for the three stories of blackened windows at the top, you would scarcely have been able to tell where the fire had happened. The walls stood firmly. A thin tongue of flame now and then licked around a window sash. On the ledge of a ninth-story window two girls stood silently watching the arrival of the first fire apparatus. Twice one of the girls made a move to jump. The other restrained her, tottering in her foothold as she did so. They watched firemen rig the ladders up against the wall. They saw the last ladder lifted and pushed into place. They saw that it reached only the seventh floor. For the third time, the more frightened girl tried to leap. The bells of arriving fire wagons must have risen to them. The other girl gesticulated in the direction of the sounds. But she talked to ears that could no longer hear. Scarcely turning, her companion dived head first into the street. The other girl drew herself erect. The crowds in the street were stretching their arms up at her shouting and imploring her not to leap. She made a steady gesture, looking down as if to assure them she would remain brave. But a thin flame shot out of the window at her back and touched her hair. In an instant her head was aflame. She tore at her burning hair, lost her balance, and came shooting down upon the mound of bodies below. From opposite windows spectators saw again and again pitiable companionships formed in the instant of death—girls who placed their arms around each other as they leaped. In many cases their clothing was flaming or their hair flaring as they fell.

By eight o'clock the available supply of coffins had been exhausted, and those that had already been used began to come back from the morgue. By that time bodies were lowered at the rate of one a minute, and the number of patrol wagons became inadequate, so that four, sometimes six, coffins were loaded upon each. At intervals throughout the night the very horror of their task overcame the most experienced of the policemen and morgue attendants at work under the moving finger of the searchlight. The crews were completely changed no less than three times.

Wages and Unemployment in New York

In a letter from New York, published in *Der Yiddisher Emigrant* (vol. 5, no. 22, 1911), an American correspondent sought to dispel the fantasy that "the worker in New York 'lives like a count,' he has a fine and comfortable dwelling, eats the finest foods, and can afford all luxuries." The following extract was translated by the editor:

If one examines the true conditions with open eyes, one sees a completely different picture. The dwelling is neither nice nor comfortable, the food is not too tasty, and the pleasures are few . . . we speak of the great mass of Jewish and non-Jewish laborers, especially those who dwell in the tenements. Even if we take $12 as the average wage, it is still far too little to support a family in the larger cities, where rent and food are so high. According to the research of another expert, a family in New York, or in another large city, needs $18 per week, for a more or less respectable living. . . .

Often young children need to work to help the family make ends meet. Despite the law which prohibits children under fourteen to work, we find thousands of young boys and girls in factories and stores, selling papers and sweets and the like. . . . Thousands of young children work in their tenement apartments on work brought home from the shop by their parents.

The above is about the fortunate who have work. The plight of the large army of unemployed beggars description. In our city, even in the "busy" seasons, there are thousands of unemployed, ready to do the hardest and most menial labor for a day's wages. Tailors, cobblers, carpenters, typesetters and the like wander about for months without work. The smallest ad asking for a "hand" attracts hundreds of the unemployed, and the employer can choose the best at the lowest price. A middle-aged, unskilled laborer has little chance to find employment. It is a fact that a person past the age of forty can rarely find a position. If he has one, he is kept on, but if he leaves it, it is almost impossible to find another.

Reports issued by organized labor disclose the rate of unemployment in New York of 400,000 union members; 62,851 were employed in 1910; and 190 labor unions reported the unemployment rate to the Bureau of Labor Statistics in the first half of 1911 as 24 percent.

In 1910, 500,000 persons received charitable help in New York. Most of these are tenement dwellers driven to charity requests by high rents.

Jewish Workers Beyond New York

Nor were conditions for Jewish workers better outside New York. Even in Bradford, Connecticut, a relatively small town, life was difficult. The following account appeared in *Ha-Magid*, February 11, 1889 (translated by the editor):

We born in Russia, who left that land during the pogroms, had our full share of troubles till we got here. But even here we did not find the peace and quiet we were seeking. In Bradford, there are twenty Jewish families. All work in the factories and earn from seven and a half to nine dollars a week.

The work we do in the factories may be compared to the labor of our ancestors in Egypt—hard drudge toil. . . . In America, the life of the laborer is regulated by his work schedule. If he comes a few minutes late to work, he finds the doors closed and he loses a day's wages.

The same happens to the worker who stops working a minute before the designated time. The worker spends his days and years running to work and working. Even when he is ill, he pushes himself to work, fearing that his absence will be used as cause for dismissal.

Even after six days of toil, on the American sabbath, which is on Sunday, we have no respite from pain and remorse. No sooner does the Jew appear on the street—even if elegantly dressed—the cry goes up from all sides, "Here comes the sheeny!" Sometimes, boys run after him and throw stones. Only in one way is it better here than in Russia—our homes are not attacked, the window panes are not smashed and we are not robbed, but troubles and pain we have enough. If a Jew appears for employment at a factory and they know he is a Jew, he is turned away.

The need to move from place to place in search of jobs is illustrated in the early memoirs of Harry Germanow (*Harry Germanow . . . My Own Story,* published privately in Rochester, New York, in 1967), who became the founder and the head of one of the world's largest manufacturers of crystals and crystal machines in Rochester, New York. During the first decade of the century, when he was eighteen years old, he was already working long hours:

I left Bethlehem by trolly-car for Philadelphia, which was not too far away, and rented a room over a grocery store. . . .

After several days of knocking myself out from one place to another, I accepted a job at Baldwin Locomotive Works for $9.00 per week. I worked there for two weeks and did not like it. The building was 8 or 10 stories high. The ceilings were very low. The machines were very crowded and dangerous. People were getting hurt every day, so I quit and got a job at Crane Shipyards for $9.00 a week. The place was an hour's walk from where I stayed. I walked back and forth every day to save 20¢ car fare.

One morning, about 10 o'ciock, I met with an accident. Working on a drill press trying to change a belt from a slow speed to a faster one, my second finger of my right hand caught in open gears and chopped a piece of my finger off. In those days machines were not guarded as now. There were no labor inspectors. I was taken to a hospital where my finger was trimmed and bandaged. I was paid for the day's work till 10 o'clock only.

I went back to Bethlehem and applied for a job in another building. There were several buildings doing different types of work in each building. My first job was in building 2. The second was in building 4, the work consisted of parts for automobiles. It was very interesting. The year was the beginning of the automobile industry. The regular daily hours of work were 10. We worked overtime every day until 10 o'clock except Saturdays. I used to go to New York every other weekend to meet some boys and girls who came from Pinsk. I was very friendly with one of the boys before we came to this country. His name was Joe Gottlieb; he worked as a machinist for the Singer Sewing Machine Co. in Elizabeth, N.J. We used to talk about the different type of work we were doing. One day he quit his job and came to work in Bethlehem to be together with me. It was very nice. After a while, he changed his mind and wanted to go back to his first job and he said to me, "Harry, I came to Bethlehem to be with you, how about you coming to Elizabeth to be with me? Elizabeth is much nearer to New York and at Singer you do not have to work overtime, and we will have more time to enjoy ourselves."

I agreed with him and quit my job and went to Elizabeth trying to get a job with the Singer Sewing Machine Co. . . . It was not easy. The Singer Co. did not care to hire Jewish people. The way my friend got his job was through a Jewish man in New York by the name of Barondess, a very well-known personality. I tried the same way. At first I was refused. After considerable appealing he consented and gave me a letter of recommendation, and I got a job at Singer's at $12.00 a week, 55 hours' work, Saturday one-half day off, and being not far from New York, we used to go together every weekend, meeting with some boys and girls we used to know in our home town.

I was very happy with my new job. . . . I worked in a toolroom, making tools to make sewing machine parts. It was so interesting that

when the day was over, I felt sorry and was very anxious to come
back the next morning to start over again. . . .

In the year of 1907 there was a terrible depression in this country.
People were losing their jobs by the hundreds of thousands. At Singer's
where I worked a great many were laid off.

Economic Conditions of
Immigrant Jews in Chicago

In Chicago, similar difficulties were to be found. A 1905 report by
Abraham Bisno, who had served as State Deputy Inspector of Work-
shops and Factories for Illinois, described the trades immigrant Jews
pursued and also analyzed why most did not support trade unions to
the same extent as other nationalities. His report, which appears in the
collection *The Russian Jew in the United States,* also discussed the
reasons why Russian Jews would not continue to labor in factories but
would sooner or later go into business, distributive occupations or professions:

Probably among no nationality does the economic condition change
more rapidly than among the Russian Jewish people in the United
States. The transition period from the junk peddler to the iron yard
owner, from the dry goods peddler to the retail or wholesale dry goods
merchant, from the cloak maker to the cloak manufacturer, is comparatively short. True, the same causes which influence trade and industry
in the economic world about them also influence this population, yet
they seem able to develop business methods of their own, which, in
many instances, successfully defy or modify well established economic laws. They can do business with little money, or practically no
money, right next door to a large house, ignoring the economic rule

that the latter, through competition, drives the smaller house out of business. They continue to hold their own in the trades in which they engage, growing in strength as the years go on. . . .

Scattered through the industries in this large city, Russian Jewish people are to be found in a large variety of occupations, from the common laborers to the highly skilled mechanics. I find them employed as iron molders, machinists, locomotive engineers, sailors, farm helpers, boiler makers, butchers at the stock yards, street sweepers, section hands on railroads, motormen and conductors on the street cars; a number as building laborers—brick layers, carpenters, steam fitters, plumbers; in bicycle plating shops; in manufactories of electrical appliances, of iron beds and springs, of shoes, of wood work, and of upholstery; in tin, mattress and picture frame factories; and in bakeries. But the industries in which they are employed in the greatest numbers are the sewing and cigar trades.

I gather from my connection with the trade union movement and from my observation while inspecting factories for the state of Illinois for four years, that the Russian Jewish people in Chicago have not nearly so great an influence on the sewing and cigar trades as in the east, particularly in New York. There are eight non-Jews to one Jew employed in the needle industries in Chicago. The proportion of non-Jews to Jews among the cigar makers is not quite so large. It can only be said, therefore, that the Russian Jews are an important factor in these trades. Among the mattress makers, too, concerning trade regulations, they must be regarded as an element to be reckoned with. . . .

One of the main reasons why they do not support trade unions and labor organizations to the same extent as other nationalities seems to be that most of them do not believe themselves to be working men for life, nor do they think that they will leave as a heritage to their children the lot of a wage-worker. A very large number speculate on the notion of opening, in course of time, a shop for themselves or going into business of some kind, or educating themselves out of the condition of the working classes. A large part of the tolerance of low wages, long hours of work, and unsanitary condition of the shops, that is, of the tragedy of economic servitude, of poverty, and of suffering, is to be ascribed to this state of mind. . . .

In the professions, there are a number of physicians, dentists, lawyers and teachers.

There are also mail carriers, post-office clerks, and holders of office under the state and city governments.

Perhaps from 2,500 to 3,000 are clerks in stores and offices, book-keepers, stock keepers and in kindred occupations, ranging from the lowest paid shipping clerk to the high-salaried department store manager. One is supposed to attain business training in the stores and offices, and there is a tendency to overstock this class of help, so the good salesman or good book-keeper is likely to receive smaller salary than an experienced mechanic or worker at a trade.

Among the peddlers and small store-keepers, the rag peddlers form the largest group. Most of them are very poor and hard working; they earn a precarious livelihood. I am told there are about 2,000. Very few of their children follow in their footsteps: most work in stores and some in factories. From the rag peddling business about 200 have become rag store-keepers. A large proportion of these own their own homes. The wealthiest is said to be worth about $20,000. The rag store cannot well be established with a capital of less than about $400.

Some 95 percent of the peddlers own their own horse and wagon; some of them, however, are so poor that they live partially on charity. The majority work in the city, but a portion ply their trade in the neighboring country towns.

Closely related to the above are the old iron dealers and peddlers. In fact, a rag dealer will often also deal in old iron, furniture, clothing, etc. But the old iron dealer is a sort of merchant, buying and selling iron and metal only. There are several hundred of these. Their earnings are higher than those of the rag peddlers. A number own their own homes and are quite prosperous. In their case the children are generally absorbed into other occupations.

The iron yard owners are a prosperous class. Some are reputed to be worth over $200,000. They do an extensive business. They are generally former iron or junk dealers.

Dealers in old bottles buy their goods from the rag peddlers. Their business has been developed only in the past few years. There are but 15 or 20 in the city and they are doing well, several being worth as much as $20,000, I am told.

Second-hand furniture store-keepers buy their goods, too, mostly at the rag peddlers. There are about 20 or 30 and they are making a fair living.

Of the fruit and market peddlers there are about 1,000. As they have not much to do in the winter, many go into the delivery business. In season they can earn from $20 to $35 per week. But as they are idle a great part of the year their average earnings are very low, and they are really poor people. Only a few are comparatively well-to-do, and own their homes. Some develop into grocery store keepers. Very few of the children of these peddlers follow the occupation of their fathers.

Jewish Farmers

Some groups of Russian Jews sought to establish themselves as farmers in New England, New Jersey, and other places. They received aid and encouragement from the Baron de Hirsch Fund, whose objective was to disperse Jewish immigrants and thereby lessen the congestion in the New York ghetto. In 1899, M. T. McKenna reported in *Our Brethren of the Tenements and Ghettos* that the Fund had "a special pet in the colony at Woodbine, New Jersey":

It is indeed a model colony, and all the other American-Jewish colonies look to it for agricultural education. Russian-Jewish farmers were unacquainted with the methods of American farmers, and the Fund established an agricultural and industrial school, where the best knowledge of theoretical and practical farming can be taught to the young Jews. The boys and girls who are without means can work for a part of each day on the premises, and this enables them to earn their expenses and gain experience at the same time. The school has enough land and all the buildings to be found on a model farm to provide for laboratory work. The object of the school is to make the boys intelligent and successful farmers, and the course of study covers three years. In the first year, physics, chemistry and botany are taught, with English, mathematics, history and geography. In the next two years the more advanced studies in agriculture are taken up, as horticulture, landscape gardening, care and management of cattle, dairy, milk testing, comparative zoology, market gardening, and everything else that is included in the advanced agricultural courses. The result is that the boys begin to love country life, and a number of the graduates are now employed as head gardeners by private parties. All who have places in the country will appreciate the advantage of trained help, particularly for the care of horses and choice cows. Three of the graduates, who were more ambitious than their fellows, completed their courses in agricultural colleges, and one of them received an appointment of special assistant from his Alma Mater, while the other two are teaching in the Woodbine school.

The educational work of the Woodbine school is not confined to the Jews, for members of the faculty hold offices in the various agricultural organizations, and are invited to read papers upon useful subjects. Many letters of inquiry are received from local farmers, and they are promptly answered. The superintendent of the Woodbine colony is a competent educator, a graduate of the Zurich College of Agriculture in Switzerland. He educates the Jewish farmers by giving lectures, accompanied by stereopticon views, on agricultural subjects. As the Jewish farmer has commenced work where American farming was practically dead, the result of the new methods of work will be watched for with interest.

The farmers are not the only Russian Jews who have been hampered by the present economic conditions, and the Baron de Hirsch Fund may be called an anti-sweatshop association, for it is the only one that is able to apply a practical remedy to the root of the sweatshop evil. It works to educate the older Russian and Romanian Jews out of that groove, and to start the little ones out in such a path that they may not fall into it.

Entry into the Professions

In "The 'Classes' and 'Masses' in New York" (which appears in *The Russian Jew in the United States*), Isaac H. Rubinow discusses the movement of the Russian Jews from the skilled workers class into the professions. While the masses of Russian Jews remained industrial laborers, the significant upward rise took place in a relatively short time:

Medicine has remained one of the favorite professions . . . Probably from four hundred to six hundred of the seven thousand physicians in greater New York are Russian Jews. Though of late symptoms of over-supply in the market have been noticed, the influx into the profession does not show any signs of abatement. The economic status of the majority is fair; many older members are well-to-do. In the real estate business of the East Side the medical man plays a part by no means unimportant. The dentists, less numerous, are much more prosperous. In the legal profession, on the contrary, the Russians cannot boast of any great success, either financial or otherwise. Pharmacy, on the border line between profession and business, has also attracted a large number of Russian youths, but the returns are far less satisfactory than those of the other occupations.

The teaching profession has probably provided a livelihood for more Jewish families than the others which we have enumerated. For obvious reasons, only the second generation, i.e., those born on the American soil, or those who had emigrated at a very early age, are fit for the profession; but it will certainly be a revelation to many an American to learn how many Russian Jewish young men and girls are doing this work of "Americanization," not only of Jewish, but of Irish, German, and Italian children. There is no doubt that the Jews have supplied a greater proportion of public school teachers than either the Germans or the Italians. The profession has never been a road to fortune; yet with the latest salary schedule, a very comfortable living has been provided for several thousand families.

The important position which the Russian Jew occupies in the professions of New York City is more significant because he entered them but a short time since. Ten years ago, a Russian Jewish journalist found only a few dozen representatives of his race in medicine and law, a few individuals in dentistry, and hardly any in the teaching profession, or in municipal service. These dozens have grown into hundreds, and even thousands, within the following decade. With a remarkable display of energy and enterprise, the Russian Jew was ready to grasp the opportunity whenever and wherever it presented itself. . . .

7. Education, Religion, Culture

In the *shtetl* culture which had shaped the Old World Jew, learning was the vehicle for social mobility, desirable marriage partners, community status, influence. The same obtained in the immigrant ghetto, with some variation. *Heder* learning gave way to public school education; the *yeshiva bochur* of Europe became the college student in America.

The immigrant Jew kept dawn-to-dark hours in his grocery or candy store, or coughed out his lungs in sweatshops, to afford the schooling for his sons that would free them from store counter and shop bench. His children (including daughters, when they could be spared from piece-work or housework) took to public school and college with a passion; these institutions for Americanization were the vehicles to economic opportunity and social status. The education the public school provided liberated the offspring from the immigrant status of their foreign-born parents:

EAST SIDE LOVE OF LEARNING
(*New York Tribune,* September 18, 1898)

The people of the East Side are again confronted with the problem of how to educate their children, and the limited capacity of the city schools, which is evident again this fall, is once more a cause for keen disappointment and unfulfilled hopes. Those who do not know the inner life of the tenement-house dwellers can hardly realize the general extent of this disappointment or the acute suffering which it entails for parents and children alike.

There were several cases brought to public notice last fall where boys who had been denied school advantages committed suicide. In other cases similar disappointments resulted in insanity. Such facts can only occasion surprise to those who are unfamiliar with the intense craving for knowledge which prevails in that part of New York where "the other half" lives. It will astonish many people to learn that the average small boy of the ghetto has none of the commercial instinct which is ordinarily taken as a sign and heritage of his race. There, boys want to become doctors and lawyers—some look forward to a political career—and social questions fill their young lives with restless longing. It is a peculiar fact, too, that the fathers of these boys, who spend their days in the ill-smelling fish market of Hester Street or live their lives haggling over the price of pushcart wares, encourage the younger generation in their desire for knowledge.

"It is enough that I am a merchant," said a long-gabardined peddler yesterday. "What is such a life? What can I do for my people or myself? My boy shall be a lawyer, learned and respected of men. And it is for that that I stand here, sometimes when my feet ache so that I would gladly go and rest. My boy shall have knowledge. He shall go to college."

College! That is the aim and ambition of hundreds of them. The father, bent beneath the load of coats he is carrying to the factory or trudging along with his pushcart, dreams of a better life than his own for the boy or girl who is so dear to his heart. When evening comes and the day's work is over, he sits in the little tenement, at the doorstoop or on the sidewalk, and instills into his children's minds the necessity for knowledge. He points to his own life—how meager, sordid, and poor it is—and he tells them that to avoid it they must study hard and learn much.

The classroom teacher was respected by parents and pupil alike, and the school principal was a figure of majestic status and influence. The veneration of the public school continued beyond the immigrant generation. No group labored more in its behalf than the organized Jewish community, jealous for its status, solicitous for its welfare. It was surely no accident that the world's largest public school should be situated in the world's largest Jewish community:

THE LARGEST PUBLIC SCHOOL IN
THE WORLD
(*New York Tribune*, September 16, 1906)

Public School No. 188 is the largest public school in the world. In the great play yard in the central court the children were romping about so noisily that the two men had to cease talking. They could not hear each other. Then, of a sudden a gong sounded, and the hubbub was hushed. The boys on one side of the yard, the girls on the other, fell into lines, each representing a class and slowly and noiselessly, save for the shuffling of feet, they marched away to their classrooms. "You won't believe it, perhaps, but that little army you have just seen contained five thousand children, or as many as attend all the schools in the entire State of Nevada. Under this roof there are a quarter of a thousand more pupils than in all Columbia University. Indeed, there are seats enough for the students of Yale, Brown, Amherst, and Bowdoin combined."

Following the boys upstairs, the two men met Mr. Mandel, the principal, whose face brightened as soon as he was asked if they might visit the classrooms. "I guess you won't have time to go into all of them," he said, as he led the way. "You see there are ninety-six altogether." Turning through a door the visitors found themselves confronted by forty lads poring over a history lesson. In the teacher's chair a boy had been left in charge. "A small-sized republic," remarked the principal. "You see how well they can govern themselves.

They have elected this president to administer affairs in the interim.''

"They do maintain good decorum to be sure," said the writer, "although there must be some tough rowdies among them. They doubtless go to school because they have to, and so when they get through the slums will swallow them up again. I suppose there is hardly one of them who has in view any definite vocation.''

"I'd be glad to take a census of the class to find out," said Mr. Mandel, and, turning to the teacher, who had just returned, he asked him to call the roll. Of the thirty-nine present, only one was undecided as to his life work. Eleven wanted to take up various business careers. Nine intended to be lawyers, six civil engineers, three dentists, three doctors, two teachers, and one each for the various callings of mechanic, engraver, designer of clothes, and electrical engineer. Of the thirty-nine, the majority were Jewish. . . .

The class of foreign girls was hard at work learning such words as "head," "hand," and "foot" when the visitors arrived. After this drill the teacher took a crayon and, holding it up, said slowly, "I have a piece of chalk." Pupil after pupil took the chalk and repeated the same words. "Now," said the teacher, "I am going back to our old lesson," and patting the head of a little girl, she asked her what part of the body it was. With a serious, almost sad, look the child faced the class, and tapping her curly locks she said, "Dis ist my piece of head." But her classmates never showed the slightest trace of a smile. Even if any of them noticed the mistake, the language was all too foreign and too strange to contain any humor.

All of the thirty-three girls were Hebrews. Twenty were born in Russia, seven in Hungary, and six in Austria. Half had arrived in New York in the last six months and had fled from Russia to escape the torch and the saber. Several of the girls were thirteen or fourteen years old, and, according to their teachers, they were proficient in arithmetic and Russian literature. "But do they appreciate the opportunities of this country?" asked the author. "Ask that little one whom you call Rosie how she regards America." In Yiddish the teacher asked the question, and Rosie's answer, translated, was, "I love sweet America. They are kind to me here."

The pressure of Jewish children on the schools in New York—and their passion for learning—are described by J. K. Paulding in his essay that appears in *The Russian Jew in the United States:*

The preponderance of Jewish pupils over all others in the schools situated below Houston Street on the East Side is so overwhelming as to render of comparatively little value questions directed to the teachers concerning the relative scholarship and aptitude of Jewish and non-Jewish pupils, unless these teachers have had experience elsewhere. Nevertheless, there is much in the testimony of teachers to confirm the prevailing impression that these pupils—the children, for the most part, of poor Jewish immigrants from Russia—are among the brightest in attendance at the public schools. Certainly they rank high in all examinations for advancement to the secondary institutions of learning such as the high schools and city college—and this not merely, it may be believed, because of a keener instinct of competition. . . .

In spite of the bad industrial conditions prevailing among the Jews of the lower East Side, the parents, or if not the parents, the children themselves are quick to avail themselves of whatever privileges their new surroundings extend to them. Among these the privilege of most worth is the education offered them, and they are not slow to appreciate its advantages. The children begin their attendance at the public school within a very short time after their arrival here, the younger ones finding their way into the numerous kindergartens connected with private institutions. Very soon, especially to the little girls, the public school teacher becomes a strong, in many instances the strongest influence in the lives of those children. They learn to look upon her as a model of good taste—first, it is true, chiefly in external things, such as clothes and manner of speech—but afterwards, very often, as a pattern of deportment as well. Happy the teacher who can "live up to" the ideal that has been formed of her! These children, most teachers report, are singularly docile—not the girls only, but the boys as well. . . .

Of the interest and ability displayed by these children of the public school age, let some of their teachers speak:

"Jewish children, as a rule, are bright, attentive and studious."

"They are generally anxious to learn, and except in English, compare favorably with other nationalities."

"They rank among the highest. They are far more earnest and ambitious [than other scholars] and many of them supplement their school work with outside reading."

The author goes on to report on the heavy attendance and achievement records of Jewish students in both the high schools and at New York's two major institutions of free higher education—the City College and the Normal College.

The Russian Jews were not only interested in educating their children; they also eagerly sought schooling for themselves, attending evening schools and classes in settlement houses to learn English, civics, and related subjects that would better equip them for life in their new country. In *Between Two Worlds,* Dr. Benjamin Gordon, who graduated from the Jefferson Medical College of Philadelphia in 1896, tells of his efforts to begin his American education shortly after his arrival in New York:

I registered at the Henry Street evening school. I was not fortunate in my early schooling in America, however. I found the classroom attended by elderly men of many nationalities, most of whom chewed tobacco and spit profuse streams of repulsive brown juice into cigar boxes filled with sand. I found the atmosphere of this house of education unbearable, and I left the evening school on the same night I entered it.

Not being successful with public education, I made up my mind to educate myself. I picked up a small Webster's dictionary in a second-hand bookstore, and a work by Oliver Goldsmith, *The Vicar of Wakefield*. At first, I found this book very difficult reading. I had to consult the dictionary at every third word, and frequently I had to use my German dictionary to understand the English dictionary. As I struggled through *The Vicar of Wakefield,* I marked down the meaning of every word I did not know. It took me six weeks to complete the book, and, when I was through, my *Vicar of Wakefield* looked like an interlinear translation of some old Greek text.

The worst development of this reading was that I valiantly tried to use Goldsmith's vocabulary in my daily conversations. This, coupled with my heavy accent, made my English into a new language! Some of my closest friends advised me that I should give up talking "dictionary language." The other books I read in my new home were *Robinson Crusoe* and *Tom Tracy's New Boy*.

I soon realized that there was little use in acquiring a vocabulary if I could not pronounce the words properly and if none of the people to whom I spoke understood the meanings of the words. I therefore made up my mind to enter a day school. I saw the principal of the Henry Street School, but he discouraged me from registering, saying that I would not feel at home among children of six to ten years of age and that my very attendance might even cause a disturbance in the classroom. He suggested that, since I had a fair knowledge of English, I would accomplish more by mixing with non-foreign Americans than by attending school. "It might be best," he said, "to rent a room among Americans, where no Yiddish would be spoken." I took his advice and on the next day found a room with an Irish family where only English was spoken.

True enough, within six months, my accent was greatly improved. I not only learned the ordinary vernacular but also the Irish accent and slang—perhaps I learned the latter first. I soon became so accustomed to speaking English that when I went into the chief rabbi's house, I unintentionally spoke that language.

Nor were Benjamin Gordon and the persistence that eventually resulted in his becoming a doctor unique. Abraham Cahan, editor of *Der Forverts*, devoted an entire article in *The Atlantic Monthly* (July 1898) to "The Russian Jew in America," the main thrust of which was to extol his passionate concern to educate and Americanize himself and his family:

This country, where the schools and colleges do not discriminate between Jew and Gentile, has quite another tale to tell. The several public evening schools of the New York Ghetto, the evening school supported from the Baron de Hirsch fund, and the two or three private establishments of a similar character are attended by thousands of Jewish immigrants, the great majority of whom come here absolutely ignorant of the language of their native country. Surely nothing can be more inspiring to the public-spirited citizen, nothing worthier of the interest of the student of immigration, than the sight of a gray-haired tailor, a patriarch in appearance, coming, after a hard day's work at a sweat-shop, to spell "cat, mat, rat," and to grapple with the difficulties of "th" and "w." Such a spectacle may be seen in scores of the class-rooms in the schools referred to. Hundreds of educated young Hebrews earn their living, and often pay their way through college, by giving private lessons in English in the tenement houses of the district—a type of young men and women peculiar to the Ghetto. The pupils of these private tutors are the same poor overworked sweat-shop "hands" of whom the public hears so much and knows so little. A tenement house kitchen turned, after a scanty supper, into a class-room, with the head of the family and his boarder bent over an English school reader, may perhaps claim attention as one of the curiosities of life in a great city; in the Jewish quarter, however, it is a common spectacle.

Nor does the tailor or peddler who hires these tutors, as a rule, content himself with an elementary knowledge of the language of his new home. I know many Jewish workmen who before they came here knew not a word of Russian, and were ignorant of any book except the Scriptures, or perhaps the Talmud, but whose range of English reading places them on a level with the average college-bred American.

The easy accessibility of secular education for Jews—most of whom had been confined to religious schools in the Jewish Pale of their settlement—inevitably led to a lessening if not an actual forsaking of strictly Jewish studies. Rabbis and Hebrew teachers could not at that time compete as models or exemplars with the secular schoolteacher. The plight of the rabbis on New York's East Side was noted by Hutchins Hapgood in *The Spirit of the Ghetto:*

The rabbis, as well as the scholars, of the East Side of New York have their grievances. They, too, are "submerged," like so much in humanity that is at once intelligent, poor and out of date. As a lot they are old reverent men, with long gray beards, long black coats and little black caps on their heads. They are mainly very poor, live in the barest of the tenement houses, and pursue a calling which no longer involves much honor or standing. In the old country, in Russia—for most of the poor ones are Russian—the rabbi is a great person. He is made rabbi by the state and is rabbi all his life, and the only rabbi in the town, for all the Jews in every city form one congregation, of which there is but one rabbi and one cantor. He is a man always full of learning and piety, and is respected and supported comfortably by the congregation, a tax being laid on meat, salt, and other foodstuffs for his special benefit.

But in New York it is very different. Here there are hundreds of congregations, one on almost every street, for the Jews come from many different cities and towns in the old country, and the New York representatives of every little place in Russia must have their congregation here. Consequently, the congregations are for the most part small, poor, and unimportant. Few can pay the rabbi more than three or four dollars a week, and often, instead of having a regular salary, he is reduced to occasional fees for his services at weddings, births, and holy festivals generally. Some very poor congregations get along without a rabbi at all, hiring one for special occasions, but these are congregations which are falling off somewhat from their Orthodox strictness.

The result of this state of affairs is a pretty general falling-off in the character of the rabbis. In Russia they are learned men, know the Talmud and all the commentaries upon it by heart, and have degrees from the rabbinical colleges; but here they are often without degrees, frequently know comparatively little about the Talmud, and are sometimes actuated by worldly motives. A few Jews coming to New York from some small Russian town, will often select for a rabbi the man among them who knows a little more of the Talmud than the others, whether he has ever studied for the calling or not. Then, again, some mere adventurers get into the position—men good for nothing, looking for a position. They clap a high hat on their heads, impose on a poor congregation with their up-to-dateness, and become rabbis without learning or piety. These "fake" rabbis—"rabbis for business only"— are often satirized in the Yiddish plays given at the Bowery theaters. On the stage they are ridiculous figures, ape American manners in bad accents, and have a keen eye for gain.

Similarly, the communal Talmud Torah, the Hebrew school, labored valiantly to inform Jewish boys of their heritage and instruct them in the ways of the tradition. But it was a school supplementary to the public school, and had to compete for the student's time, interest, and devotion. Additionally, its financial situation was always critical, the faculty beleaguered, and the students often rebellious:

A SCHOOL FOR HEBREW
(New York Tribune, November 12, 1899)

One of the schools of New York which is unknown beyond the Russian district has recently been enlarged and improved, and the building which it occupies, Nos. 225 and 227 East Broadway, has been changed into one of the most attractive structures in that part of the city. Many educational and charitable institutions in that neighborhood receive contributions from members of the Jewish community living in the upper part of the city, and some of these institutions could not exist without the support desired from that quarter. But the Machzikay Talmud Torah School depends for funds entirely on the Russian-Jewish population. This seems only natural when one knows that the school is maintained for the purpose of teaching the Hebrew language and Hebrew literature. . . .

The school was established about fifteen years ago, and has grown with the Jewish population from one class of twenty-five pupils to twenty-two classes having about eleven hundred pupils ranging in age from six to fifteen years. There are no charges for instruction, and besides being a free school in all that the term implies, needy children who attend are supplied with shoes and clothing. The money for maintaining the institution comes from the annual dues of the members, of whom there are about two thousand, and from contributions from Russian Jews who wish to pay more than the stipulated $3 a year. There is probably no schoolhouse in New York in which less money has been expended for interior decoration than this Hebrew school. The rooms are absolutely bare except for the plain benches and chairs and the desks of the instructors. The pupils are for the most part children of poor parents, and as a class would not bear close inspection for neatness, but they display an earnestness in their work which shows that they share, even in a childish way, the sentiments of their parents and regard the tasks set before them as more than ordinary school work. In order that the work required of them in the Hebrew school may not interfere with their regular school duties, the sessions are from four to seven o'clock on weekdays and from nine to one o'clock on Sunday. "We take no pupils," said Mr. Robison, the head of the school, "who do not attend the public schools, and the translations which the children make are from Hebrew into English."

The problems of assimilation and secularization were analyzed by Dr. David Blaustein, head of the Educational Alliance, the most celebrated of the East Side settlement houses, in an interview appearing in the *New York Tribune* on August 16, 1903:

It is impossible to understand the Lower East Side . . . or the attitude of the people there toward American institutions without knowing the conditions from which these people came in Eastern Europe. For instance, the average Russian Jew of the Lower East Side will declare that there is more religious liberty in Russia than in America. He cannot understand the state's interfering with marriage and divorce, which in Russia are left entirely to the rabbi. He is especially puzzled by the state's attitude toward divorce. There are more divorces on the Lower East Side in proportion to the population than in any other part of the city, and far more than among the Jewish population of any other country on the globe. . . .

As a matter of fact, there is perfect liberty in Russia so far as the exercise of his religion is concerned. The Jew is never interfered with in his religious observances. He simply loses, on account of them, all civic and economic rights. He pays for his religious liberty with the latter. His church has infinitely greater power and importance in Russia than in America. The rabbi keeps all the vital statistics. The rabbi marries and divorces. The rabbi has charge of all education. He also acts as a court in both civil and criminal cases. Formerly, Jewish contestants in Russia were compelled by law to take their cases to the rabbi. In certain classes of cases they may now go before a general court. If they agree to take the case to the rabbi, they are required by law to abide by his decision.

At every turn of the road the Jew's religion is recognized. He is taxed as a Jew, enlisted as a Jew. No matter how many Jews there may be in a city, or how many synagogues they may have, representing as many different shades of religious opinion, they are all lumped together as one congregation. One man represents this congregation to the government. He is responsible to the government for their taxes. The government will support him in any attitude he may take toward any individual in the matter of taxation. He is responsible for the number of soldiers required, fifty or one hundred, as the case may be. He can decide what young men shall be chosen.

This representative to the government is elected by the Jews of the city. Their choice may be rejected by the government, but once it is confirmed, the people cannot change their representative. One can easily see in this method a fertile opportunity for tyranny and oppression.

You can imagine the confusion in the immigrant's mind when he reaches America. He finds his church of no account whatever. No one cares what church he belongs to or whether he belongs to any church or not. The state delegates no rights or powers to the church. All that is asked is whether he is an American or not and whether he is loyal to his adopted country. No one cares anything about his loyalty to his church or regards his religious belief as a matter of any importance to anyone but himself. In place of finding the congregation all powerful and all embracing, he finds when he joins a congregation that he has simply joined a liberal society.

There are 332 little congregations east of Broadway and south of Houston Street. They are founded not on differing shades of belief but merely on the fact that the members came from different towns or villages in Eastern Europe. Each congregation is a mutual benefit society. It has a sick benefit and in many cases free medical treatment. The rooms serve as a clubroom where the men meet to talk over old times, read letters from home, discuss politics and current events, or study the Talmud and other religious writings. Religious services are

also held, with one of their number, not necessarily an ordained rabbi,
acting as leader.

The continuing genteel social discrimination against a rising Jewish
middle and upper class in the 1870s and 1880s became overt acts of
anti-Semitism with the influx of Jewish immigrants from eastern
Europe. Jewish peddlers were routinely harassed, stones and filth were
thrown at them by "playful" boys, their beards were pulled.

As the following newspaper article reports, Jews were not spared
even at their religious devotions. Rowdies took every occasion to bait
and annoy, while the police chose to close their eyes:

ROWDIES ANNOY JEWS
(*New York Tribune*, October 2, 1905)

Another instance of police inefficiency or indifference was yesterday
given on the East Side where Orthodox Jews in the observance of the
New Year ceremony were assaulted and mocked by gangs of ruffians
along the river front. Although the Jew baiting and intermittent riots
continued from two o'clock until nearly sundown, the blotter of the
7th Precinct Police Station in Madison Street showed only three arrests.
Of these, two were effected by a special officer. Not only were the
police precautions entirely inadequate, but the few policemen who
were assigned to the work of protecting the thousands of Jews in the
observance of the day refused on several occasions to make arrests.

The Tishri * ceremony at the river front followed the services in the
synagogues, which terminated with the blowing of the *shofar* or ram's
horn. None of the symbolical ritualism of *Rosh Hashanah* is more interesting than Tishri.* The Jews from now until Yom Kippur prepare
for the forgiveness of their sins. Yesterday's ceremony in this connection consisted of casting their sins into the sea. Many of them carry

* The ceremony referred to by the reporter is *Tashlich.*

with them crumbs with which to feed the fishes, and they throw these out in token of the unloading of their sins into the water.

From early afternoon until evening there was an incessant flow of the devout sons of Israel to points along the water front. Thousands of them were along the docks from the Brooklyn Bridge to Houston Street while many performed their religious duties on the two East River bridges. The even more than congested condition of the East Side streets caused by this great outpouring of worshipers made them almost impassable. It was during this part of the observance of the Jewish ritual that the Jew baiting occurred. Most of the trouble took place at Pike's Slip where members of the Cherry Hill gang pulled the beards of the worshipers and in other ways maltreated them. Other ruffians from the trestle used in extending the Delancey Street approach to the Williamsburg Bridge pelted the men, women, and children with stones. Several of them were injured. There were several fist fights, and several of the policemen who were on duty refused to make arrests when appealed to.

Internal Religious Conflicts

Religious conflicts within Jewish families were also a problem. From Philadelphia, for example, comes a report by Julius Greenstone (in the collection *The Russian Jew in the United States*) that tells of the sadness of old parents brought over by grown children already established in the New World:

The old mother immediately assumes the duties of the household, and her husband, after a few days of sight-seeing, is either initiated into some easy labor, or is left alone to spend his time as he sees fit, his support being provided for by his children. Glad as they are of the fine appearance of their children, of their modern ways and their business successes, they cannot suppress a sigh at beholding their shaved chins or at seeing them eat their breakfast without having put on their phylacteries, prayed, washed their hands and pronounced the blessings before and after the meals—customs which they held sacred and inviolable. Their religious sentiments are constantly outraged by the actions of their children, and their cup of sadness and disappointment is filled to overflowing, when, on the first Sabbath, they behold their children depart for their daily occupations. Who can measure the misery and wretchedness of the parents, strangers in a strange land, at seeing that which they regarded as dearer than life violated, voluntarily, by their own children? Many a father spent his first Sabbath in America in weeping and lamentation, many a mother turned hers into a day of mourning, a real *Tisha Bov* (the ninth day of the month of Ab, the anniversary of the destruction of Jerusalem; the Jewish memorial day of mourning). They could not command as they would have done in their old home, for they are dependent upon their children. They cannot argue, for their arguments are met either with ridicule or with explanations of inexorable, unanswerable problems of economy which they do not understand. They can only silently weep at their misfortune and regret the day that they set foot in this *trafa medina,* "this unclean land."

Outright Jewish hostility to religion was also manifest. Chief Rabbi Jacob Joseph had been brought from Vilna to reign over immigrant religious life, and the High Holy Days in 1888 served to welcome him and to present him to his constituency. Large enthusiastic crowds had greeted his arrival, and the Days of Awe presided over by a chief rabbi seemed to exude a heightened sanctity.

The anarchist Jews of New York decided to use the occasion to demonstrate their hostility to religion. From London, they imported the concept of the Yom Kippur Ball. On the eve when *Kol Nidre* was being chanted in the synagogues, the Pioneers of Freedom and other groups gathered in meeting rooms and dance halls for celebrations of desecration. The balls remained a feature of immigrant life for many years.

The following advertisement appeared in the *Freie Arbeiter Shtimme*, September 21, 1900:

YOM KIPPUR AT KOL NIDRE

ALL FREETHINKERS WILL MEET IN THE BEAUTIFUL HALL, 116 13TH STREET
WHERE SONGS, DECLAMATIONS AND PRESENTATIONS APPROPRIATE TO THE
OCCASION WILL TAKE PLACE.

And yet, of course, there were many Jewish families that continued to practice Judaism and observe its commandments. As noted earlier, synagogues had been established throughout the land during colonial times, including the Spanish-Portuguese Shearith Israel in New York and the celebrated congregation in Newport, Rhode Island. Reform Judaism got an early foothold during the mid-nineteenth century, Dr. David Einhorn providing the ideology and Dr. Isaac Mayer Wise the organizational structure.

By the early nineteenth century, Ashkenazi synagogues had started to dot the landscape, beginning with the establishment of Rodeph Sholom in Philadelphia. The first east European synagogue, the Beth Hamidrash, was founded in New York in 1852. A contemporary report in *The Occident* states:

Its founders were few, and they established it in poverty. . . . in affliction, deprivation and straightness they watched over its early rise . . . Now [1857] it is supported by about eighty men in Israel. . . .

Like a typical east European synagogue

it is open all day . . . There is daily a portion of the law expounded publicly . . . every evening, when the people rest from their daily task . . . there are persons who study the law for themselves, either in pairs or singly . . . it is filled with all sorts of holy books. . . . on Sabbaths and festivals, in the evening and morning . . . the house is full to overflowing . . .

Even on the remotest frontier, Jews gathered for prayer. In *The Occident,* December 22, 1859, is the report:

> . . . *in this town and county of San Diego, there number some twelve or fourteen Israelites. These scattered few of God's chosen people agreed to unite in the observance of the sacred festival of the New Year, as well as in the solemnities of the Day of Atonement. . . . On the eve of that memorable day, a worthy citizen, named M. Manasse, journeyed fifty miles to be with us, and complete the number designated and requisite to form a congregation.*

In order to bring order into the religious scene, pleas began to be voiced for one uniform American Judaism. In 1870 one such entreaty came from Jacob Goldman, who had traveled widely in the United States and who argued for unity in his *The Voice of Truth:*

> *The Jehudim of the different parts of Europe, etc., have brought into this country their different "minhagim"* [local religious practices] *. . . Our Rabbis, D.D.'s Reverends, Preachers . . . are holding on to their various minhagim . . . In the name of God, in the name of all Israelites whose hearts are still accessible . . . in the name of all Jewish American citizens, prepare . . . a code of minhagim common to all, and to be adopted by all of us survivors of the year 1870! Look upon our posterity! They are no longer Polander, German, Russian, English, Portuguese; they are Americans, and will and can have nothing more useful than "a Minhag of America . . ."*

The Union of American Hebrew Congregations, established in 1873, and its Hebrew Union College, founded two years later, were intended to serve all of American Israel. The break was, of course, long in the making. For three decades there had been division between Reform Jews and traditionalists. Within the group there were further division between moderate and radical reform, and between west and east European traditionalists. The ever-increasing immigration of Jews from eastern Europe caused a restructuring. The Reform groups drew closer together in their desire for separation from the new immigrants.

The east European immigration had its effect on the traditionalist camp as well. The west Europeans were not at ease with the east European Orthodox Jews, and they in turn would not look for religious leadership to Sephardim or moderate reformers. The west European traditionalists and the moderate reformers of the "historical school" (spiritual disciples of Zachariah Frankel, principal of the Jewish Theological Seminary of Breslau), repelled by the increasing radicalism of American reform, now joined in a common endeavor to found, in 1886, the Jewish Theological Seminary, dedicated to "the preservation in America of the knowledge and practice of historical Judaism as ordained in the Law of Moses and expounded by the prophets and sages of Israel in Biblical and Talmudical writings . . ."

The east European Orthodox Jewish community was growing in size and self-awareness. For a quarter of a century, since 1860, its leading rabbinical figure had been Rabbi Joseph Asch. With his death in 1887, an Association of the American Orthodox Hebrew Congregations was organized "in order to create an intelligent orthodoxy." This task was to be entrusted to a Chief Rabbi, who would "be the leader in the battle which must be waged to keep the next generation faithful to Judaism in spite of the educational, social, and business influences which, in America, are so powerful as to make our sons and daughters forget their duty to . . . [their] religion. . . ." Rabbi Jacob Joseph of Vilna came as Chief Rabbi to a community fired with great hopes and high enthusiasm. Ill-conceived and utterly mismanaged, this proved to be an ill-fated undertaking in every way, arousing antagonisms and rivalries in the community and bringing personal tragedy to the rabbi. But it also marked Orthodox Jewry in America as an independent, self-conscious force, jealous of its place and prerogatives.

The tripartite American Jewish religious community became institutionalized in the twentieth century as Orthodox, Reform, and Conservative Judaism. Each group had its rabbinical seminary, its lay and rabbinic organizations. American Judaism was on its way.

Social Life and Amusements

American Jewish life had its lighter side as well. All was not just long hard toil, educational pursuits, and intergenerational conflict over religion and other issues. A rich and varied cultural life was available to the immigrant and his family. Foremost was the Yiddish theater, which offered escape and provided social activity. It gave the ghetto heroes and heroines to adore and idolize; their romantic exploits provided delectable gossip. Historical dramas were popular because they lifted the harried immigrant to pride through memories of Jewish sovereignty and victories. Contemporary melodrama brought the release that free-flowing tears provide. And what better topic for discussion and argument than the quality of the writing and the acting?

Coffee houses were the locale for discussions political and ideological; decisive analyses of Marx, lectures on the great Russian and Yiddish novelists, practical advice for reigning monarchs and heads of government filled these social centers.

A charming description of the "amusements and social life" of the immigrant is to be found in an article by A. H. Fromenson, editor of the English Department of the *Jewish Daily News* of New York, which appears in *The Russian Jew in the United States,* and which is excerpted below:

It is in the "coffee saloon"—where many times more tea is consumed than the beverage from which it takes its name—that the East Side finds recreation. Whether it is to play chess or checkers, or to discuss Karl Marx or Bakounine, or to analyze Tolstoi or Ibsen, or to debate the relative merits and demerits of the naturalistic or romantic drama—or the wonderful coloratura of the last night's prima donna at the Metropolitan—(for all of these are included in the light converse of the East Side), or to denounce the critics of Adler, the actor, or to excoriate the traducers of Gordin, the playwright—these topics are handled best, thoughts come lucidly and words eloquently, over the glass of tea *a la Russe*—with a floating slice of lemon, and the cigarette.

It is estimated that there are between 250 and 300 of these coffee and cake establishments on the lower East Side, which figure is the best proof of the popularity of these "workingmen's clubs." Unlike the occasional liquor saloon on the East Side, they are absolutely independent of transient trade. The chance passer-by does not enter into the calculations of the proprietor, and is stared at as an intruder by the regular habitués. We have called these places "workingmen's clubs." They answer that description more truly and more pleasantly than the Bishop's tavern, for here there is an absolute guarantee of sobriety, and a free, democratic foregathering of kindred spirits. If one is up in the coffee and cake geography of the district, he knows where he may find the social and intellectual diversion most to his liking. It is each to his own; the Socialist has his chosen headquarters, the chess-crank his, the music-lover his, and so on right down the line. Some, indeed, combine two or three cults or fads, but even these have a *tendenz* which stands out clearly after the first clash of impressions.

Two or three of these "clubs" have considerable life in the afternoon, especially those in which the radical *literati* and journalists, the compositors on the Yiddish dailies, and students and insurance agents and others who have a few hours of the day to kill congregate. But, for the most of them there is no life until late in the evening. It is generally ten o'clock before the social phase manifests itself; if the "popular price" performance at the Metropolitan Opera House is a worthy one, or if there is something worth while on the boards in the Yiddish theatre, it may even be later before the roll-call would have a full response in certain of these places. The resort of the chessplayer is naturally quiet enough, but the philosophers and critics are oracular and demonstrative. Often it is "mine host" who leads the discussion, or sits in judgment of the pros and cons. When he says his say, it is boldly, recklessly almost, viewed from the mercenary aspect of retaining his patronage. Nor does he fail to castigate a stubborn adherent of a contrary view. But the heat of controversy never assumes a petty, sulking character; to tear "mine host's" arguments to tatters, to utterly rout him at every point, is no mean accomplishment and worth hazarding many defeats, for generally he is very well informed on the topic under discussion. In fact, it is his known views and predilections that decide the character of his patronage. Thus, if his establishment is frequented by Socialists, it is fair to assume that he belongs to that political school; if his clientele is made up largely of musicians, he is an amateur critic or patron of the liberal art.

The Yiddish theater was a major cultural force at the turn of the century. Hapgood, in *The Spirit of the Ghetto*, is again the best recorder of its centrality:

In the three Yiddish theatres on the Bowery is expressed the world of the Ghetto—that New York City of Russian Jews, large, complex, with a full life and civilization. In the midst of the frivolous Bowery, devoted to tinsel variety shows, "dive" music-halls, fake museums, trivial amusement booths of all sorts, cheap lodging-houses, ten-cent shops and Irish-American tough saloons, the theatres of the chosen people alone present the serious as well as the trivial interests of an entire community. Into these three buildings crowd the Jews of all the Ghetto classes—the sweat-shop woman with her baby, the day-laborer, the small Hester Street shopkeeper, the Russian-Jewish anarchist and socialist, the Ghetto rabbi and scholar, the poet, the journalist. The poor and ignorant are in the great majority, but the learned, the intellectual and the progressive are also represented, and here, as elsewhere, exert a more than numerically proportionate influence on the character of the theatrical productions, which, nevertheless, remain essentially popular. The socialists and the literati create the demand that forces into the mass of vaudeville, light opera, historical and melodramatic plays a more serious art element, a simple transcript from life or the theatric presentation of a Ghetto problem. But this more serious element is so saturated with the simple manners, humor and pathos of the life of the poor Jew, that it is seldom above the heartfelt understanding of the crowd.

The audiences vary in character from night to night rather more than in an up-town theatre. On the evenings of the first four week-days the theatre is let to a guild or club, many hundred of which exist among the working people of the east side. Many are labor organizations representing the different trades, many are purely social, and others are in the nature of secret societies. Some of these clubs are formed on the basis of a common home in Russia. The people, for instance, who came from Vilna, a city in the old country, have organized a Vilna

Club in the Ghetto. Then, too, the anarchists have a society; there are many socialistic orders; the newspapers of the Ghetto have their constituency, which sometimes hires the theatre. . . .

On Friday, Saturday and Sunday nights the theatre is not let, for these are the Jewish holidays, and the house is always completely sold out, altho prices range from twenty-five cents to a dollar. Friday night is, properly speaking, the gala occasion of the week. That is the legitimate Jewish holiday, the night before the Sabbath. Orthodox Jews, as well as others, may then amuse themselves. Saturday, altho the day of worship, is also of holiday character in the Ghetto. This is due to the Christian influences, to which the Jews are more and more sensitive. Through economic necessity Jewish workingmen are compelled to work on Saturday, and, like other workingmen, look upon Saturday night as a holiday, in spite of the frown of the orthodox. Into Sunday, too, they extend their freedom, and so in the Ghetto there are now three popularly recognized nights on which to go with all the world to the theatre.

On those nights the theatre presents a peculiarly picturesque sight. Poor workingmen and women with their babies of all ages fill the theatre. Great enthusiasm is manifested, sincere laughter and tears accompany the sincere acting on the stage. Pedlars of soda-water, candy, of fantastic gewgaws of many kinds, mix freely with the audience between the acts.

Literary Life

In July 1898, Abraham Cahan could boast in the *Atlantic Monthly*:

The Russian Jews of New York, Philadelphia, and Chicago have within the last fifteen years created a vast periodical literature which furnishes intellectual food not only to themselves, but also to their brethren in Europe. A feverish literary activity unknown among the Jews in Russia, Roumania and Austria has arisen here among the immigrants from those countries, educates thousands of ignorant tailors and peddlers, lifts their intelligence, facilitates their study of English, and opens to them the doors of the English library. . . . Truly, the Jews "do not rot in their slums, but, rising, pull it up after them."

At the turn of the century, the Yiddish newspapers and periodicals could begin to boast of purity of language and quality of content. The works of leading European writers began to appear, notably that of Mendele Mocher Sforim and J. L. Peretz. The reader of Yiddish could choose between four dailies, the Orthodox *Tageblatt,* the right-wing socialist *Der Forverts,* the left-wing socialist *Abend-Blatt,* and the nonpartisan *Yiddisher Kurier* of Chicago. These were soon joined by another Orthodox daily, the *Morgen-Zhurnal,* and the *Varheit,* and still later by the nonpartisan, cultural *Tag.* In 1910 *Der Forverts (The Jewish Daily Forward)* had a circulation of 175,000, the *Varheit,* 108,000, the *Morgen-Zhurnal* 106,000, and the *Tageblatt* 66,000.

In *The Spirit of the Ghetto,* Hapgood offers a perceptive appreciation of the role newspapers played in the life of the immigrant Jew. They helped in his education and Americanization, and served to direct his passions and marshal his social consciousness:

Yiddish newspapers have, as compared with their contemporaries in the English language, the strong interest of great freedom of expression. They are controlled rather by passion than by capital. It is their joy to pounce on controlling wealth and to take the side of the laborer against the employer. A large proportion of the articles are signed, a custom in striking contrast with that of the American newspaper. The prevalence of the unsigned article in the latter is held by the Yiddish journals to illustrate the employer's tendency to arrogate everything to himself and to make the paper a mere organ of his own policy and opinions. The remark of one of the Jewish editors, that the "Yiddish newspaper's freedom of expression is limited by the penal code alone" has its relative truth. It is, of course, equally true that the new freedom of the Jews, who in Russia had no journal in the common Yiddish, runs in these New York papers into an emotional extreme, a license which is apt to distort the news and to give over the editorial pages to virulent party disputes.

Nevertheless, the Yiddish press, particularly the socialistic branch of it, is an educative element of great value in the ghetto. It has helped essentially to extend the intellectual horizon of the Jew beyond the boundaries of the Talmud, and has largely displaced the rabbi in the position of teacher of the people. Not only do these papers constitute a forum of discussion, but they publish frequent translations of the Russian, French, and German modern classics, and for the first time lay the news of the world before the poor Jewish people. . . .

The make-up of the Yiddish newspaper is in a general way similar to that of its American contemporary. The former is much smaller, however, containing only about as much reading matter as would fill six or eight columns of a downtown newspaper. The sporting department is entirely lacking, the Jew being utterly indifferent to exercise of any kind. They are all afternoon newspapers and draw largely for the news upon the morning editions of the American paper. The staff is very limited, consisting of a few editors and, usually, only one reporter for the local news of the quarter. They give more space proportionately than any American paper to pure literature, chiefly translations, (though there are some stories founded on the life of the East Side) and to scientific articles of popular character. . . .

The Weekly anarchistic paper, the *Freie Arbeiter Stimme*, prints about seven thousand copies. Out of this circulation, with the assistance of balls, entertainment, and benefits at the theaters, the paper is able to exist. It pays a salary to only one man, the editor, S. Janowsky, who receives the sum of thirteen dollars a week. He is a little dark-haired man, with beautiful eyes and a soft persuasive voice. He thinks that government is so corrupt that the anarchists need do little to achieve their ends, that silent forces are at work which will bring about the great day of anarchistic communism. In his newspaper he tries to educate the common people in the principles of anarchy. The aim is popular, and the more intelligent exploitation of the cause is left to the monthly *Freie Gesellschaft* which with the same principles as the *Freie Arbeiter Stimme*, has a higher literary and philosophical character. The editors and contributors are men of culture and education, and work without any pay. It is still gentler and more pacific in its character than the weekly *Freie Arbeiter Stimme* of whose comparatively contemporaneous and agitatory method it disapproves calmly; believing, as the editors of the monthly do, that a weekly paper cannot exist without giving the people something other then the ideally best. . . .

The talk of these anarchists is distinguished by a high idealism and an unpractical and devoted attitude. One of the foremost among them (they say they have no leaders as that would be against individual liberty) is Katz, literary editor of *Der Forverts,* contributor to the anarchistic monthly, a former editor of the anarchistic weekly, and a recently successful playwright in the ghetto. His play, *The Jewish Don Quixote,* was produced at the Thalia Theater on the Bowery. Not since Gordin's *Siberia* has a play aroused such intelligent interest. The hero is a quixotic Jew, full of kindness, devotion, and love for his race and for humankind.

8. Community: Jews
Helping Jews

With the beginning of emigration, established Jews came to the aid of the Jewish immigrants. The Jews of western Europe formed a network of organizations to help the Jews of eastern Europe emigrate to America. While the main motivation was to come to the aid of brethren in distress, self-interest was a not insignificant factor. The Jewish communities of Germany, France, and England preferred to serve as bridge and conduit rather than as place of final residence for the growing emigration from the Russian and Austro-Hungarian Empires in the last three decades of the nineteenth century.

The Alliance Israelite Universelle took the lead in organizing aid for the east European Jews, who were being uprooted by economic and political pressures. Initially a twofold program was suggested: to encourage migration from the Jewish Pale of settlement (the western provinces of the Russian Empire) to the interior, and to facilitate emigration to the countries of the west. Once the Russian government ruled out the former, all attention turned to the latter. As Elias Tcherikow discusses in "Jewish Immigrants to the United States" (*YIVO Annual of Jewish Social Science,* vol. 6, 1951), the Jews of western Europe were

. . . *anxious on the one hand to help the victims of the pogroms, and, on the other, afraid that they might engulf their countries. They therefore seized upon America as an ideal solution and resolved to direct the stream of immigrants to that "vast free and rich country, where all who want to work can and will find a place."*

A division of responsibility was arranged. The journey westward across Europe became the responsibility of the German Jews. The London Manor House Committee was to get the immigrant to his destination, America. On arrival, his settlement and integration were the responsibility of American Jewry.

The Jews of America were no more anxious to have a mass of Russian Jews settle among them than were the Jews of western Europe. A spokesman for the United Jewish Charities of Rochester expressed the fears of many, calling the Russian Jews "a bane to the country and a curse to all Jews. The Jews have earned an enviable reputation in the United States, but this has been undermined by the influx of thousands who are not ripe for the enjoyment of liberty and equal rights, and all who mean well for the Jewish name should prevent them as much as possible from coming here."

Nonetheless, American Jewry did assume responsibility and began to organize philanthropic aid for its persecuted brethren. The Board of Delegates of American Israelites and the Russian Emigrant Relief Fund in cooperation with the more permanent and more inclusive Hebrew Emigrant Aid Society gave extensive help in the 1880s. But even the organizations formed to aid the newcomer urged that immigration be selective and controlled.

Among the documents from the *Publications of the American Jewish Historical Society* (vol. 40, March 1951), is a letter from the Russian Emigrant Relief Fund in New York, dated October 31, 1881, and addressed to the Alliance Israelite Universelle. The letter sums up American Jewry's concerns for and problems with the increasing number of Jewish immigrants:

The recital of the outrages in Russia, of which our unfortunate brethren have been the victims, have excited in us the deepest sympathy, and an earnest desire to alleviate their condition as far as lies in our power.

We are compelled to state that we cannot agree with you, that emigration to America is the great panacea for the woes of the Russian Jews. The number of persons whose condition can be bettered in this way is comparatively small.

It was understood that you were to send us only the strong and able-bodied, willing to work and possessing a knowledge of some handicraft; no others have a possible chance of supporting themselves here; and their coming over here in any number would only lead to prompt action being taken to secure their return to Europe. . . .

You will doubtless share our disappointment and vexation when you learn that fully one-third of those who have arrived thus far possess none of the requisite qualifications, and that their unfitness must have been apparent to your agents, if they exercised any discrimination whatever, and that not over one-third are really desirable emigrants.

Most that we have seen are clerks or tradesmen; they know no handicraft and wish to peddle. We are overrun with peddlers already, who have become a source of much annoyance to us. Several have been theological students merely. It is impossible to find positions here for clerks or tradesmen who are ignorant of our language, of our methods of conducting business, and of the commercial requirements of America, and to teach them trades takes considerable time and involves a large outlay of money for their support while learning; besides, many of the clerks and tradesmen who have arrived are too old to learn any trade, and not a few of them are burdened with large families. . . .

There are not over four hundred thousand Jews in this country—not one per cent of the population—seventy-five thousand of whom live in this city, about as many more in Philadelphia, Chicago, Cincinnati, St. Louis and New Orleans combined, and the balance are scattered in smaller cities; very few are agriculturists.

The position of the Jews in this city is peculiar as all the emigrants are landed here. The few who have means, frequently, on their arrival, seek homes in the West or South as they may be advised by their countrymen who have preceded them to those sections; but the great bulk settle in this city and crowd the filthy tenements in a certain section on the East Side.

In this connection, as you may not know what a tenement means in this vicinity, we would state that it is a house built on a plot of ground usually 25 feet wide by 100 feet deep, part of which is occupied for an open yard and outhouses; upon the small space left a tenement is built five or six stories (étages) in height, with about twelve small rooms on each floor; and two to three rooms are rented to each family. There are frequently twenty-four families in one house; occasionally two or three families occupy the same room or rooms for sleeping, cooking, sitting, working and every possible purpose. Decency suffers, and morality is undermined. The squalor, misery and dirt of some of these tenements, and their insufficient sanitary appointments must be seen to be understood. . . .

The natural influx of Jewish emigrants is probably from three thousand to five thousand annually, and any large increase in the number, especially if of the character of the majority of those already sent by the Alliance would render the burden upon us absolutely intolerable. . . . Many of these are sent over here purposely, merely to relieve the European Communities; then there are constantly arriving widows with small children, and also deserted wives and children seeking their husbands and fathers, but without any definite idea where to find them. . . .

Local Committees have been formed in Philadelphia, New Orleans, Houston (for the State of Texas) Milwaukee (for the State of Wisconsin) Louisville, Albany, Rochester, Quincy and other cities, all of which are co-operating with us. We are also in correspondence with the United Hebrew Relief Associations of Chicago and St. Louis and numerous prominent Israelites in various parts of the Union. Your letter has been printed, and will be circulated among these local Committees, both for their information, and for the purpose of eliciting their views on the points you discuss. These Committees are sending us orders for mechanics, farmers and laborers, but they have had their patience sorely tried by some of the emigrants refusing to accept employment, when offered, and demanding to be sent back to this city, and in some cases, begging to be returned to Russia. . . .

Please bear constantly in mind that the position of the Jews in America is not such that they can well afford to run any risk of incurring the ill-feeling of their fellow citizens.

It is not so much a matter of religion, but of race and of habits. We appreciate your remark that "the situation of American Jews may be deeply influenced for better or worse according to the manner in which they behave in this emergency," and while we will make every effort to induce our brethren here to realize the gravity of the case, we trust you will assist us by diffusing abroad correct information as to the probable consequences of flooding this country with Jewish paupers.

The Relief Fund sent word to Europe that immigration must be limited because "the number of persons whose condition can be bettered in this way is comparatively small." On January 8, 1882, the Hebrew Emigrant Aid Society of New York appointed a delegate, Moritz Ellingers, to visit Europe and to present the various aid organizations in London, Paris, Berlin, and Vienna with suggestions for the settlement of Russian Jewish immigrants. The main proposal was to create a special fund of at least one million dollars for dispersing the new arrivals throughout the country. Stress was placed on rigid selection:

The selection of emigrants must be systematic, and must be controlled by the European Committee from the departure from the Russian town until the arrival at an American port. The shipments must be regulated according to the ability of the American Committee to receive and distribute emigrants. Only those having a trade, or able and willing to settle on the lands of the Society, or to work as laborers on railways and otherwise, should be selected for emigration. The aged and helpless should remain in Europe, at least until those on whom they are dependent have been successfully established in their new homes. Absolute paupers must on no account be chosen for emigration. Before sending emigrants to America, the difficulties of settlement in a new country must be clearly set forth, and only the willing must be transported. And these must abide by the decisions of the American Committee as to provision for their settlement.

The same year the Aid Society sent an even sharper warning: "We will not receive another refugee . . . Emigration must cease."

Emigration not only did not cease but the trickle of the 1880s grew into giant waves in the 1890s and the decades beyond. And as the immigration increased, so too did the scope and intensity of the organized efforts of aid.

The American Jews feared that the east European Jews, whose dress, habits and way of life were so unlike those of the west, would act as a detriment to his acceptance by and integration into American society, and might cause a growth of anti-Semitism. The resident American Jew was not at all agreeable to the coming of the Russian Jew, but once he arrived he was aided in his settlement and adjustment to American life by those who had opposed his arrival in the first place.

It was the Russian Jewish immigrants themselves who ultimately took leadership in organizing aid for the new arrivals. One of the first organizations offering direct aid to the arriving immigrant was the Association of Jewish Immigrants of Philadelphia. The nature of its activities is described in the President's report offered at its Second Annual meeting on November 7, 1886:

During the past year we have actively continued the work of our organization. We have assisted immigrants to reach other points to which they were destined, and have provided them with food on their route. We have lodged and fed those who remained in the city until their friends were found, or work obtained for them, or decent homes secured. We have hunted up lost baggage, rescued some from the thieves who frequent the wharves, and redeemed it when held for unpaid freight. We have procured tickets in place of those run out, and tickets for distant cities where none had been obtained prior to shipment.

We have notified friends by telegraph and otherwise of the arrival of immigrants who had claims upon their care and attention. We have guarded their rights so that they would not suffer through ignorance or the bad advice or evil designs of others. We have protected them against thieving innkeepers, imposters under the guise of co-

religionists, agents of haunts of vice, and others whose vocation it is to rob, swindle and mislead ignorant and unsuspecting foreigners. We have procured employment for many, homes for some and have aided in furnishing rooms and in starting others in business suited to their abilities.

In this and subsequent reports concrete illustrations of work done were cited under the following headings: Telegrams and Letters; Advertisements (for lost relatives); Reshipments; Distribution; Baggage; Rooms Rented; Care of the Sick; and so on. The Miscellaneous category in the 1887 report suggests the range of personal problems with which the Association had to cope:

A young man sixteen years old, who arrived at Baltimore in August, 1886, from Russia, was sent to the house of our Agent, on the 27th May last, with a letter from Rev. H. Ungerleider of Lancaster, requesting him to obtain work for the applicant. He was supported for five days on the society's account until work was obtained for him on a farm. . . .

A girl of 12 years, with frozen feet, so much swollen as to be unable to wear her shoes, could not proceed with her father to their destination, although their tickets were already changed and the train about ready to start. Our Agent's attention was called to the case, and with some trouble he induced the dispatcher to detain the train a few minutes until he could procure a pair of shoes for the sufferer. This was reluctantly done and the shoes were purchased to the delight of the poor family, who feared they would be separated.

A family consisting of a husband, a wife and four children, arrived on the 28th of July. Even in their downcast and wretched state, traces of a noble, honest and charitable life could be seen. For fourteen years they had lived peacefully and happily together, the husband cultivating the soil, and dwelling in perfect harmony with his Christian neighbors. The poor of all denominations had found under his roof shelter, in him a father, and in his family friends. Suddenly the decree of expulsion reached him, forcing him to leave his happy home and beloved soil, and with his wife and little ones to endeavor to begin life

*anew in a strange land. "Do not despair, my friend, take my advice
and go west, where you must learn tailoring through which to earn a
livelihood. This trade you will pursue for a year or two, until you have
acquainted yourself with American life and the English language.
Then you can again return to your former vocation. May Israel's Re-
deemer, for whose religion you suffer, lead you in the path of comfort
and prosperity." Thus spoke the Agent. The man then produced 100
rubles, and two tickets were purchased for him and his wife at a low
rate for Indianapolis. It was arranged that the children should go free.
Provisions for the journey were given them and the address of the Rev.
Messing in Indianapolis. . . .*

By 1889, the President was able to report:

*The gravity of the condition which so strenuously demanded our atten-
tion heretofore has gradually lessened, partly through the decreasing
numbers of immigrant Jews, and more especially by reason of the better circumstances of the new arrivals.*

*This condition of affairs is traceable to two causes—first, the general
relaxation of the rigors of political persecution, more especially in the
Slavic districts not included in the Russian Empire, and second, to the
effects of the dissemination through both the Jewish and secular press
of Europe of correct information regarding the economic conditions
on this side of the water.*

It was early recognized by leaders in the organized immigration aid
effort that one of the chief problems was the concentration of the immigrant population in the port cities of the eastern seaboard, most particularly in New York. This presented a twofold evil: it was a hindrance in the social integration of the resident population, and it
worked unusual hardships (economic, social, moral) on the immigrant.
A constantly increasing population made for job competition which
kept wages low and production expectancy high. The sweatshop
worker was driven by the fear of loss of employment to a newcomer
ready to take a job at minimum pay for maximum hours. The crowded
ghetto environment was a health hazard, physically and morally. Un-

ventilated sweatshops and dark tenements brought the incidence of tuberculosis to epidemic proportions. Life in crowded cities made prostitution and crime not only prevalent but also highly visible. The concentration of the immigrant population in self-contained communities prevented a more rapid rate of acculturation and integration, which drove an ever wider wedge between the immigrant and his Americanized children.

One suggested solution was dispersal of population and diversification of occupations. The largesse of the Baron de Hirsch Fund was used to establish training schools and agricultural settlements. Efforts in these directions had been anticipated in the Russian Jewish community. Schools to teach a trade were set up by the Fund in Russia, and young Russian Jewish idealists, influenced by the back-to-the-soil movements in Russia, organized the *Am Olam* to settle in America in cooperative colonies. Members of *Am Olam* did arrive and did found settlements in the South and in the West, but these were short-lived due to the lack of practical experience and knowledge of agriculture. The Baron de Hirsch Fund colonies fared better, but large-scale colonization of the immigrant Jew in America was never realized.

The efforts at dispersal were more successful. The Jewish Alliance of America undertook to promote colonization, but lack of success forced it to change its emphasis and enterprise to the resettlement of immigrants in the American hinterland.

In the year 1891 the First Convention of the Jewish Alliance of America was held in Philadelphia. Organized at the initiative of Russian Jewish immigrants "for the purpose of more effectively coping with the grave problems presented by the enforced emigration of Hebrews from proscriptive countries," the goals were spelled out by its first president, Dr. C. D. Spivak:

What do we want to accomplish by this Alliance? We want to secure for those of our brethren who overflood the market of hands some honest work. We desire that the Jewish immigrant shall not crowd into the large seacoast cities; we want to exterminate peddling and petty trading; we purpose, in short, to give a possibility to the immigrant to

*make a living for himself and his family—not to fall a burden upon the
various Jewish charitable institutions—and to become an independent,
self-supporting citizen of this republic.*

*How are we to accomplish this? By directing and leading the im-
migrant in the way of acquiring new trades apart from the needle that
has pierced many a heart, and outside of the basket under whose burden so many have succumbed.*

*Agriculture, in the opinion of my co-laborers and myself, ought to
be the mainspring of the future activity of the Alliance.*

Bernhard Marks of California, an authority in colonization, was
then called upon by the Convention to present a plan for the Russian-
Jewish immigrants:

*I will endeavor to state briefly the foundation principles which, in my
opinion, should be considered, and some of which should govern in
the agricultural colonization of the Russian Hebrews.*

*The first great principle is this, and to it I ask your earnest atten-
tion: The colonist must become a farmer, and not a specialist. What is
a farmer? The man who raises a single product, and therefore depends upon the sale of his crop for the means to purchase what his
family needs to eat, is not a farmer, but a specialist. If he raises
wheat, he is a grain producer; if butter and cheese, he is a dairyman;
if vegetables, he is a gardener; if fruit, he is a fruit-grower; if trees,
he is a nurseryman; if cattle, he is a stockman; if sheep, he is a wool-
grower. But none of these are farmers. They all buy flour, meat, milk,
butter, cheese, veretables, fruit, eggs, just as the lawyer, doctor, or
storekeeper buys them. . . .*

*A farmer is a practical, non-speculative, independent man who
raises on his farm, as nearly as conditions permit, all the necessaries
and as many of the luxuries as his family is provided with, and who
relies on the excess of his productions to obtain by exchange or sale
what he cannot produce. That is, he occupies his land with diversified
farming. His first care is to ascertain how he can produce food all the
year round for one or two cows. He violates an important principle if
he counts on buying a single pound of miller's stuff. No matter what
kind of soil or climate he may have to deal with, he can raise some*

kind of hay, stimulate some kind of pasture, raise some kinds of roots and produce some kind of grain. It will resolve itself simply into a question of how many acres he must devote to the maintenance of each cow he may elect to keep. And a cow is the foundation of the farmer's wealth. She is the farmer's most accommodating banker. She will sometimes honor his check when he knows he does not deserve to have a dollar in bank. A cow furnishes milk for the children, buttermilk for a beverage, butter and cheese for the family, pot-cheese for a delicacy, and sour milk for the pig or the hens.

In my examination of the Hebrew colony in New Jersey I was amazed, almost horrified, to ascertain that the entire colony went almost wholly without milk, and of course without butter, for longer than two years. That was a great mistake, and it was a principal reason of their long and unnecessary suffering.

An appeal for funds went out from the American Committee for Ameliorating the Condition of Russian Refugees the following October:

They do not come in quest of charity; they come not as paupers, seeking alms; they come in search of means to subsist by their own efforts, under the favorable conditions which our country offers to every honest toiler and worker. Nor is there any lack of opportunity. Our country is large and wide enough, and has employment for all who are willing to labor.

The problem which presents itself is to find proper fields wherein the immigrants can procure the work they are in search of, and they are fitted for the varied handicrafts and agricultural pursuits. They must not be allowed to crowd special localities, but should be dispersed over the whole land. Thus they will be easily absorbed, and, what is all important, will become Americanized more readily, and in less time than if permitted to aggregate in a few large cities.

The people of the United States, ever in sympathy with the oppressed of all nations who come to our shores with the determination of securing an honorable existence by their own efforts, will stand by us in our exertions for the aid and relief of our unfortunate brethren. We may also feel confident that the public authorities, as far as it lies within their power, will assist us in a task, which, in its result, will prove a benefit to the whole country by enriching it with the product of the labor of honest and useful citizens.

Let us, then, go to work, singly and unitedly, with warm hearts and cheerful willingness, young and old, rich and poor; let each contribute according to his means; let each and every one strive to find employment, to find a home for at least one family. The opportunity is given to assist in this philanthropic work by taking part in the formation of local societies now forming in every city, town and village in the country. Remember that a heavy responsibility rests upon us all alike, and we must be ready to assume our share of the burden.

LEWIS SEASONGOOD	*Cincinnati, O., President*
LAZARUS SILVERMAN	*Chicago* ⎫ *Vice-Pres.*
JOSEPH FOX	*New York* ⎭
JACOB H. SCHIFF	*New York, Treasurer*
ADOLPHUS S. SOLOMONS	*Washington, D.C.* ⎫ *Secs.*
BERNARD HARRIS	*Philadelphia* ⎭

Dispersion of Immigrants

By the end of the nineteenth century, after attempts at colonization had largely failed, it was decided that a more determined effort for the dispersal of Jewish immigrants had to be made—particularly to divert or remove them from New York City. For this purpose the Industrial Removal Office was created in 1900. New York was ready to send the newcomers, but "host" cities refused to accept; also, immigrants once arrived in New York were loath to leave.

In the first five years some 40,000 immigrants were relocated, but it was felt that a new scheme or plan was needed. In response, the Galveston Immigration Plan came into being. Galveston, Texas, a port city far distant from the eastern seaboard, seemed an ideal portal to the communities of the South and Midwest. The report of Rabbi Henry Cohen, the leading spirit in the Galveston plan, indicates that this effort was not without success. In a note dated December 1, 1913, he can boast, "8,150 immigrants distributed to date."

But New York remained the main port of entry, and the chief city of settlement as well. Two decades of Jewish immigration from eastern Europe made it the largest Jewish city in the world.

About a million Jews arrived in the United States in the first decade of the twentieth century. The great majority were aided in their journey through Europe at immigrant centers founded and maintained by the Jews of Europe in such immigration depots as Brody in Galicia, Koenigsburg, East Prussia, and the port cities of Germany, France, and England. When they arrived in the United States a network of immigrant aid societies helped them at the port of entry, and a variety of charitable organizations lent a helping hand in their settlement, employment, and acculturation. The organized immigrant aid effort as it existed in 1911 is summed up in the report that appeared in the *Yiddisher Emigrant* (vol. 5, no. 13, 1911):

THE WORK OF THE JEWISH IMMIGRATION SOCIETIES IN NEW YORK

In the center of the United States, toward which there has been flowing for a long time now the great immigration wave, there exist a number of societies laboring for the benefit of the Jewish immigrants. The most important of these is the Hebrew Sheltering and Immigrant Aid Society. An acquaintance with the multifaceted work of this society will give us a full understanding of what is being done for the immigrants. The other two societies, The Industrial Removal Office and the Clara de Hirsch Home, have specific purposes: the former, to develop and aid the dispersal of Jewish immigrants throughout the land, and the latter to protect Jewish immigrant girls against falling into the nets of the white slavers. . . .

Before the present special Jewish immigrant aid societies were established, the work of representing the interests of the immigrant was done by the United Hebrew Charities. Its representative in the old Castle Garden had the responsibility to provide information; to place advertisements in the press about detained immigrants who had lost the addresses of their relatives; to appeal the decisions of the Board of Special Inquiry (which determines the fate of the detained immigrants). This was done only in rare cases, and relatives had to pay for it.

It did not undertake to see the newcomer to his destination. But it did arrange to have a private individual, approved by the Commissioner, chaperone the immigrant to his address, for which he was charged a dollar or dollar and a half. When an immigrant could not reach his relatives and had to be on his own for a few days, the Charities provided lodging in a private hotel.

Thus the work continued until nine years ago, when the Hebrew Immigrant Aid Society was organized. It undertook to intensify and widen immigrant aid. Another Jewish representative was placed on Ellis Island and many more appeals were made on behalf of the detained newcomers. The task of delivering the "tired" detainees to their relatives was undertaken as a responsibility. Eventually the Hebrew Immigrant Aid Society came to be recognized as the only Jewish official presence on Ellis Island. The founders of the society are almost all Russian Jews, and have thrown themselves into immigration work with great energy.

Two years ago there took place an important change, which made for a major expansion of the work. This was its amalgamation with the New York Hachnasat Orchim. Now possessed of its own building and expanded facilities and resources, it began to develop to its present stage of effectiveness. The work of the new organization can be divided into the following eight categories: 1) Information Bureau; 2) Ellis Island Bureau; 3) Bureau of Dispersal—which sends the newcomers to their destinations; 4) Bureau to provide hospitality and lodging; 5) Employment Bureau; 6) Education Department; 7) Religious Department; 8) Bureau of Statistics.

The Information Bureau daily answers hundreds of inquiries by relatives and friends about arriving immigrants. It gives advice on how to deal with the variety of problems faced by the newcomers, informs the interested parties about the detained, the quarantined, the deported, etc. etc. The released immigrants are advised how to claim their baggage from ship and train. When baggage is late or if it was pawned on the way, the Bureau helps in regaining possession. The Bureau also carries on an extensive correspondence. It maintains constant communication with committees and organizations in the large centers in Europe, searching for the husbands, abandoned wives, children for parents, and the whereabouts of relatives. It also publishes articles in newspapers touching upon various immigration matters as well as warnings and notices to the relatives of immigrants. It keeps the public constantly informed as to the changes in immigration policy of the administration.

The most important and most useful work of the Society is done on Ellis Island. The Bureau maintains offices on the Island. Its object is to protect the rights of the interned and rejected immigrants and to care for those permitted to enter whose destination is beyond New York. It has all the needed information with which it can keep relatives and friends informed. It teaches the immigrants how to cope with the problems facing them, it unites them with friends, arranges for meetings with the proper authorities, obtains for the immigrant, when necessary, a new examination, and wherever possible it undertakes appeals to highest governmental authorities in behalf of those marked for deportation. Each case receives individual attention, and everything possible is done to enable the immigrant to remain. The interned are visited daily and their daily needs are provided. Recently, with the approval of the Commissioner, a kosher kitchen was established on the Island, and those immigrants who formerly had to make do with little now can enjoy a warm kosher meal daily. . . .

The immigrant aid societies dealt with many heartrending personal problems, one of which was that of the *agunot* or abandoned wives. The *Yiddisher Emigrant* (vol. 5, no. 15, 1911) reported on the Conference of Sheltering Societies in New York, in which "over one hundred delegates from various parts of the country and Canada participated." It was decided that each sheltering society should have a special department to deal with wives seeking their husbands, and that these departments would receive a description and picture of the husband being sought. It was also decided that each society should undertake to promote legislation similar to the law in New York State which makes abandonment of wife and children a criminal offense.

The magnitude of the immigration from eastern Europe in the two decades which concluded the nineteenth century and the two which opened the twentieth demanded a heroic effort of immigrant aid. Organized Jewry in Europe and in America matched need with generosity in the expenditure of funds and energies. While the Alliance Israelite Universelle, the Baron de Hirsch Fund and the Hebrew Immigrant Aid Society (HIAS) must be singled out for special attention and commendation, the greatest effort was made by the immigrant himself. The *landsmanschaft* groups, organized according to towns of origin, made the immigrant feel welcome among people he knew from his former community. He found a sense of security in their friendship and concern, and received ready aid from them in time of need. *Landsmanschaft* congregations gave the immigrant a feeling of continuity in a world in which everything was in flux. The same synogogal melodies, the same vying for honors, the meetings without end with those whom he could address with Old World nicknames—all these made him more at home in the strange new land.

Beyond all organized aid was the everyday help given by one member of a family to another, by one newcomer to his neighbor. The door of an immigrant home open to the newer arrival, a welcome place at the family table, a timely loan—these helped forge American Jewry into the largest, most affluent and influential Jewish community in the four millennia of Jewish history. They cared about one another, as the marchers for the victims of the Kishinev pogroms indicate:

50,000 MARCHERS MOURN KISHINEV MASSACRE
(*Evening Post*, December 4, 1905)

Previous demonstrations in this city in mourning for the victims of the recent anti-Jewish outbreaks in Russia were eclipsed today by an immense parade of Jewish organizations through the East Side and the wholesale district in Broadway, ending with a meeting and the adoption of resolutions in the plaza at Union Square. The demonstration was the most impressive ever attempted by the Jews here, not excepting the great procession of mourners at the funeral of Rabbi Joseph four years ago. Nearly a hundred organizations, labor, benevolent, and charitable, religious, socialistic, and revolutionary, took part in the parade, and not less than 50,000 persons were in line. More than 10,000, it was estimated, came over the Williamsburg Bridge from Brooklyn.

The demonstration was under the direction of the Jewish Defense Association, the body which has raised a fund of above a million dollars for the relief of the Jews in Russia. . . .

At the head of the parade, following a squad of mounted police, marched members of the Theatrical Musical Union, playing solemn music and accompanied by the Choristers Union, the Boy Synagogue Singers, and the Cantors Union. There was music, instrumental and vocal, in every division and all mournful and dirge-like. In line also were the Manhattan Rifles and Zion Guards, semimilitary organizations. A detachment of the Zion Guards from New Haven marched with them, and the Kishinev Organization, made up of survivors of the Kishinev massacre, was another notable part of the parade. Black and white crepe draped the houses and stores all along the line of march. The banners of the various organizations were also draped with black flags signifying mourning for the dead. American flags draped in black and the Zion flag, a blue six-pointed star on a white field, were numerous. Several times as many people as were in the parade watched its progress from sidewalks, windows, and roofs. One thousand patrolmen and 300 mounted men, under Inspectors Schmittberger and Hogan, kept the crowds in order and forced a way through the throngs. The officers and executive committee of the Jewish Defense Association inspired the demonstrations, and, headed by the chairman, Dr. J. L. Magnes, marched in the parade.

PART THREE

*From Immigrant
to American Jew:
Four Remember and Recall*

Della Rubenstein Adler was born in Buffalo and lived there for eighty of her almost one hundred years. Abraham Goldman was born in Neustadt, Lithuania, and lived in central New York State. The Hebrew poet Ephraim Lisitzky and the philosopher Morris Raphael Cohen were natives of Minsk, White Russia, and came to America as young men. All lived through the turn-of-the-century Jewish immigrant experience and recorded their impressions.

Mrs. Adler's memories are of the east European Jewish community of Buffalo in its early days. Goldman's is a simple, unpretentious narrative prepared mainly for his own family. Those of Lisitzky and Cohen are literary works by men who achieved fame in their respective fields. Taken together, these four memoirs offer a mosaic of the diversified experiences that went into the making of the American Jew.

9. Della R. Adler, Girlhood Memories

In her ninetieth year, Della Rubenstein Adler recalled her girlhood in the east European immigrant community in Buffalo. She was born there in 1876 to Louis W. and Catherine Rubenstein, both east European Jewish immigrants. In 1907 Della was married to Joseph Adler, who had come to Baltimore from Bavaria fourteen years earlier. On his death in 1926 she returned to her native Buffalo, where she lived until her death in 1975. This selection from her memoirs, "Immigrants in Buffalo," appeared in *American Jewish Archives,* vol. 18, no. 1, April 1966:

SIX SILVER SPOONS

Grandfather—Jacob H. Mayerberg—came to this country in 1867, from a small place in Lithuania called Volkovisk. His original mission was a business one, and he expected to return. Destiny decided otherwise.

He had heard that the U.S.A., especially New York City, was perishing from a need for *seforim*—Hebrew books of learning. So, the idea was to come here with a stock of books, sell them at a good profit, and return.

Poor Grandfather! On the way over, every book—plus all else he possessed—was stolen, and he arrived in Castle Garden, destitute.

He did what he was totally unequipped for—physically and by nature—he peddled. What with, I do not know, but I do know he peddled through New York State in deep, drifted snow and icy winds and finally reached Buffalo and settled down as a *melamed*, a Hebrew teacher. The late Willard Saperston was one of his *talmidim*, his students. He thus eked out a pathetic living in bleak, dreary surroundings, and there Grandmother Hennie and their four children found him when they arrived in this country some three years later.

Grandma's comment on first seeing him was, "Yankov Hirsch, what happened to you? In three years you have become an old man." He was then forty-seven years old.

Grandmother was not one just to sit and do nothing. Her first effort was to find respectable living quarters. To pay the rent, she sold her most valuable possession, six silver spoons. The day came when there was no money to pay another month's rent, and Yankov Hirsch and Hennie assumed a "the Lord will provide" attitude; and the Lord, blessed be He, did provide.

Came a knock on their door, one fine day. A man of friendly mien stood there and asked—did they have one large or two small rooms to rent to six men who peddled in the country and came home just for *Shabbos* [the Sabbath]? There were five married men whose wives were awaiting the necessary *Schiffskarten* to come to America, and there was one twenty-one year-old unmarried youngster who was being petted and spoiled by the older men. Each Thursday, one of the six came home to cook for *Shabbos*. The other five came home on Friday.

The Mayerbergs could, and did, rent them rooms, and this miraculously solved the rent problem for them, until they could scramble to their feet. The single man, Louis Rubenstein, married the eldest daughter of the Mayerbergs, Kate—Chayeh—and they became my parents.

This all happened in the very long ago. Both the Mayerbergs and my parents prospered in a very modest way, and thereafter needed no crutch.

Today, I am the last living member of the Louis Rubenstein family, and the memory of the six silver spoons still lingers.

THE EARLY BALLABATTIM OF
BUFFALO

Thoughts come to me of my young days and the men I used to know, most of them members of the then young Clinton Street *shul,* Congregation Beth Jacob. This *shul* was the brainchild of Grandfather Mayerberg, who needed a place to worship in his own righteous, traditional way. He needed to be abetted by his own type and wanted no hindrance, either to his traditionalism or in the worship rite. So, aided by his son-in-law, my father Louis, they set out ambitiously enough to build the *shul,* which flourished and became well-known in later years as a bulwark of traditional Orthodoxy.

It was a goal for *meshulahim* [itinerant fundraisers], *hazzanim* [cantors], an outstanding *maggid* [preacher] now and then, and altogether a charity target. Here the pleas for *yeshivot,* orphan asylums, homes for the aged, Jerusalem charities, and so on, were heeded and supported to the best ability of the members, none of whom had much of worldly goods. If misfortune befell, such as the loss of a peddler's horse which was indeed a calamity, or a dowry was needed to marry off a daughter, a special meeting was called, and therewith the horse or dowry was provided by contributors, each as he could give. In the case of the horse, this was also a sort of mutual insurance, as no one knew when his horse might be the next to fall. This seems like true charity and was practiced whole-heartedly by this group of men who had so little, yet could always spare a little.

Perhaps the most affluent one was Joseph—Yossel—Saperston, who was a joiner, either for *shuls* or organizations, and a flitterer—here awhile, there awhile, but, when there, was a prominent member, had a say-so and a following. He had come to Buffalo before the other members and was well-established in a fine home with his wife, Shamie, and their large family.

Grandfather Mayerberg and my father were great friends and did things together, including the building of the *shul* and holding up the righteous pillars to keep a traditionally Orthodox congregation in the way of upright Lithuanian *mitnagdim* [non-mystics].

I do not remember all of the original members, but there was Sholem Cohn, who later became father's business partner. At that early time, he plodded through the world, driving his old white horse till midnight as his day began at noon, scrupulously saving every spare penny until he became quite a wealthy man. He was honorable to a degree, a religious man but dour—I think I never saw him smile. Not a colorful man, but he did well enough to help run the *shul*.

Then there was Harris Cohen—a quiet, unobtrusive, fine little man whose ayes and nays were also valuable. He, who died tragically at an early age, lived with his wife Rachel a block away from the *shul* and raised a large family of well-doing people—one son, Dr. J. Y. Cohen, a prominent physician here; the late Frank L., a road builder; and a daughter, Etta, a high school English teacher.

Schmerl Brumberg, the brother-in-law of Harris Cohen, was an individualist and something of a nonconformist—in theory, if not in practice—but evidently he did not succeed in shaking the roots of the *shul*. It stayed steadfast despite Schmerl. He, too, was a scrupulously honest man. The story was that, when Schmerl's day went well, the family ate, and when it didn't, they subsisted. He and his very good, but subservient wife Maryasha raised a fine family, three of whom were physicians of repute.

Levine, the oil man, as he was called, peddled kerosene oil from a truck, and I remember him well. A fine, thoughtful man, he often stopped at our house for a cup of coffee on the day he delivered the oil to fill our five or six lamps. The chore of filling these lamps, polishing the glass globes till they shone, and wiping off the surplus smelly oil was a burdensome job that, in itself, would make me remember Levine, the oil man. But I liked him for himself. He inspired me with his honesty, integrity, and faith.

Then there was Uncle David Shepsel Gottlieb, who really had the attributes of a successful man and never, never was. He was a short, squat man with a nice face and humorous, twinkling eyes, had a fine Hebrew background, was a well-known lay *hazzan* as he possessed a beautiful voice, and also had a repertoire of songs which no one could sing as he did. I still remember them. I also remember his daily pilgrimage to our house from *shul* and the daily *schnapps* he and my father took from a brown crockery jug which stood behind the pantry door. No fancy labeled bottles in those days—when the jug was empty, the liquor delivery man filled it.

There was also one S. Cohen, known as Schmuley der Yoven, a man of firm convictions which he made no attempt to conceal. Far from polished, but a good and honorable man, he ran a peddlers' supply store, where the *ballabattim* [synagogal pillars] congregated to argue "pro and con" about what they wanted and what they didn't want. His wife Fagie was a character, no match for witty and outgoing Schmuel. One of their descendants is a brilliant lawyer.

I must not leave Israel Friedlander out. He had ideas on every subject—some good, some not so good, but all expressed in a loud, booming, convincing voice. He was a natural orator, and on each and every occasion, he aired his talent. He and his wife Hadassah lived a turbulent life. They had a large family, one of whom is a college professor. I believe none married, and the Israel Friedlander dynasty is ended.

Later, there was one member who owned a horse by the name of Chaim. Chaim was a knowledgeable animal—on *hol ha-moed Pesach*, the intervening days of Passover, Chaim trotted smartly by the saloons which his owner regularly, if unsteadily, patronized on weekdays. At these times, Chaim came to a full stop of his own accord. This gentleman wasn't the only one who had a weakness for the bottle. There was Abram Salinski, the Jewish town drunkard, whose poor wife Mindel, a wonderfully good soul, spent most of her time trying to sober him up as unobtrusively as possible. Not a word of complaint, but we all knew it. They raised a large family in dire, but immaculate poverty. The children all went to work at an early age and had no schooling; nevertheless, all of them possessed an elegance of bearing, a surprisingly fine diction, and a dignity all their own. A relative was a very well-known, highly successful English teacher in the high school.

In the category of inebriates, I cannot omit Chaikel, the carpenter. He really was superior in mind and wit, also in his chosen field. A humorist and philosopher, a sort of Jewish Will Rogers, yet he often had to be dragged out of one saloon after another. He did many a little job to the exacting specifications of my mother—from a just-so rolling pin to a folding table to be set by the then tiny sink as an aid in dishwashing. This table had two fitted boards, one for dairy dishes and one for meat—it was a real convenience. Later Chaikel was the architect and builder of our North Division Street home, which had to be remodeled after father's untimely death when mother had to pull the reins tight.

And now comes Uncle Saul Rubenstein, who lived to be very old and was so well-known on William Street after the influx of the 90's and later. There was scarcely a refugee family from the Old World's tyranny who did not feel the sympathetic, philanthropic touch of Saul Rubenstein and his son Emil H., who so ably carried on. Emil it was who had the proper contacts, so the people here would be assured that their scraped-up, hardearned money would reach father, mother, wife, and so on, in American dollars of full value. Then they engaged in the *Schiffskarten* business on the installment plan—so much down and, thereafter, weekly payments to speed the bringing over of relatives from the hell that was theirs. This was philanthropy of a high and unusual order and I pay tribute to the memory of Uncle Saul, and I honor my cousin Emil for his untiring zeal. In his later years, this fine old man's philanthropy took the turn of selling tickets for charity—it mattered not what kind of charity, as long as it was a ticket and needed to be sold, he was there to do it. He had his "customers," traveled many miles to reach them, was always warmly welcomed, had his hearing—and the tickets were sold. The Rosa Coplon Home was one of his pets—he did very much for it and his efforts were appreciated and are remembered. My son [Dr. Selig Adler], in his book, *From Ararat to Suburbia,* wrote of Uncle Saul as an earthy man and he was—he loved the outdoors, the growing of things, animals, especially horses. He once shocked his wife almost unconscious by bringing a foal into the living room. He smiled much, loved a game of cards, talked with everyone and everyone talked with him—he was a character and a well-beloved one.

These were all the early men of the Clinton Street *shul*—it served its purpose well for many years until the changing neighborhood closed its doors and caused its abandonment.

10. Abraham Goldman, Boyhood Memories

Abraham Goldman, a Jewish businessman in Utica, New York, remembers his life as an immigrant son of immigrant parents in upstate New York at the turn of the century. His simple memoirs (*The Goldman Family Saga*, privately printed in Rochester, New York, 1961) offer glimpses of the hard work, the family solidarity, and the adaptability demanded of Jewish immigrant life:

Now, Dad is leaving Neustadt [Lithuania] coming to America because he has a brother and sister here. It must have taken every dollar he had to pay for his passage because he was stone broke when reaching New York.

Upon arriving in Castle Garden, there were some Lithuanian farmers on the ship, and they had quite a sum of Russian Rubles which they wanted to exchange for American dollars. They could only speak Litvish but the custom officers could only speak German. As Dad could speak both Litvish and German, he acted as an interpreter for both parties, and in the exchange from Russian rubles to U.S. money Dad made U.S. dollars.

Uncle Hyman Weinberg met Dad at Castle Garden and took him to his apartment on Orchard Street. The next day Dad said he took a walk to see what New York looked like. On East Broadway he saw a bank with a sign printed in Yiddish. It read "Jarmulowsky Bank, Money sent to all parts of Europe."[Sender Jarmulowsky was the leading Jewish banker on the Lower East Side of New York.] Dad went in and sent the $15.00 he made to Mother in Neustadt.

Dad had no intention of remaining in New York, even though Uncle Hyman assured him of a job in the clothing factory where he could learn the trade of a tailor. Dad wanted no part of working for someone else. He was determined to get to Syracuse and start out for himself.

Uncle Hyman advanced Dad the price of a railroad ticket. Upon arriving in Syracuse there was a Jewish truck driver, with a one-horse truck at the station. Dad showed him Uncle Ralph's address and asked how much he would charge to take Dad and his burlap sack to that address. At this point he had exactly 27 cents. After some dickering they agreed on 25 cents.

Now, here is Dad in Syracuse with no trade and no money, but, thanks to God, with good health and a strong body. So, what is there to do but to become a pack-peddler? A Mr. Shimberg had a wholesale notions and dry goods store where most of the peddlers traded. He advanced Dad $35.00 worth of credit, mostly in notions, and with that Dad started peddling. With so little merchandise he confined his travels close to Syracuse. This he did for about six months, until he accumulated a little capital, which enabled him to start out on the road with a fairly complete line of dry goods.

Dad had a special harness built for himself. On his back was the big pack. On both sides of his chest were hooks where small cases were hung; and he had a satchel in each hand. Picture a setup like that, walking from five to ten miles a day over rough country roads. I've had big strong farmers come into our store in Rome and tell me they remembered that when Dad carried the pack it was so heavy that they, as young men, could not lift it off the floor.

I once asked Pa, "In those days horses were cheap, so why didn't you buy a horse and wagon instead of playing the part of a horse?" His answer was that he was so lonesome for Mother and the children that all he could think of was to return to Neustadt. He did not want to tie up any of his money in rigs. He carried the pack for three years and nine months, and then decided that he is in this country to stay, so he swapped or traded three second-hand watches with Dad Fox, the old horse trader, for a small horse and Democrat wagon. . . .

How hard Dad worked no one but he knew, but he had a supreme purpose for working and saving. His dream and goal in life was to bring Mother and us three children here so that he could enjoy the pleasure of being with his family. In those days the average man earned 10 cents per hour. Milk was 3 cents per quart. Men's socks were 2 for 25 cents. I mention these facts to show how hard a man had to work in order to accumulate any amount of money. So, with the dollar so hard to come by and with Dad here but four years as a pack-peddler, he had saved and had on deposit in the Onondaga County Savings of Syracuse $1400.00.

Now he considered himself an established traveling merchant, for over the wide stretch of territory which he covered he was already acquainted with people and had regular customers. So, he buys steamship tickets and sends for his family.

As there was no railroad in Neustadt, we were all loaded into a horse-drawn wagon and taken to the nearest railroad station in Germany, where we were put aboard a train for Hamburg, the seaport. We had a two day lay-over before the ship sailed, and were housed in army-like barracks. . . .

Dad had purchased steamship tickets for a fast boat, which was to make the trip in seven days, but instead we were put on a slow boat which took three weeks. Dad was very angry over the error and received a cash rebate.

Uncle Hyman met us at Castle Garden and took us to their apartment. The next day we were put on the train for Syracuse. Mother knew a few words in English, and on the train was teaching us children what to say. . . .

Dad met us at the R.R. station in Syracuse, where he had a hack "carriage" engaged, and we were taken to Uncle Ralph's home. Dad had an apartment rented and furnished ready for us to move into. They were nice rooms but with no inside plumbing, but homes without plumbing were the regular way of living in those days. We had a hand pump in the kitchen which supplied wash water from a cistern in the cellar. There was an open well a short block from our house, so once every day I or Eli would go to the well and bring back a pail of drinking water. . . .

Eli started school one term ahead of me. We both started in the Adam Street School, probably one of the oldest school houses in Syracuse. It was a wooden building with a big, pot-bellied coal burning stove in each room and with a Chick Sales outhouse privy in the yard. I was in the third room, grade 2B, when we moved from Adam to Jackson School, a new modern brick building, with steam heat in each room and flush toilets in the basement. As soon as we became settled, the principal, a motherly woman, went in each room and cautioned us all not to use more than two sheets of tissue paper when we went to the toilet. . . .

One day, in 1900, Tanta Zlatta and her husband were to our house visiting on a weekend when Dad was at home. Mr. Salinger was also a peddler but not a successful one, like Dad. He peddled close to Syracuse and was telling Dad some of his experiences. Amidst the conversation I heard Mr. Salinger say to Dad, "Jake, sometimes in a little town you can pick up a couple of dollars." In a sense, that's a classic and I've had many occasions where that saying fitted in very well. Mr. Salinger did not peddle for long. He and Tanta Zlatta opened a second-hand furniture store in Syracuse.

When I was 12 and 13 years old, during vacation, afternoons I worked in the store. Tanta Zlatta wanted me around for company's sake. To make it look like a job, she paid me 50 cents a week and supper. One afternoon, late in the summer of 1901, someone came into the store and said the news just came over the wire that President Wm. McKinley was shot in Buffalo, while attending the Pan American Exposition. Everyone felt very bad because President McKinley was liked by all, for he was a non-controversial peaceful kind of a gentleman. He died shortly after school opened in September, and in class we sang "Nearer My God to Thee." Theo. Roosevelt became President and in so doing was the youngest President ever to enter the White House and a rip-roaring President he was, full of pep and go. He coined the famous saying, "Speak softly but carry a big stick."

Syracuse was known among wholesale houses and clothing manufacturers as a city having many peddlers, and Dad was considered one of the best. The New York Mfgs. used to bring their sample line to Syracuse twice a year, Passover week and during our High Holy period in September, for the exclusive purpose of selling to the peddlers. They would headquarter at the old Globe Hotel. Two other successful peddlers were the Isaac Brothers, Henry and Isaac. Mrs. Isaac Isaac was a Shubert, a sister to the famous theatrical Shuberts, but in those days Isaac was looked upon as the rich man and the Schubert Boys, Sam, Jake and Lee, were peddling newspapers in Syracuse.

One day when Dad was home, Isaac Isaac came to our house and tried his best to get Dad to go into partnership and open a store in northern New York. Dad said no, for he did not want any partners. Dad said the only partners he ever wanted were his wife and children. . . .

Mr. Clint Smith owned the general store in Point Rock. He was appointed Superintendent of the Oneida County Home in Rome so he wanted to sell his store. Dad made a special trip home to talk it over with Mother and Uncle Ralph. They decided that Point Rock was no place to bring up Jewish children. It was entirely too far away from a *shul,* from a *heder,* and from everything *kosher.* . . . So, we continued living in Syracuse and Dad continued peddling, coming home only once in three weeks, and that wasn't pleasant for any of us. . . .

The year 1901 rolled on till the approach of my *Bar Mitzvah,* which was on the Sabbath of Hanukkah. Activities around the house reached a high pitch. In those days there was no such luxury as a caterer. The women all pitched in and a perfect chicken dinner was served to about 30 people. One of the highlights of the affair was the visit of Uncle Max Jacobs and his mother, our grandmother, Bubbie Simie, from Detroit. It was appreciated by all members of our family for that was some distance to travel for a *Bar Mitzvah.* However, Uncle Max was pretty well off financially at the time and to him it was a reunion with his relatives whom he hadn't seen since leaving Neustadt.

My *Bar Mitzvah* was an event which made Mother and Dad feel very proud. I read my portion of the Torah, chanted the *Haftarah* and delivered a ten minute speech quoting several lines in Hebrew. The manner in which I acquitted myself was hardly a surprise for I attended one of the best *heders* in Syracuse; Rebbe Levi was known throughout central New York as one of the best Hebrew teachers. Most every successful business and professional Jewish man in Syracuse of my generation attended Rebbe Levi's *heder*. . . .

As time went on life became harder for Dad to be on the road away from home and family. It must be remembered that he was a very religious man. In all of his years on the road, living entirely with Christians, he never ate non-*kosher* food. The only time he knew the taste of meat or chicken or home-made soup was when he would get home, one weekend in three or four weeks. I can well remember Mother's answer to us children when we complained about our dinner, "If only Pa could have a dinner like this."

In the fall of the year Dad would send about 20 geese or ducks to Syracuse, keep them in the crate for several weeks, feed them all the corn they could eat so as to make them fat. Then the *shohet* would come to kill them, the women would get together in our house to pluck the feathers, and then the dressed carcasses were given to Blumberg the butcher to cut in quarters and smoke. Now Dad would have *kosher* meat to eat on the road during the winter. Mother would bake many loaves of home-made black bread, and that would be his noonday meal on the road. The reason for this routine was that the days were short in the fall and winter so Dad could not afford to take the time out to stop to eat. The horses were fed in the nose bags, and business went on without interruption.

When on the road Dad never worked on the Sabbath, but he also respected his neighbor's Sunday, thereby traveling only five days a week. Throughout his territory he had special farmers with whom he stayed on weekends. As the neighbors heard that Jake was among them, many would come on Sunday to buy. . . .

1903 was the year of an important milestone in the lives of our family. Dad decided to move to Rome. Mother and the rest of us were happy and excited about moving to a different city, but our main happiness sprang from the fact that, at long last, we would have Dad at home a few days of each week.

What a layout we had! Almost a miniature farm, an acre of land, a large two-story barn, henhouse, a good size strawberry patch and flower garden.

There were six Jewish families living in Rome, and we made the seventh. Dad had had a meeting with these families and told them that he would not move to Rome unless they agreed to organize a *shul*. This they were very happy to do. Our first *shul* was in the front bedroom of Max Altman's house. It was close counting for a *minyan* requiring most every man and *Bar Mitzvah* boy to be present. That was the humble beginning of the Jewish community of Rome, N.Y.

During our early years in Rome, in the summer our relatives from Syracuse spent weeks at a time visiting us with the feeling that they were in the country. Dad had an aunt in New York, his mother's sister, whose name was Goldstein. She had a son, Paul, a big strapping single man who spent weeks at a time visiting us. He was a typical East Side New Yorker, not overly ambitious but very good company, and he and Eli had a lot of fun together. . . .

Dad was becoming tired of the road and felt that some day he would open a store in Rome, but not until he had his own help. He was not going to trust his store to strangers. Well, there were Eli, 18 years old, and I, 16. But Eli never wanted to work with Dad; he always wanted to work for himself, so Dad pinned his hopes on me.

There was a store in the Wiggins Block that would be available in August, 1905, and Dad rented it. This was in January of 1905 and I was in the second year of high school. After a brief conference between Mother, Dad and myself it was decided that I would go to business college in Syracuse for 6 months, which was the regular length of the course, and upon my return I would be qualified to assume the management of the store. No complications to life in those days; a 16-year-old boy without experience was to manage the store. In all my years of affiliation with Dad I was never afraid as long as Dad was around. He was a tower of strength.

The school I went to was the Henley Business College, considered the business school for Syracuse U. in 1905. Many of the fellows who went up the hill took their business course at Henley's. . . .

In the 6 months, twice I went home for a visit, for Passover and

Shevuoth. Not that I wasn't plenty homesick, but the train fare from Syracuse to Rome was 75¢, and I had to count my pennies.

I graduated in September 1905, and returned home with a diploma big enough to cover half of a wall. Dad already had the store open and in addition to clothing and jewelry, which was always his line, he added a full line of men's and boy's footwear. . . .

Now we were all happy. Dad retired from the road and was at home all of the time. Eli decided that since Dad had the peddling cart and the team of horses and since he knew all of Dad's customers, he would take up the peddling where Dad had left off. Until he was able to establish a line of credit in the wholesale market, Dad supplied him with merchandise from our store.

Present day storekeeping from 9:00 a.m. to 5:00 p.m. is a joke compared to the hours we used to keep. 8:00 to 8:00 every day with the exception of Wednesday, when we kept open until 10:00, and Saturday till 11:00 or 12:00, and then Sunday forenoon. No one complained. We were all happy to get along.

11. Ephraim E. Lisitzky, Poet

Ephraim Lisitzky was born in Minsk in 1885. At the age of fifteen he came to America to join his father, who was eking out a poor existence in Boston. Forced at an early age to seek out his own livelihood, he turned to *shehita* (ritual slaughtering) and Hebrew teaching, which eventually took him to Central Canada, Buffalo, and Milwaukee. In 1918 he settled in New Orleans, where he became principal of a Hebrew school, which he soon fashioned into a model of its kind; it came to be considered one of the best schools in the United States.

By vocation an educator, he was a poet by avocation. His major works are marked by deep feeling and spiritual searching: *Ki Teko'a Shofar* (1922) celebrates the rich spiritual life of the Jew in eastern Europe and laments the arid life of the American Jew, and *Naftulei Elohim* is replete with mythology and aspects of Jewish, Christian, Islamic, and Buddhist doctrine. In 1960 he published his reflections on the Holocaust, *Bi-Mei Sho'ah u-Meshu-ah.*

Significantly, he used American themes in two of his outstanding works. *Medurot Do'akot* (Dying Campfires), published in 1937, is about two Indian tribes and is filled with Indian legends and lore. *Be-Ohalei Kush* (In the Tents of Kush), issued in 1953, concerns the American Negro, demonstrating Lisitzky's rich knowledge of Negro folktales, spirituals, and customs.

Lisitzky the man and poet had two identities, as Jew and American.

In the Jewish world he had his associations and found his life work. As for American life, he most closely identified with the uprooted Indian and the exploited Negro, themes reminiscent of his own immigrant experience.

His autobiography, *In the Grip of Cross-Currents* (New York: Bloch Publishing Company, 1959), which may well be his most distinguished literary creation, is marked by the twin themes of alienation and exploitation and a quest for both roots and liberation, a quest characteristic of the immigrant Jew in America:

"IN THE DUSK MY FATHER'S FACE . . ."

During all of my trip to America my imagination kept conjuring up a picture of my encounter with my father. The image of my father's face, which had dimmed in my memory, shone through a haze of eight and a half years as it had registered in it the night before his departure, as I lay at his side holding him in tight desperation. Only now, his melancholy look of compassion had brightened. Anticipation of reunion softened the trials of the journey—stealing across the border, wandering through thick forests in the dark of night, the ship tossed about by storm for three consecutive days.

The picture of our reunion became sharper when, in New York, I boarded the train for Boston. The entire trip I visualized my father at the station, waiting for the train to pull in. When the train arrived and I got off, he would rush over and embrace me. I could see him standing there and hear the clatter of the train wheels bringing his greetings to me: "Welcome, my son!" And my heart responded in joyful tones: "Papa! Papa!"

The train slowed down to enter the station and my heart beat faster, as though to prod the train to hurry. Through the coach window I could see faces and eyes happy, trembling with anticipation. I searched for my father but he wasn't there! I descended from the coach, still looking and my heart scrutinizing every face in the crowd. But my father was nowhere in the crowd! I trudged to my father's home stopping passers-by on the street to show them the crumpled address transcribed in my strange tongue. When I finally got there he was not in—he had gone to work early, as he did every day, for the telegram from New York announcing the time of our arrival in Boston had been misaddressed and had not reached him.

At the entrance to the hall of a house populated with poor tenants, with one of whom my father roomed, I stood tense with anticipation. My eyes scrutinized every passer-by; perhaps father would be there, for his landlord had gone to look for him in the street to tell him of our arrival. The din of the city filled the street. Foot and wagon peddlers shrilly announced their wares. An Italian ground his organ as girls danced on the sidewalk and in the street. Boys skated madly along, holding on to one another's back in a long line that twisted and straightened, broke apart and joined again. In passing they glanced mockingly at me, eyeing my Slutzk garb which branded me as a "greenhorn," and my strange hat—a stiff Homburg acquired in Belgium after I had lost my Slutzk cap en route. They laughed and hurled at me names, which, though uttered in a foreign tongue, were clearly not complimentary.

Many tedious hours I stood and waited, rejecting the pleas of my stepmother and my father's landlady to eat and rest from the journey. I was not going to put off for one moment the anticipated meeting with my father. The hours passed. Standing there, all tensed up, my nerves on edge, the effects of the two weeks at sea overcame me and I swayed and sank to a step near the entrance to the hall. I fell into a kind of exhausted faint which lasted many minutes.

Suddenly, a figure came towards me through a rosy mist. As it approached, the mist lifted and I saw it, radiant and compassionate. I leaped up—it was my father.

In the dusk my father's face loomed up from the street. He walked heavily bent under a sack full of rags and bottles. His face was dark and hard, with an expression of mingled humiliation and forgiveness. I shrank back, offended and silenced.

At midnight, lying on the bedding they had laid out for me in a corner of the kitchen floor in the apartment where my father roomed, I cried in silence over the alienation that screened me from my father.

"AN AUTUMN DRIZZLE FALLS OUTSIDE"

The question of my future began to vex me. My attention was diverted from my Talmudic problems to a much more serious one whose solution could not be postponed: What was to become of me? My father sought the advice of our fellow Slutzk immigrants who used to drop in. They thought it over, discussed it among themselves and concluded that my salvation lay in becoming a custom-peddler. They preached the advantages of peddling:

In the first place it gives you a livelihood, meager to begin with, but eventually plenteous. It does not require you to desecrate the Sabbath or holidays; if you want to, you can observe them. At the same time, you get an opportunity to learn the language and ways of America. To be sure, it's a small beginning—but many people began carrying a peddler's notions basket and ended up owning a business or a factory—and it wasn't a matter of luck either. . . .

I nodded involuntary affirmation mingled with self-pity: so this is the end of the great achievements you aspired to—to be a door-to-door peddler!

Still, repugnant as the prospect was, I decided to try peddling and see whether I was fit for it. I talked to one of my acquaintances, a boy my own age, who was a peddler himself, and he consented to lend me for a day his notions basket with the understanding that we would share the profits. I chose Tuesday, a lucky day in Jewish tradition, to embark on my peddling experiment.

It was a rainy autumn day. The wind shook my basket and whipped the shoelaces dangling from my hand into my face. I trudged down the street like a doomed man on his way to the gallows. Whenever anybody looked at me I lowered my eyes in shame. I approached a house whose number was the numerical equivalent of a verse of Scripture I had in mind, timidly mounted the stairs—and couldn't bring my hand to knock at the door. At last I knocked diffidently. The door opened. I stood in the doorway with downcast face, and inquired clumsily in a low voice:

"Maybe the lady wants matches?"

"Matches?" The woman at the door responded sardonically. "Come in and I'll show you the piles of matches the peddler already supplied me with—enough to burn up all the houses in Boston!" . . .

That evening I went back to my acquaintance's house, and returned the basket with all the merchandise intact—not a thread or shoelace was missing. He checked his merchandise and gave me a scoffing and pitying look. I scoffed at myself: "Oh, you Slutzk unworldly idler, you good-for-nothing yeshiva student—there's no hope for you!"

I plodded wearily to the synagogue and stayed after the evening prayers to study my daily portion of Talmud. Mutely I looked at the Talmud, afraid to open my mouth lest the suppressed cry within me, about to burst forth, erupt.

The synagogue emptied. The distinguished scholars who had finished the portion of their nightly study left. Only an old Slutzker, Artche, the Hebrew teacher, remained to finish his study. He sits at his Mishnah, intoning sadly, reading every chapter once in the book through a magnifying glass, and repeating it twice by heart. He is losing his eyesight, and before losing it entirely he is laboriously fortifying his memory with portions of Mishnah, food for his soul in the days of blindness that were closing in on him. Upon completing his daily portion he shuts his feeble eyes, and ends his study with a portion of Psalms chanted in a melancholy undertone. Suddenly his voice rises and he begins to groan and cry out into the stillness of the synagogue: "My heart flutters, my strength fails me, and the light of my eyes is also gone from me—O God, my Light and my Salvation, the light of my eyes is gone from me!"

An autumn drizzle falls outside and covers the panes of the synagogue with tear-like drops. The synagogue sheds tears out of compassion for Artche, the Hebrew teacher, whose light of his eyes is dimming and for me, whose light of my life likewise is dimming, and for both of us, our world turns dark. . . .

YESHIVA OR UNIVERSITY?

[Learning, education, was the key that opened the golden door. A young man coming from Slutzk, a city steeped in the Torah tradition of Talmudic study, naturally turns to yeshiva learning. Lisitzky studies for a time at the Rabbi Isaac Elchanan Yeshiva in New York City.]

The Rabbi Isaac Elchanan Yeshiva's beginnings were modest. Its first location was the women's gallery of the Anshei Kalvariah Synagogue on Pike Street in New York City. There was housed a small group of boys and young men who had brought their baggage of learning with them across the ocean. Few were the students, and most of these had chosen the yeshiva as a stopping-off place. Actually they were seeking a way in the American labyrinth of life, stopping for provisions at the yeshiva, which they viewed as a kind of stocking-up point on the way to Americanization.

During the time I studied at the yeshiva, I fulfilled the saying of the Sages about the true scholar: "You shall live a life of hardship and toil in the Torah." I came to New York without a penny to my name, for I had refused to take from my father more than I absolutely needed for a ticket. I was dependent upon the yeshiva for support: $2.75 a week—$1.75 for food, twenty-five cents for three meals a day—if they could be called "meals"—and seventy-five cents for a room, and the balance for all my other needs, largely drugs for my ailing stomach; these I bought very cheaply at a nearby hospital. The room, which cost me more than 25 per cent of my stipend, was a tiny back room which was always dark, so that it was difficult to distinguish between day and night. It had a window of sorts that faced on a high and narrow space between which was like a chimney hole, admitting no sunlight—only the noise of the nearby elevated train. It was summer, and the sun's heat was absorbed during the day by the brick and stone of the buildings, at night they exuded a sweaty vapor. I was nearly suffocated; the vapor combined with the clatter of the nearby elevated line to deprive me of sleep most of the night.

A *SHOHET* I WILL BE

[After six months at the yeshiva, Lisitzky decides to abandon plans to become a rabbi. He wants instead to get a secular education and study at a university.]

When I told [my father] my decision to abandon the rabbinate, he became frantic with grief. At first he tried to persuade me to return to the yeshiva: didn't I know I was ruining my life and his by this decision? Here was our chance to rise in the world together and I was throwing it away! Since when was secular school more important than a sacred Jewish one? True, every Jew in America had to know the vernacular—but a scholar like me could master it easily in my spare time. When he saw that gentle persuasion was no use, he became grimly silent. Dejectedly resentful, he would return from his daily labor and sit down to eat supper with knit brow and downcast eyes. Having eaten and recited grace, he would open his notebook, and examine his accounts in a mournful exclamation, "Father-in-Heaven!" Mine was another account that didn't balance, another one of his bubbles that had burst! . . .

The combination of my father's grim silence and my stepmother's scolding caused me to defer entering school. I decided to leave home and find an occupation that would put me on my own feet. I would rather do the most menial work than continue to be dependent on my father's charity. But I wouldn't work on the Sabbath, and the only occupation I know that did not require that was peddling. But I had already failed at peddling. After much contemplation, I made a final decision: I would become a *shohet,* a ritual slaughterer. True, like the rabbinate, it was not highly respected in America, but it would be only temporary. I would be a *shohet* for a few years, until I could qualify for admission to a university, and save up enough money to go. . . .

When the time came to slaughter my first chicken, my heart pounded. I was terrified at the prospect of shedding blood. Up to now, *shehitah* had been only a theoretical matter for me, studying the rules and practicing sharpening the knife. But now that I was about to apply the theory, I trembled all over. I had a tender nature, full of pity for all living creatures. At an early age I had seen an alley cat that had pounced upon a chick that had fallen out of his nest and dragged it off, quivering and bleeding in the cat's mouth. I cried all evening and my parents were unable to console me. Well into the night I lay sobbing in bed, all the while hearing the sad twittering of the bereft mother bird at the top of the tree in our courtyard. . . .

The High Holy Day season approached and the sound of the *shofar* announced the arrival of judgment day, rousing all to penitence. I was aghast at the thought that the eve before Yom Kippur a rooster and a hen would be slaughtered, one in expiation of my sins, and one of my stepmother's. I was ashamed to look at them like a guilt-laden criminal standing before his victims. The night before Yom Kippur, when the rooster and the hen lay bound under the table, I tossed and turned in bed: Why should these unfortunate creatures be slaughtered so that we may live? Early the next morning I hurried to the synagogue, where I stayed a long time to avoid seeing them, all blood-stained, their throats slit, when my stepmother brought them home from the slaughter house. . . .

"LIKE A FOUNDLING BANISHED BY HIS FOSTER PARENT"

[America was not waiting for another *shohet*. Boston had more than it could use, "seven to every chicken." The father's anticipation and the son's ambition came into conflict, the former advising marriage, the young man eager for education and opportunity.]

Difficult days followed, heart-sickening days of disappointment, until rescue came from an unexpected source: I got a job in Auburn in New York State. This job had a slight drawback: it involved being a teacher half time and a *shohet* half time in a little community with only fifteen families. These two half-time jobs between them didn't offer half a decent salary. Nevertheless, I jumped at the opportunity for I felt a small job was just right for me; it wouldn't keep me busy all day and I would have time to study English and the other subjects I needed to qualify for admission to a university. My father was angry at me. One of the veteran *shohatim* and *mohalim* of Boston had become interested in me as a match for his daughter, a job as assistant *shohet* at the slaughter-house promised, and here I was throwing away this chance by taking a job and burying myself in some remote village. It was sheer spiteful stubbornness! I begrudged him the little joy that this match might bring him!

My heart went out to my father. I wanted to explain to my father why I had to refuse the offer, so he would understand it was not out of spite, but I knew he would be unable to understand and I would only be aggravating his pain, so I kept quiet. He returned silence for silence, and we each were further offended by the other's silence. . . .

The train pulled out. Slowly it moved off to be swallowed in the dark winter night. Slowly I rode away from Boston without a word of goodbye from my father. For the second time my father and I had separated without a word. Ten years before he had stolen away from me in Slutzk, and now I was leaving him behind in Boston—leaving him without his farewell blessing, like a foundling banished by his foster parent.

"Standing at the Door of Life a Beggar . . ."

The "rich relative" was part of the immigrant experience. Every family had one. He had come a bit earlier, had worked a bit harder, cut corners a bit more freely and suppressed compassion a bit more easily. The very qualities which made for his "success" in the New World made him a source of pain and humiliation to those relatives who turned to him in need. He helped; he gave a little money and a lot of advice and abuse. Lisitzky turns to such a relative for the eight dollars he needed to go from New York to Auburn.

He counted eight silver dollars into my hand. I felt like a Slutzk beggar standing at the door, with trembling hand outstretched for a dry crust. I accepted the money; I didn't throw it back in his face, as I felt like doing. I had long ago come to accept humiliation as inevitable. I put the money in my pocket—it was "hot money," glowing coins, scorching at their touch, an illustration of the Midrashic phrase: "A coin of fire." I felt their scorching even after I had spent them on a ticket. These "coins of fire" were branded on my soul.

The train pulled into Auburn at night in the middle of a snowstorm. I picked up my bundle and got off. The Auburn trolley cars had stopped running, so I had to walk. The streets were buried in snow and empty. I walked ankle-deep in snow; there was no path. The wind shrieked, icy flakes hailed against my face. My feet were freezing. I kept sinking into the snow. My eyelashes were coated with hail which pricked my eyeballs when I blinked. The world was inundated and all dimensions of space were obliterated, and I wandered in this turmoil, and it seemed to me that I would always wander thus, pathless and aimless. I had only one urge: to sink down upon a mound of snow, stretch out there and freeze, congeal into the eternal, infinite conglutination, repose in the redeeming Sabbatical peace, cease in the divine nullity.

"BE ANYTHING BUT A HEBREW POET"

[The leading Hebrew literary figure to come to America was Menachem Mendel Dolitsky. He had already attained some fame in Russia and was of such promise that Yehudah Leib Gordon, reigning poet, pointed to him as his crown prince. But America had little need of Hebrew poets. Lisitzky describes their meeting.]

When I was a yeshiva student I thought there was nothing grander than an author. I saw the square letters of the Hebrew book as godly letters, which were handed down from Sinai, and its author as a sublime, almost divine, superhuman being. The only Hebrew author I had ever met was the Ridbaz, author of a commentary on the Jerusalem Talmud; I imagined every other author would be a man of God, like the Ridbaz. Even after I had given up my religious studies, books and authors remained sacred to me.

I had never even hoped to see a Hebrew writer in person, and here I was to greet a poet! A poet was something of a prophet, I had learned from *Ha-Igron*, the Hebrew-writing primer. Like the prophet, the poet received his inspiration in nightly visions, in meditations, amid fear and trembling and perception of still voices. And the author of this book is none other than Dolitzky, the poet, who had certainly experienced the poetic inspiration he describes, as I had myself, in small measure, at dusk along the banks of the Charles River. In those days I was enthusiastic over the newer Hebrew literature. Still, I remained true to the Haskalah writers, principally J. L. Gordon. It was enough for me that Gordon approved of Dolitzky.

The reception turned out to be a dismal affair. Entering the hall I felt the melancholy that had settled everywhere—on the sooty walls, the dim gaslights, the chandeliers and globes, covered with cobwebs and fly offal. The same melancholy sat on the faces of the *Maskilim* who comprised the audience. They were gloomy because the occasion reminded them of vanished dreams and days and climes of long ago, when they were young, from which they were banished. . . .

Dolitzky had agreed to see me in his hotel the next evening. It was a dilapidated building, in one of the narrow streets in the Jewish West Side of Boston neighborhood. I found him sprawled out on a threadbare couch, tired and depressed after a day spent going from house to house soliciting subscribers for his Yiddish book. He looked grim. It had been a hot summer day; towards evening the air was stifling and humid. Dolitzky lay there sweating and panting. Outside, the heat rose from the pavement in waves, streetcars clattered back and forth over the iron tracks, and wagons and coaches rattled across the cobblestones. Dolitzky's books lay on a bench in the corner opposite the couch next to an open valise; the gilded letters of his name on the bindings stared at the exhausted poet.

While I struggled to overcome my shyness and hand him the poem I had written on the banks of the Charles River, for his opinion of its merits, he smiled sarcastically. . . . Dolitzky was silent a moment, then asked: "You told me last night you wanted to talk to me. What about?"

I handed him the poem and asked him to read it and give me his opinion of it.

I studied Dolitzky's face intently as he read, to get his reaction. My heart was pounding. He looked at me, the same sarcastic smile as before creasing the corners of his mouth.

"Stop it," he said bitterly. "There's no glory in it. The devil with poetry! Don't be a fool poetaster! You know what happens to Hebrew poets in this country: First stage—Hebrew poet. Second stage—Hebrew teacher—or rather cattle herder, with the children in the role of unwilling cattle. Third stage—you write trashy novels for servant maids and teamsters. You're young, you can get into the university here. Learn an honorable profession that will give you a decent living. Do anything, be anything—peddle candles and matches—sell windbags and bubbles, if you must. Be a tailor, a shoemaker, a cobbler—anything but a Hebrew poet in America!"

12. Morris Raphael Cohen, Philosopher

Morris Raphael Cohen was a legend in his own time. A philosopher and teacher of philosophers, admired for his keen intellect, revered for his devotion to truth, feared by intellectual foes and respected by all who were committed to the life of reason, he was one of the foremost intellectual influences in the period between World Wars I and II.

Born in Minsk in 1880, Cohen came to America at the age of twelve, studied in New York's City College, and took his Ph.D. at Harvard. He returned to teach at his alma mater, with the most enthusiastic recommendations that Harvard's greats—William James and Josiah Royce—had ever issued. He was an awe-inspiring teacher—students flocked to his classes and quaked in his presence.

He served as president of the American Philosophical Association, and was accorded many honors by the American academic community. His interest in the working class led him to legal philosophy, which combined his social concern with academic distinction. Among his major works were *Law and the Social Order* (1933), *Preface to Logic* (1945) and *The Meaning of Human History* (1947).

His interests in the welfare of Jewish people were an important part of his life and work. He was a founder of the Conference on Jewish Relations, devoted to the scientific study of Jewish problems, and of its *Jewish Social Studies Quarterly*. *Reflections of a Wondering Jew*, his essays on Jewish themes, were published posthumously in 1950. The following selections are from his autobiography, *A Dreamer's Journey* (Boston: Beacon Press, 1949):

THE NEW WORLD

What I first saw of America did not come up to the high expectation which popular accounts of its unlimited wealth and radical difference from the Old World had led me to entertain. Almost all the people I met in the street and in the stores, with the exception of some children, spoke Yiddish; and though their dress had a somewhat different tone from the one to which I was accustomed, it did not seem much richer in quality. Grand Street, which at that time was the great business thoroughfare of the East Side, and still had department stores such as Ridley's and Lord and Taylor, did not seem so much grander than the great mercantile streets of Minsk, such as the Franciscaner.

The most marked outer difference was the uniformity of the many-storied houses and the absence of any wooden ones. . . .

On the inner side of life, the chief characteristic difference was the greater intensity and hurry. At six o'clock in the morning the alarm clock would wake us all up. My mother would prepare breakfast, my father would say his prayers and after a hurried meal my father and my brother Sam would leave the house so that they could begin their work at the moment when the clock struck seven.

I had occasion to visit my father's "shop" and I was impressed with the tremendous drive which infiltrated and animated the whole establishment—nothing like the leisurely air of the tailor shop in Minsk where my Uncle Abraham had worked and where the men would sing occasionally. Sometimes my father and another presser would start a competitive drive to see who could press the largest number of jackets during the day. We all knew by his appearance that this had happened when he came home at seven o'clock in the evening. It was hard to dissuade my father from engaging in such drives, for he was paid according to the number of jackets pressed.

I soon understood why the unions were fighting so hard for a weekly wage to take the place of payment for piece work. That experience made me realize what later my friends educated in economics could not see, namely, the wisdom as well as the humanity of some limitation of output. For, in the long run, excessive work diminishes the effective life span and thus reduces the chief productive power of the nation. Even a machine cannot be economically run if it functions always at maximum speed. What good is it to a nation to increase the number of its commodities if it exhausts and brutalizes its human beings?

When later I learned of the large profits that the manufacturers were making and how lavishly they spent their money, I could not dismiss as mere rhetoric the complaint against the harsh injustice of the distribution of wealth under capitalism. But at first I knew only that my father worked in a "shop" in the rear building of a yard on Ridge Street, and that his boss, a certain Mr. Riemer, received the cloth all properly cut, ready to be sewed up into garments, after which it was returned to the manufacturers, who were referred to as "the warehouse" and who sold the product to distributors. Mr. Riemer, as the boss, was an Olympian figure to us. He was the one who paid my father. But the Sampters, who paid Mr. Riemer, were dim figures whose magnitude I had no opportunity to measure. . . .

On the religious side there was at first much less difference than I had expected. All the people that I knew (with the exception of my brother Tom who was a clerk in a shoe store on the Bowery) refrained from working on Saturdays, and all the stores in our immediate neighborhood were closed on that day. On Friday nights, on Saturdays and on holidays I would accompany my father to a hall on Broome Street where the Neshwieser Verein held religious services in the regular Orthodox manner. It differed from a regular synagogue in the old town only in not having daily services, a library of sacred books, or any rabbi to preach and expound the Torah after the prayers were finished. At these services on Broome Street I found myself in Neshwies again. There were not only two of my uncles, who had changed their names from Farfel to Aronson and Jackson respectively, but three of my former classmates at my first *heder* in Neshwies. . . .

I continued to attend religious services with my father up to 1899 although I had drifted away from my religious Orthodoxy long before that. In the first place there was no incentive and little opportunity for me to continue my Hebraic and Talmudic studies. There were no suitable books in our house and no one urged me to continue such study. It was taken for granted that in a few years I would join my father in some phase of tailoring, for I had no desire to become a rabbi. I did, indeed, once go to the synagogue on Norfolk Street where I found some tractates of the Talmud, but I lacked the ardor to engage in such study by myself long enough to surmount the difficult places.

A more important factor, however, in my drift from religious Orthodoxy, was provided by a conversation which I overheard between my father and a certain Mr. Tunick, in the fall of 1892. Mr. Tunick's brother had been a neighbor of ours in Minsk, and my father had helped him to come to this country. Our visitor challenged my father to prove that there was a personal God who could be influenced by human prayers or deeds, or that the Jewish religion had any more evidence in favor of its truth than other religions. To this challenge my father could only answer, "I am a believer." This did not satisfy my own mind. And after some reflection I concluded that in all my studies no such evidence was available. After that I saw no reason for prayer or the specifically Jewish religious observances. But there was no use arguing with my father. He insisted that so long as I was in his house I must say my prayers regularly whether I believed in them or not. Such is the Orthodox conception. I had to conform to it until I was in a position to refuse to obey and tell my father I would leave his house if he insisted. This occurred in the fall of 1899.

Though my father respected my independence it came as a heavy blow that I should desert the only intellectual life we had ever shared. To him the synagogue meant a great deal. He would go to services every morning and in addition would attend the class in Mishnah on Saturday afternoons. He was a devout believer in all the teachings of Orthodox Judaism and conformed to all its laws in most faithful fashion. In later years the synagogue at Bensonhurst became almost the center of his life. He had no doubt about a life after death but was not certain as to what punishment would be accorded to his son who was morally good (according to his view) but religiously an infidel.

My abandonment of Judaism as a religion was later reinforced in my mind by my scientific, historical and philosophical studies. Although I never abandoned my interest in the history and in the welfare of the Jewish people, I ceased to read Hebrew, so that after many years it became almost a foreign language to me. . . .

In September, 1892, my sister and I were sent to public school. In those days there were no special provisions for older and more advanced immigrant children unfamiliar with English; and so I was put into the beginners' or ABC class. I do not recall that I was particularly embarrassed by being placed among small children, but I was dazed because I understood little of what it was all about. Despite all that, in the course of a few weeks I was promoted several times from one class to another—probably to make room for new entrants. Thus I soon reached the third grade. (In those days the classes in public school were numbered not according to the progress of the pupil, but in the reverse order so that the final or graduating class was called the first.) The teacher of this grade seemed sympathetic and showed considerable patience at my inability to answer in English.

After a month or two, the principal, Miss Byrnes, came in, wrote a problem in subtraction on the blackboard, and asked how many could solve it. I volunteered to do so, and together with several others, I was again promoted in the middle of the term. . . .

My intellectual life before I could read English books with understanding would have tapered off to nothing, had it not been for the stimulus of the little Yiddish literature at home which I devoured as one famished for food. . . .

But for intellectual stimulus I turned every week to the *Arbeiter Zeitung,* the Jewish organ of the Socialist Labor Party. In its columns I read translations of Flaubert's *Salammbô,* and of Smolenskin's *Kevuras Hamar* (disgraceful burial). The former stirred me by its military narratives, the latter by the revelations of the chicanery and corruption of the old fanatical leaders of Jewish communities. I was, moreover, seriously interested in the news of the week and in Abraham Cahan's articles on socialism, which were in the form of addresses like those of the old Hebrew preachers. The early numbers of the Socialist monthly *Die Zukunft* also gave me much mental nourishment. . . .

As soon as I learned to read English, I began to borrow books from the Aguilar Free Library, which was located on the top floor of the Educational Alliance (formerly the Hebrew Institute) building. Unless I am mistaken my first book was called *A Child's History of the Civil War*. The only other books that I remember of that period were Abbott's biographical histories of Hannibal, Alexander the Great, Pyrrhus, and Cortez. Alexander the Great had been a familiar figure to me through the reading of Josephus, and Hannibal through the Yiddish translation of Flaubert's *Salammbô*. But it was the book on Cortez that stirred me most and my remembering its contents helped me considerably on a later occasion . . .

BROWNSVILLE

Brownsville was at that time a Jewish boom town, whose bloom had been nipped in the bud. It had a number of newly built houses, as well as a scattering of houses belonging to old settlers. Everywhere there were vacant fields and in the direction of Canarsie, meadows, woods, brooks and marshes. Almost all of the natives, old and young, played baseball and so did the Jewish boys of my age.

At the time we moved into our house on Rockaway Avenue my father had some hope of finding work in Brooklyn or in New York, but this turned out to be illusory. He once tried his hand as a glazier, but on his first job he got into some difficulty with the owner of the house where he was to put in a window pane and the latter called him a "sheeny" and threatened to beat him up. My father came home terribly depressed, and though it was Friday night and mother tried to provide the usual Sabbath cheer, father broke down after saying *kiddush* and wept bitterly. After that he was more or less reconciled to the fact of unemployment. Nor was my brother Sam much more successful, though for several weeks during the winter he did find some work. We lived on the little rent that we were occasionally able to collect from some of the tenants, one of the stores being almost always vacant. Despite my mother's wonderful management we often arrived at the state of not having any money or food in the house. I would then walk to New York over the Brooklyn Bridge and ask my brother Tom, who had not lost his position as clerk in Kaufman's Shoe Store, for money to buy bread.

When I applied for admission to the Brownsville Public School I was asked in what grade I had been in New York, and when I told them the truth, that I had just been promoted into the grammar department, they told me that the Brooklyn schools were more advanced and that I would have to enter the last primary grade. This seemed to me an intolerable humiliation, and so I walked a considerable distance to a Brooklyn school on Chauncey Street and applied for admission to its grammar department. When the assistant principal asked me in what class I had been in New York I told her that I had been in the seventh grade, thinking that I would then be placed in the eighth and so avoid losing a grade. She, however, wanted to make sure of my qualifications and asked me what I knew in arithmetic. I told her that I could do fractions and so to my great elation she put me into the seventh grade. My elation, however, subsided when I entered the classroom. A grammar lesson was in progress, and each pupil in turn was called upon to parse certain words in sentences which were on the blackboard. ... .

For the first half-year I was the only Jew in the school; however I got along fairly well with my schoolmates. Two of them, Mosher and Meyer, invited me to their homes and presented me to their mothers as the brightest boy in the class. But on the way to school I had difficulties. Beyond Dean Street I passed a number of houses inhabited by Germans who delighted to set their young children on me, yelling "sheeny," and running after me as if they were going to attack me from the rear. When I turned around they would retreat, but as soon as I resumed my walk they would return to their annoying pastime. One day I became so irritated that I ran after one of the youngsters and slapped his face. At once, his older brother came out of the house and gave me a good thrashing for hitting someone below my size. But the

total result was satisfactory, for the youngsters thereafter left me
alone.

I DISCOVER ENGLISH LITERATURE
AND OTHER THINGS

[Many years later] we went up to the City College to take our entrance
examinations. I thought I did fairly well in arithmetic, history, geography and drawing, but during the grammar examination I got into a
nervous stew. I wrote, not on both sides of the paper, but on what I
supposed to be the wrong side of the paper. When I discovered my
mistake, I hurriedly began to rewrite the whole thing. Naturally I
could not finish and I was certain that I had failed. During the two
weeks or so before the results of the examinations were announced,
I was downcast and stayed awake at night, forming all sorts of plans
as to how I might continue my education. . . .

On the afternoon when Mr. Adams was to inform us of the results
of the examination, I came to school in a resigned mood. To my utter
amazement Mr. Adams announced that "the highest mark was attained by Morris Cohen, who is thus entitled to the Adams gold
medal." He asked me to come up and be congratulated. I looked
sheepish; I could hardly believe that this was true. Even when I went
home I could not realize that I had actually passed. My mother at that
time was bed-ridden, and when I told her that I had passed the examination and was thus admitted to college, a flood of tears came into her
eyes. She was not at all interested in the fact that I had received the
gold medal. It was only later that I appreciated her discriminating wisdom. The medal made little subsequent difference, except that occasionally we were able to borrow a few dollars on it. However, my
admittance to college did make a tremendous difference. When one of
my aunts remonstrated with my mother, "You cannot afford to send
your boy to college," she replied, "If need be I'll go out as a washer-
woman and scrub floors so that my Morris can have a college educa-

tion.'' For people who had all their lives been scrupulously careful not to incur any expense which could possibly be avoided, this was a lavish luxury. But by a rare good fortune it proved the best investment that my parents ever made.

The academic year of 1894–95 marked not only the completion of my school career and entrance into college, but also my arrival at what may be called mature manhood. It was one of great intellectual as well as physical awakening. Through books like Hilliard's *Sixth Reader* I became acquainted with great masterpieces of English and American literature and became interested not only in classic stories and novels, but in essays, histories, and lyric, as well as narrative, poetry. In the grammar book which we used, Gould Brown's, there was a large number of quotations from the classics and they stimulated my interest in the great poets. I cannot say that I then appreciated the real beauties of Shelley or Keats—that came later; but I read the narrative poems of Scott and Byron, and many of the shorter lyrics of Wordsworth and others in Palgrave's *Golden Treasury*. Among the essays were many of Macaulay's and Carlyle's, some of Addison's and Emerson's. I am sure that at that time I did not understand fully the mood which binds together Emerson's disparate, atomic sentences. But at the end of the year I was thrilled to read Plato's shorter dialogues and the first two books of the *Republic*. The years since have convinced me that they can be appreciated by, and serve as proper food for, ordinarily intelligent young people of fifteen. Perhaps they gave me an undue taste for Socratic questioning, but on the whole I think it was unfortunate that my reading of Plato was interrupted and not resumed until five years later.

The book, however, which exercised the most practical influence on me at the time was Franklin's autobiography. The notion of keeping a check on yourself through an account of your thinking in a diary appealed to my critical bent and to my introspective mood. I soon developed the habit of jott.ng down the day's reflections on scraps of paper—I did not think I could afford to buy a diary or notebook for the purpose. Franklin's diary was an acknowledged model in some of my earliest jottings.

COLLEGE DAYS

In September, 1895, I entered the college which was to nurture and sustain me through the major part of my life. City College then, as in later years, offered a frugal though nourishing intellectual diet. Since the College was free, attendance brought no social prestige. Since admission was not limited by race, class, creed, or social status, it had to be limited by rigorous scholastic standards. Social life, sports, social polish, and the other superficial attractions of American college life were neglected. The consequence was that those to whom these extracurricular goals mattered found their way to other more congenial colleges and universities. Those who chose City College did so only because its courses seemed to offer a key to a wider intellectual world. It was thus the student body rather than the faculty that created the intellectual tone of the College. . . .

In my undergraduate years, and even more in later decades, an increasing proportion of the students was Jewish, many of them foreign-born, and very many of the others children of foreign-born parents. Many of us, therefore, were familiar with what are today provincially called "un-American" ideas. Certainly, a large part of the student body of the College has always been peculiarly open-minded and critical towards the accepted commonplaces of the complacent. These students came prepared to weigh and consider new, as well as old, ideas, and their intellectual eagerness was encouraged rather than restrained by home conditions.

It was hard for a teacher who was not a master of his subject to survive this sort of intellectual climate, but many did. In this, worthy pedagogues and scholastic drill masters were protected by a tradition of military discipline which had been fixed upon the college by its first two presidents, both West Pointers—Dr. Horace Webster and General Alexander S. Webb. Rigid discipline and pursuit of marks were more important to most of the teaching staff than love of learning. But what the professors lacked in love of learning, the student body made up.

There was no need to preach to us the importance and value of scholarship, or to instill in our hearts a love of learning. That was why we were there. There was nothing else that we could hope to get out of the College. The intellectual companionship of my fellow students thus came to mean a great deal to me.

Because the College made no effort to impose a single pattern of social behavior upon its graduates, its militarism was not tainted by totalitarianism. Many of its graduates have become rabbis, others have become Christian ministers, communist leaders, financiers, and distinguished statesmen and jurists. The College thus, despite the mediocrity of its teaching staff in those days, embodied what has always seemed to me the essence of liberal education as opposed to dogmatic indoctrination. I do not know of any charge that has been brought against our Jewish boys of the City College that could not have been brought against me personally, at the comparable age, and yet the College was willing to ignore or forgive my defects in the social graces, as well as the unorthodoxy of many of my views. That the College tolerated me became, to me, a symbol of liberalism in education. It gave me a sound education in mathematics, languages, and the natural sciences and thus opened the gates to a wider intellectual world than I had dreamed of.

Further Reading

Antin, Mary. *The Promised Land*. Boston: Houghton Mifflin Co., 1912.

Bernheimer, Charles S., ed. *The Russian Jew in the United States*. Philadelphia: The John C. Winston Co., 1905.

Cahan, Abraham, *The Rise of David Levinsky*. New York: Harper & Brothers, 1917.

————. *The Education of Abraham Cahan*. Philadelphia: Jewish Publication Society, 1969.

Epstein, Melech. *Profiles of Eleven*. Detroit: Wayne State University Press, 1965.

Feinstein, Marvin, *American Zionism, 1884–1904*, New York, Herzl Press, 1965.

Goodman, Henry. *The New Country, Stories from the Yiddish about Life in America*. New York: Ykuf, 1961.

Handlin, Oscar. *Immigration as a Factor in American History*. Englewood, New Jersey: Prentice-Hall, 1959.

Hapgood, Hutchins. *The Spirit of the Ghetto*. Edited by Moses Rischin. Cambridge, Mass.: The Belknap Press, 1967.

Hirshler, Eric G. *Jews from Germany in the United States*. New York: Farrar, Straus & Cudahy, 1955.

Howe, Irving. *World of Our Fathers*. New York: Harcourt, Brace and Jovanovich, 1976.

Kohler, Max J. *Immigration and Aliens in the United States*. New York: Bloch Publishing Co., 1936.

Lifson, David S. *The Yiddish Theatre in America*. New York: T. Yoseloff, 1965.

Marcus, Jacob R. *Early American Jewry*. 2 vols. Philadelphia: Jewish Publication Society, 1951–1953.

Memoirs of American Jews, 1775–1865. 3 vols. Philadelphia: Jewish Publication Society, 1955–56.

Rischin, Moses. *The Promised City: New York's Jews 1870–1914*. Cambridge, Mass.: Harvard University Press, 1962.

Schoener, Allan, ed. *Portal to America: The Lower East Side 1870–1925*. New York: Holt, Rinehart and Winston, 1967.

Tcherikower, Elias, ed. *The Early Jewish Labor Movement in the United States*. Translated and revised by Aaron Autonovsky, from the original Yiddish. New York: Yivo Institute for Jewish Research, 1961.

Index

Acknowledgment is made to the following for permission to reprint:

AMERICAN JEWISH ARCHIVES: The Joseph Rosengart letter, "The Departure" by Basil Dahl, and "Immigrants in Buffalo" by Della Rubinstein Adler.

AMERICAN JEWISH HISTORICAL SOCIETY: *The Jewish Experience,* edited by Abraham J. Karp; "The Early History of the Jews in New York, 1654–1666" by Samuel Oppenheim; "New Light on the Jewish Settlement of Savannah" by Malcolm Stern; "A Memorial Sent by German Jews to the President of the Continental Congress" by M. Kayserling; *The Russian Jew in America* by George M. Price, translated by Leo Shpall.

BLOCH PUBLISHING COMPANY: Material from *In the Grip of Cross-Currents* by Ephraim E. Lisitzky.

LEON GERMANOW: Material from *Harry Germanow . . . My Own Story* (privately published), Rochester, N.Y., 1967.

JOHN L. GOLDMAN: Material from *The Goldman Family Saga* by Abraham S. Goldman (privately published), Rochester, N.Y. 1961.

HARCOURT BRACE JOVANOVICH, INC.: Material from *The Autobiography of Lincoln Steffens.* Copyright 1931 by Harcourt Brace Jovanovich, Inc.; Copyright 1959 by Peter Steffens. Reprinted by permission of the publishers.

HEBREW PUBLISHING COMPANY: Material from *The Days of Our Years* by Israel Kasovich, translated by Maximillian Hurtz. Copyright by Hebrew Publishing Co., reprinted by permission.

THE JEWISH PUBLICATION SOCIETY OF AMERICA: Material from *Memoirs of American Jews,* edited by Jacob Marcus, and from *Selected Papers and Addresses of Louis Marshall.*

JOHNSON REPRINT CORPORATION: Material from "The East European Hebrews" from *The Old World in the New* by Edward Alsworth Ross.

MACMILLAN PUBLISHING CO., INC.: Material from *A Dreamer's Journey* by Morris Raphael Cohen. Copyright 1949 by The Free Press.

YIVO INSTITUTE FOR JEWISH RESEARCH: Material from *The Early Jewish Labor Movement in the United States* by Elias Tcherikower, and from "Source Material on the History of Jewish Immigration to the United States" by Rudolf Glanz, *Yivo Annual,* Vol. VI, 1951.

Thanks to the Morris Adler Publications Fund of B'nai B'rith's Commission on Adult Jewish Education for making the Jewish Heritage Classics Series possible as a memorial to the late Rabbi Morris Adler, former Chairman of that Commission.